Rethinking Law, Regulation, and Technology

RETHINKING LAW

The Rethinking Law series is a forum for innovative scholarly legal writing from across all substantive fields of law. The series aims to enrich the study of law by promoting a cutting-edge approach to legal analysis.

Despite the old maxim that nothing is new under the sun, it is nevertheless true that laws evolve and contexts in which laws operate change. Law faces new and previously unforeseen challenges, responds to shifting motivations and is shaped by competing interests and experiences. Academic scrutiny and challenge is an essential component in the development of law, and the act of re-thinking and re-examining principles and precepts that may have been long-held is imperative.

Rethinking Law showcases authored books that address their field from a new angle, expose the weaknesses of existing frameworks, or 're-frame' the topic in some way. This might be through the introduction of a new legal framework, through the integration of perspectives from other fields or even other disciplines, through challenging existing paradigms, or simply through a level of analysis that elevates or sharpens our understanding of a subject. While each book takes its own approach, all the titles in the series use an analytical lens to open up new thinking.

Titles in the series include:

Rethinking US Election Law
Unskewing the System through Law and Politics
Steven Mulroy

Rethinking Law and Language
The Flagship 'Speech'
Jan M. Broekman

Rethinking the Law of Contract Damages
Victor P. Goldberg

Rethinking Environmental Law
Why Environmental Laws Should Conform to the Laws of Nature
Jan G. Laitos

Rethinking Comparative Law
Simone Glanert, Alexandra Mercescu and Geoffrey Samuel

Rethinking the Regulation of Cryptoassets
Cryptographic Consensus Technology and the New Prospect
Syren Johnstone

Rethinking Law, Regulation, and Technology
Roger Brownsword

Rethinking Law, Regulation, and Technology

Roger Brownsword

Professor of Law, King's College London and Bournemouth University, UK

RETHINKING LAW

Cheltenham, UK • Northampton, MA, USA

© Roger Brownsword 2022

All rights reserved. No part of this publication may be reproduced, stored in a retrieval system or transmitted in any form or by any means, electronic, mechanical or photocopying, recording, or otherwise without the prior permission of the publisher.

Published by
Edward Elgar Publishing Limited
The Lypiatts
15 Lansdown Road
Cheltenham
Glos GL50 2JA
UK

Edward Elgar Publishing, Inc.
William Pratt House
9 Dewey Court
Northampton
Massachusetts 01060
USA

A catalogue record for this book
is available from the British Library

Library of Congress Control Number: 2022931124

This book is available electronically in the **Elgar**online
Law subject collection
http://dx.doi.org/10.4337/9781800886476

Printed on elemental chlorine free (ECF)
recycled paper containing 30% Post-Consumer Waste

ISBN 978 1 80088 646 9 (cased)
ISBN 978 1 80088 647 6 (eBook)

Printed and bound in the USA

Contents

Preface		vii
1	Introduction to Rethinking Law, Regulation, and Technology	1
PART I	**RETHINKING LAW, REGULATION, AND TECHNOLOGY**	
2	Rethinking law, rethinking regulation, and rethinking technology	23
3	The new landscape of law, regulation, and governance	42
PART II	**RETHINKING LEGALITY, THE RULE OF LAW, AND LEGITIMACY**	
4	Rethinking legality	57
5	Rethinking the rule of law	72
6	Rethinking legitimacy	90
PART III	**RETHINKING LAW AND REGULATION IN PRACTICE—LAWTECH, REGTECH, AND TECHNOLOGICAL MANAGEMENT**	
7	Rethinking legal and regulatory practice and the provision of legal services	104
8	Rethinking disputes and dispute resolution	118
9	Rethinking crime, control, and channelling	138
PART IV	**RETHINKING LEGAL AND REGULATORY INSTITUTIONS**	
10	Rethinking national legal and regulatory institutions	162
11	Rethinking international legal and regulatory institutions	180

PART V	**RETHINKING THE INSTITUTION OF LAW, AUTHORITY, AND RESPECT**	
12	Rethinking the authority of law	194
13	Rethinking respect for law	201
PART VI	**RETHINKING THE LAW SCHOOL**	
14	Teaching law	218
15	Researching law	241
16	Concluding remarks	252
Index		254

Preface

Once upon a time—that is to say, when I was an undergraduate law student in the 1960s—there was a serious problem with pressure on law library resources. Both books and seats were in short supply for an expanding population of undergraduate law students.

At the London School of Economics, where I was an undergraduate, law students followed a common programme of study through their first two years. For the student cohorts of that era, the most serious pressure point was in relation to accessing the prescribed law review reading for upcoming weekly tutorials. Imagine the best part of 100 students all wanting to read a couple of articles in, say, the *Criminal Law Review*. Students resorted to self-help: enterprising students were able to find what they wanted in other law libraries; but, the pressure on the law reviews encouraged some practices that were less than model.

In retrospect, I assume that law librarians were caught on the hop by a burgeoning population of law students whose need was for a teaching resource rather than a library set up for use by researchers and the occasional practitioner visitors. One response might have been to introduce new rules (for example, to require books to be reshelved at their correct location on the library shelves) and to increase penalties for non-compliance; but, in practice, I doubt that they would have made a great deal of difference. Another kind of response might have been to improve the practical options available to students—for example, by subscribing to more than one set of the journals that were most in demand. In other words, the response might have focused on changing the 'normative coding' (the rules, the ethics, and the etiquette governing how students ought to conduct themselves in the law library) or on smarter management of the practical options (governing what students could actually do in the law library). Over time, the latter was to prove the more effective approach.

The first significant improvement came when law libraries took the teaching stock out of the main collection and put it in protected short loan collections. This eased the pressure somewhat. Law librarians, we might say, recognising that the old-school practical arrangements were not fit for purpose, took a more 'regulatory' approach.

Thus far, technology does not figure in this story. Indeed, technology was no part of any story in the law schools of that time. Law schools and the law curriculum were largely technology-free zones. However, technology can play

vii

a key role in the management of practical options: by adding to, subtracting from, or modifying the available options; and by minimising the harm or damage that might be caused by the exercise of whatever options are available. From here on, the story is about technologies that added to the practical options of law students.

An important step to easing the pressure came with the arrival of photocopying machines. To be sure, this was far from a complete answer. Seats in the law libraries were still in short supply but at least students could make their own copies of the key reading. They duly responded with gusto, copying material on an industrial scale, leading to long queues and delays at the machines. Predictably, at staff–student meetings, one of the standard agenda items was the call for more photocopying machines.

Initially, the development of electronic databases did not improve the situation; access was limited to a handful of library staff. However, with the digitisation of the stock, the world was to change. It no longer mattered how many students were trying to read the same article in the *Criminal Law Review*; the use of materials became, as it is now fashionable to say, 'non-rivalrous'. Moreover, before too long, with laptops and other devices connecting to the materials, students were able to access their reading at any time in pretty much any place. In the end, technology was the solution—the solution to both pressure on books and pressure on library seats.

If technologies can transform the way in which law students study, can they also transform the way that lawyers undertake their practice and, more generally, the way in which legal and regulatory functions are carried out? If so, will the outcomes always be positive? Does everyone live happily ever after? Of course, that would be too much to hope for. Rather, the question for our times is whether we can rethink and re-articulate the relationship between law, regulation, and technology in ways that are by and large beneficial for humanity. My hope is that this book will help lawyers to do just that.

1. Introduction to Rethinking Law, Regulation, and Technology

1.1 INTRODUCTION

There was a time when lawyers and technologists had little or nothing to say to one another. They each took an interest in their own work but not in the work of the other. This is no longer the case. The need to elaborate regulatory frameworks for emerging technologies has given lawyers and technologists a common concern (in ensuring that the regulatory environment is fit for purpose); and, an overlapping interest in 'law, regulation, and technology' has intensified as we come to appreciate the many ways in which new technologies can be applied for legal and regulatory purposes. In a general sense, this book is about a now-critical conversation between lawyers, regulators, and technologists at the heart of which is the question of the role of today's (and tomorrow's) technologies in the governance of our communities.

More specifically, this book is about the 'rethinking' of law, regulation, and technology. In particular, it is about the way in which legal and regulatory thinking does and should engage with technology. To some extent, it is a report of rethinking that has already taken (or is now taking) place; however, it is also a book about the further rethinking that is required. While this book starts with the rethinking of our ideas, it is more than that—it is also about the rethinking of our practices, our attitudes, our values, the design of our institutions, and the philosophy and practice of our law schools.

Imagine that humans thought that their world was both the centre of the universe and that it was flat, these ideas shaping not only how they conceived of their world but also what they did in it. If it were proposed that humans should 'rethink' the nature of the world—perhaps, no longer conceiving of it as flat—this might or might not have much impact on either everyday human thinking, or human practice or action. Life might continue much as before, humans working and sleeping, sitting in the sun with a cooling drink, and enjoying the company of their fellow humans—and, possibly, now feeling somewhat less anxious about the risk of falling off the planet. However, for those who took their rethinking seriously, especially if the rethinking de-centred Earth in the larger picture of the universe, this would be likely to lead to a change

1

in their ideas, their values, and their attitudes, as well as in their practice. It is in this spirit that this book invites a rethink in relation to law, regulation, and technology.

Each of the exercises in the rethinking of law, the rethinking of regulation, and the rethinking of technology can be approached as a discrete process and project: we can focus just on the one thing—on the rethinking of law, on the rethinking of regulation, or on the rethinking of technology. However, whether our particular focus is on law, on regulation, or on technology, our rethinking will have knock-on effects for our understanding of the ways in which law, regulation, and technology relate to one another.

So, how do we think about law, regulation, and technology? Traditionally, law is conceived of in a somewhat narrow and autonomous way. Law is about nation-states and their regimes of governance, about a particular institutional allocation of competence, about rules, and (implicitly but importantly) it is about a *human* enterprise. We can term this the 'Westphalian' view. In national legal systems, it is the decrees and decisions of high-level institutions (legislatures and courts) and the provisions of formal constitutions and codes that are focal; and, beyond this, there is a similar picture of international law, where the law is found in treaties and conventions to which nation-states have signed up as well as in the custom and practice of those states. Moreover, in the common law world, it is the precedents, the application of settled general principles, and the coherence of legal doctrine that occupy legal scholarship.

From this traditional legal standpoint, if any thought at all is given to regulation, it will be understood as being either external to the law or at its periphery; and, as for thinking about the relationship between law and technology, that is simply not on the legal radar—law is for lawyers and technology is for technologists. However, once we break with tradition, conceiving of law in a broader way, its relationship with regulation can be brought more sharply into focus. For example, there can be some rethinking about the distinction between principles-based and policy-focused reasoning, about the relationship between law and politics, and about the legitimacy of legal and regulatory measures. Technology, however, is still off the map.

If we are to bring technology onto the map, and if we are to triangulate law, regulation, and technology, there needs to be a quantum leap in our thinking. What is most likely to prompt that leap is the conjunction of two thoughts: first, there is the thought that the common function of both law and regulation is, as Lon Fuller famously put it, to 'subject human conduct to the governance of rules';[1] and, second, there is the thought that modern technologies offer tools that may be used to support such governance. If this does not suffice to

---

[1] Lon L. Fuller, *The Morality of Law* (New Haven: Yale University Press, 1969).

Introduction to rethinking law, regulation, and technology

stimulate our imagination, our thinking can be given a further jolt when we appreciate that some of these technologies foreshadow governance, not by rules, but by smart machines. Once we so appreciate that technology might become a major partner or even competitor to law and regulation, it will be understood why the need for rethinking is a matter of some urgency.

The book is in six parts, each involving its own exercise in rethinking. First, we undertake the groundwork in rethinking, respectively, law, regulation, and technology, as well as the relationship between (as it is traditionally perceived) law and regulation on the one side and technology on the other. This leads to a sketch of the new landscape of law. Second, given this new landscape, we undertake some fundamental rethinking of legality, the rule of law, and regulatory legitimacy. Third, with technology now a salient feature of a reimagined legal and regulatory landscape, we rethink our performance of legal and regulatory functions—in particular, we rethink how emerging technologies might be employed to guide human conduct, resolve disputes, and monitor and secure compliance. How far do we take automation? How far do we entrust legal and regulatory functions to smart machines? Fourth, we assess whether our institutions, including our traditional legal institutions, are fit to engage with emerging technologies. This assessment focuses first on the institutional design within nation-states and then considers the design of our global institutions. Fifth, in the light of new tools to be employed for legal and regulatory purposes, we rethink the ideas that we traditionally have about the authority of law and about respect for its requirements and decisions (simply because they state 'the law'). While we might question deference to the judgments of the law where this is a recognisably human enterprise, what should we make of submission to the (arguably superior) judgments of machines where humans are no longer central to governance? Finally, we reassess the philosophy and practice of our law schools—that is to say, we rethink what we teach, how we teach, who we teach, and what we research, how we research, and with whom we research.

1.2 RETHINKING LAW, REGULATION, AND TECHNOLOGY

In Part I of the book, we start by rethinking, respectively, law, regulation, and technology. In each case, our rethinking involves 'de-centring' those features that are taken to be focal or characteristic in traditional thinking. In each case, new paradigms (of law, of regulation, and of technology) evolve which, as a set, generate a radically different appreciation of the legal landscape.

1.2.1 Law, Regulation, and Technology De-centred

If law, as traditionally conceived, is to be rethought, it might be one or more of the nation-state, high-level institutions, rules, or humans that is de-centred. Such rethinking has already begun and the process of de-centring law, so conceived, has occurred in more than one way.

Coming from one direction, legal pluralists and transnational lawyers have been responsible for de-centring the traditional Westphalian model of law—a model that treats national legal systems together with international agreements made by nation-states as central. Without too much difficulty, the pluralists and transnationalists have found orders with law-like features in many other places, both within and beyond national law.[2] Coming from a quite different direction, commentators on law and technology have amplified our awareness of the significance of non-state rule-makers and dispute-settlers. Much has been made, for example, of the role played by ICANN in the governance of Internet domain names,[3] and, similarly, of governance by online intermediaries.[4] This pincer movement—on the one side, involving the pluralists and transnational lawyers and, on the other, the law and technology scholars—serves to de-centre both the state and its top-level institutions of governance.

More directly, developments in technology have been doubly disruptive. First, they have disrupted the idea that the empire of law is to be found in the courts and judicial application of historic general principles; and, with that, the idea that legal reasoning is all about doctrinal coherence has been de-centred. Then, in a second disruptive moment, technology has challenged the idea that law (even an extended idea of law), with its rules, standards, and principles, is the central instrument of social order.[5] This not only disrupts the idea that rules

---

[2]   See, e.g., Sally E. Merry, 'Legal Pluralism' (1988) 5 *Law and Society Review* 869; Hanneke van Schooten and Jonathan Verschuuren (eds), *International Governance and Law: State Regulation and Non-State Law* (Cheltenham: Edward Elgar, 2008); Roger Brownsword, 'Framers and Problematisers: Getting to Grips with Global Governance' (2010) 1 *Transnational Legal Theory* 287, and *Law, Technology and Society: Reimagining the Regulatory Environment* (Abingdon: Routledge, 2019) pp 20–22.

[3]   See, e.g., A. Michael Froomkin, 'ICANN and the Domain Name System After the "Affirmation of Commitments"', in Ian Brown (ed), *Research Handbook on Governance of the Internet* (Cheltenham: Edward Elgar, 2013) 27; Rolf H. Weber, 'The Legitimacy and Accountability of the Internet's Governing Institutions' in Ian Brown (ed) (n 3) 99; and, Chris Reed and Andrew Murray, *Rethinking the Jurisprudence of Cyberspace* (Cheltenham: Edward Elgar, 2018) Ch 2.

[4]   See, e.g., Natasha Tusikov, *Chokepoints: Global Private Regulation on the Internet* (Oakland: University of California Press, 2017).

[5]   For this thesis of the double disruption of law, see *Law, Technology and Society: Reimagining the Regulatory Environment* (n 2) and 'Law Disrupted, Law Re-imagined, Law Re-invented' (2019) 1 *Technology and Regulation* 10.

Introduction to rethinking law, regulation, and technology 5

are central; it introduces the prospect of technological governance which then de-centres humans.

Turning to regulation—understood as the channelling, directing, or guiding of human conduct, the monitoring of compliance, and the correction of non-compliance[6]—it is already recognised that governance by rules can be found beyond the nation-state.[7] Traditionally, the focal concern of regulatory thinking is the effective implementation of economic policy and the correction of market failure. This is the paradigmatic feature that has been de-centred by technology. In particular, the focus on questions of efficiency, economy, and effectiveness has been disrupted by technologies, especially by biotechnologies, that call into question the legitimacy of regulatory purposes and positions as well as the ability of regulatory measures to stay connected and sustainable as new technologies and new applications come on stream.[8]

As for technology, in regulatory thinking, technological developments first present as a challenge, as a target for regulatory measures. However, a major rethink occurs when technologies then present as potential regulatory tools, to be used in support of rules or even to supplant rules and bear the full regulatory burden—for example, as with digital rights management, and when health and safety standards are incorporated in the design of autonomous vehicles.[9] Here, we have a double de-centring: first, a de-centring of the idea that technologies are objects that need to be regulated rather than tools to be used by regulators; and, second, the de-centring of the role of humans in the legal and regulatory enterprise.

1.2.2 The New Landscape of Law

To repeat, much of the rethinking that is charted in this part of the book has already happened. For example, the idea of transnational law, of law beyond

---

[6] See, e.g., Julia Black, 'What is Regulatory Innovation?' in Julia Black, Martin Lodge, and Mark Thatcher (eds), *Regulatory Innovation* (Cheltenham: Edward Elgar, 2005), 1, at 11 ('regulation' signifies 'the sustained and focused attempt to alter the behaviour of others according to standards or goals with the intention of producing a broadly identified outcome or outcomes, which may involve mechanisms of standard-setting, information-gathering and behaviour-modification').

[7] See, e.g., Julia Black, 'De-centring Regulation: Understanding the Role of Regulation and Self-Regulation in a "Post-Regulatory" World' (2001) 54 *Current Legal Problems* 103.

[8] See, Roger Brownsword, *Rights, Regulation and the Technological Revolution* (Oxford: Oxford University Press, 2008).

[9] Compare Roger Brownsword and Karen Yeung (eds), *Regulating Technologies* (Oxford: Hart, 2008).

the nation-state, is hardly new;[10] and, it is more than 20 years since Lawrence Lessig introduced the idea of code (not text-based rules) as law.[11] However, if we synthesise these individual exercises in de-centring and rethinking, we see a radically different landscape of law. In that landscape, three paradigms (Law 1.0, Law 2.0, and Law 3.0) co-exist. Each paradigm has its own way of engaging with new technologies and its own account of what it is to think like a lawyer.[12]

Stated shortly, if we operate in a Law 1.0 fashion, we will equate 'thinking like a lawyer' with 'applying legal principles to particular fact situations' (to determine what the law is in those situations) and, where novel technologies or their applications are implicated in particular fact situations, we will continue to ask how legal principles and precedents bear on such situations. As Frank Easterbrook famously put it, from a (traditional) legal perspective, computers and software are not particularly salient or significant; for computer enthusiasts to recognise a field of 'cyberlaw' would be as absurd and inappropriate as for horse enthusiasts to recognise the 'law of the horse'; technologies and their applications are simply part of the economic and social context to which legal principles are applied.[13]

By contrast, if we operate in a Law 2.0 fashion, our thinking is more regulatory, more policy-focused. Here, we will equate 'thinking like a lawyer' with 'checking whether the rules of law are fit for purpose and, if not, revising them to render them fit'. In societies where new technologies are increasingly important for manufacture, transport, health, and so on, the regulatory challenge is to support beneficial innovation while also managing unacceptable risks of harm to humans and the environment.

By further contrast, if we operate in a Law 3.0 fashion, although our approach is still regulatory, we will now equate 'thinking like a lawyer' with 'checking whether legal and regulatory purposes might be better served by technical measures rather than by rules or principles'. Technology is viewed as more than part of the context, even a particularly salient part of the context; it is now a tool that can be employed for legal and regulatory purposes. From a Law 3.0 perspective, technology presents as a potential solution to regulatory problems.

---

[10] Philip Jessup's seminal Storrs Lectures on this subject date back to 1956: see Philip C. Jessup, *Transnational Law* (New Haven: Yale University Press, 1956).

[11] Lawrence Lessig, *Code and Other Laws of Cyberspace* (New York: Basic Books, 1999).

[12] As elaborated in Roger Brownsword, *Law 3.0: Rules, Regulation and Technology* (Abingdon: Routledge, 2020).

[13] Frank H. Easterbrook, 'Cyberspace and the Law of the Horse' (1996) *University of Chicago Legal Forum* 207.

Introduction to rethinking law, regulation, and technology 7

Putting this another way, in a world of Law 1.0, lawyers and technologists have little to say to one another; in a world of Law 2.0, they have quite a bit to say to one another, each viewing the other as potentially problematic; and, in a world of Law 3.0, the interaction and conversation is different again as they each view one another as potential partners in achieving their respective objectives.

1.3 RETHINKING LEGALITY, THE RULE OF LAW, AND LEGITIMACY

Having rethought law, regulation, and technology so that we now view the rules of a nation-state's legal system as just one element of the regulatory environment, and having brought technical measures and technologies into that environment, we need to rethink our ideas about legality, the rule of law, and legitimacy. Rethinking these ideas is the task for Part II of the book.

In particular, we need to rethink these ideas alongside three articulations of Law 3.0: first, where technologies are employed to assist governance by rules (governance by rules in conjunction with technical measures); second, where governance is by machines (with humans out of the loop); and, third, where technologies are employed in the management of the practical options that are available to human agents (i.e., the use of 'technological management'). Although governance by the management of practical options does not always involve technologies, where technologies are involved, this might be to add to, subtract from, or modify the practical options that are available or to minimise the harm or damage that might be caused by the exercise of particular options. Generally, in this book, our focus will be on 'technological management' that limits the available practical options to those which are approved by the relevant regulators[14]—for example, by employing appropriate designs of products and places and by automating processes.

1.3.1 Legality

Starting with legality, what should we now make of the well-known procedural 'laundry list' of the kind proposed by Lon Fuller?[15] The Fullerian principles presuppose a system of governance by rules (and they tend to focus on primary

---

[14] See, further, Roger Brownsword, *Law, Technology and Society: Re-imagining the Regulatory Environment* (n 2) 40–42. Compare Ugo Pagallo, *The Laws of Robots* (Dordrecht: Springer, 2013) 183–192, differentiating between environmental, product, and communication design and distinguishing between the design of 'places, products and organisms' (185).

[15] Fuller (n 1).

rules imposing duties on citizens). If we try to apply these principles to technologies that operate in support of the rules, we might be able to extend some of them so that they apply to both the rules and the technological instruments. For example, the principles that the rules should be published, should be clear, and should not be contradictory might be interpreted as requiring that citizens be given a fair warning not only about the rules but also about the use of technological instruments. In this light, regulators should declare where and when surveillance and locating technologies are in operation and, arguably, citizens should be told when they are dealing with a robot rather than a human.

That said, there is only so much that we can derive from the commitment to governance by rules, only so much that is analytically contained within that concept and commitment. Necessarily, the predicates of the legal enterprise (as a human enterprise and as an enterprise of rules) restrict what we can extrapolate from Fullerian thinking. Where governance by rules gives way to governance by machines (without humans) and to technological management (where agents are left only with practical options that are treated as acceptable relative to regulatory policy), it is hard to see what relevance the Fullerian principles of legality now have. Because the risk of citizens not being compliant has been designed out, citizens are no longer being guided by the signals given by rules. Granted, as we have said, there might be a case for requiring that citizens be given a fair warning that they are entering a technologically managed zone, but this is not in order to enable them to comply with rules. If a community insists on there being a fair warning, this is not because it is implicit in governance by technology but because the community specifies this as one of the conditions for acceptable use of this mode of governance.

1.3.2   The Rule of Law

Given that the regulatory environment is now viewed as including technical measures and technologies, given that the latter have been developed and applied by both private and public regulators, and given that the ideal of 'legality' does not in itself do much to constrain or control the drift from governance by rules to governance by technologies, the burden shifts to the rule of law; and a major rethink is called for. To this end, it is proposed that the rule of law should be rethought in the following five ways.

First, the rule of law must be understood as applying to governance and acts in both offline and online environments. An analogue-only rule of law will not do.

Second, the discipline of the rule of law must be applied to both rules and technical measures. Rulers should not be able to bypass the rule of law simply by switching from rules to technical measures.

Introduction to rethinking law, regulation, and technology 9

Third, the rule of law must be applied to both public and private regulators. Not only does exempting private regulators from the discipline of the rule of law give rise to difficult legal questions about whether a party is acting in a public or private regulatory capacity (or carrying out public or private regulatory functions),[16] it makes no sense to exempt private regulators, particularly when they are in the vanguard in developing the key regulatory technologies.

Fourth, the processual and procedural requirements of the rule of law should be applied not only to the new rules that are made but also to the making of those rules (citizens must be given a fair opportunity to participate in deliberative processes). Moreover, these requirements should also apply where there is a material change in the use of technological instruments, or when it is proposed to introduce some element of governance by technology (so that rules and humans are taken out of the loop).

Finally, the substantive authorising provisions of the rule of law must also be brought to bear on the application of new technologies for the performance of legal and regulatory functions.

If we rethink the rule of law in this way, it stretches right across the regulatory environment and it also goes a long way towards assuring the legitimacy of law. However, there is still more work to be done in rethinking legitimacy.

1.3.3   Legitimacy

Because new technologies present novel regulatory opportunities but also, particularly in communities where there is a plurality of preferences and priorities, represent a major challenge for both regulators and their regulatee communities, there needs to be some rethinking of legitimacy.[17] When both humans and prescriptive rules are de-centred by the automation of processes and reliance on smart machines, some significant rethinking is required.

If we build on a reworked understanding of the rule of law, as indicated above, two legitimacy concerns will have been addressed. First, the processual requirements will ensure that those who have conflicting and competing preferences and priorities in relation to some proposed measure will have a fair hearing. There is no guarantee that the ensuing best accommodation of interests will satisfy all parties, but it will at least be defensible. It is not as though the views of some group are being ignored. Second, the substantive provisions in the authorising rules will ensure that the fundamental values of the community

---

[16]   As exemplified in the British case law on whether, for the purposes of the Human Rights Act 1998, a body is a public authority. For discussion, see Roger Brownsword, 'General Considerations' in Michael Furmston (ed), *The Law of Contract* 6th ed (London, LexisNexis, 2017) paras 1.245–1.253.

[17]   Nb the discussion in Reed and Murray (n 3) Chs 7 and 8.

are respected by the rulers. There is nevertheless a further concern which goes deeper and beyond each community. This is the concern that no community should act in ways that might compromise the basic preconditions for human existence, human agency, and human community itself. These preconditions are applicable in all places at all times Accordingly, it is suggested that we should rethink the legitimacy of law and regulation by drawing on the idea of a 'triple licence' (the three elements of which—the global, the community, and the social—become the reference points for legitimacy).[18]

Briefly, where a particular technology or its application meets the terms of this triple licence, it confirms three things. First, the global licence confirms that the technology or its application is compatible with respect for the essential conditions for human social existence—that is, the protective and facilitative conditions that make it possible for humans to co-exist, to construct their own community orders, and to settle their conflicts and disputes. The second element, the community licence, is an assurance that the technology or its application is compatible with the community's own distinctive fundamental values. Finally, the third element, the social licence, confirms both that there has been a process of consultation and deliberation about the technology and its applications (this overlapping with the processual requirements of the rule of law), and that the position taken up by regulators is not unreasonable and is broadly acceptable to members of the community—in other words, as the Legal Services Board has expressed it, that the applications are 'socially acceptable'.[19]

1.4 RETHINKING LAW AND REGULATION IN PRACTICE: LAWTECH, REGTECH, AND TECHNOLOGICAL MANAGEMENT

In Part III, the focus of the book is on how the availability of technological options impacts on the way in which legal services are provided, how legal and regulatory functions are discharged, on the ways in which disputes are pro-

---

[18] This is elaborated in Roger Brownsword, 'Law, Technology, and Society: In a State of Delicate Tension' (2020) XXXVI *Politeia* 137, 26.

[19] See, Legal Services Board, *Striking the Balance: How Legal Services Regulation Can Foster Responsible Technological Innovation* (London, April 2021) esp. at para 4 and paras 91–99.

Introduction to rethinking law, regulation, and technology 11

cessed and prevented, and on how conduct is channelled. The focus, in short, is on LawTech,[20] RegTech,[21] and technological management.[22]

Key questions that are raised by this rethink include how new technologies might be deployed in the provision of legal services (whether the technologies are employed to monitor the providers or to interface with consumers); whether and how smart technologies might be used to minimise and resolve disputes; and, whether and how a more technological approach to the prevention of crime and the control of human conduct might be adopted. To the extent that these questions are about automation and governance by machines, they invite conversations about taking humans out of regulatory loops; and, to the extent that there are proposals to reduce disputes or use technology to prevent wrongdoing in the first place, they invite conversations about human responsibility and autonomy.

Initially, technological tools are deployed incrementally in support of rule-based channelling of human conduct and court-centred handling of disputes. Here, the primary purpose of the technology is to support and streamline traditional practice; the technologies improve the effectiveness of both the rules and the remedies as well as making legal processes more accessible and efficient. However, from this point on, our interest in technological applications becomes more radical. On the one hand, our rethinking focuses on technological management of conduct with a view to the prevention of wrongdoing, conflicts, and disputes (de-centring the idea that law acts only in a corrective mode responding ex post and introducing the idea of ex ante anticipation and prevention); on the other hand, our rethinking focuses on the automation of the provision of legal services and the use of smart machines to perform legal and regulatory functions (in both cases, de-centring humans who are taken out of the loop). While the former seeks to reduce and avoid wrongdoing and disputes per se, the latter seeks to reduce the involvement of humans in our response to wrongdoing and disputes. While the former implies that we would be better off without wrongdoing and disputes, the latter looks

---

[20] In the United Kingdom, the Law Society uses the term 'LawTech' 'to describe technologies that aim to support, supplement or replace traditional methods for delivering legal services, or that improve the way the justice system operates': see https://www.lawsociety.org.uk/en/campaigns/lawtech/guides/what-is-lawtech (last accessed 6 April 2021).

[21] According to the UK Financial Conduct Authority, the term 'RegTech' 'applies to new technologies developed to help overcome regulatory challenges in financial services': see https://www.fca.org.uk/firms/innovation/regtech (last accessed 6 April 2021). However, for our purposes, the term should be understood as applying to the use of technologies for the performance of regulatory functions in all sectors (not simply in financial services).

[22] This term should be understood in the sense indicated in 1.2.2.

to smart machines to make a better job of our ex post response to wrongdoing and disputes.

As is well known, there has already been some considerable rethinking about dispute settlement with court-based adjudication being complemented (and replaced) by less formal arbitration, less adversarial conciliation and mediation, and by various kinds of online dispute resolution systems. These are significant developments: as Ethan Katsh and Orna Rabinovich-Einy remark, 'new forms of resolving and preventing disputes will move us even further away from the idea that the legal system is at the center of the dispute resolution solar system.'[23] Where disputes are higher value, or are more complex, old-style adjudication might still be appropriate. However, in many instances, the plan will be to divert claims into regulated (no-fault) compensation schemes.

LawTech is also being employed for a range of non-contentious legal purposes by both non-professional and professional parties.[24] Moreover, law firms will be pressed to follow the example of their corporate clients by looking for opportunities to automate routine functions—disclosure and due diligence are stock examples—thereby cutting costs.[25]

In the regulatory sector, too, we can expect there to be an increasing investment in applying smart tools to facilitate the performance of a range of functions (particularly relating to monitoring, reporting, and compliance). Already the Financial Conduct Authority is in the vanguard of regulators who are developing and using RegTech; and, we can expect to see other regulators, in sectors other than financial services, following the FCA's lead.[26] Increasingly, LawTech and RegTech will be significant features of the evolving legal landscape.

On the criminal side, although there is a great deal of noise about policing and criminal justice, we can detect elements of rethinking that reflect the regulatory approach of Law 2.0 as well as an embrace of technological instru-

---

[23] Ethan Katsh and Orna Rabinovich-Einy, *Digital Justice* (Oxford: Oxford University Press, 2017) 20.

[24] See Benjamin H. Barton and Stephanos Bibas, *Justice Rebooted* (New York: Encounter Books, 2017) Ch. 8.

[25] See, e.g., Richard Susskind and Daniel Susskind, *The Future of the Professions* (Oxford: Oxford University Press, 2015). See, too, *The Future of Legal Services* (London: the Law Society, 2016) 38, where technology is said to be impacting on legal services in the following ways: enabling suppliers to become more efficient at procedural and commodity work; reducing costs by replacing salaried humans with machine-read or AI systems; creating ideas for new models of firm and process innovation; generating work around cybersecurity, data protection, and new technology laws; and, supporting changes to consumer decision-making and purchasing behaviours.

[26] See https://www.fca.org.uk/firms/innovation/regtech.

ments that is in line with the approach of Law 3.0. For example, in relation to the former, we find a rising tide of 'regulatory' crimes to set alongside what, from a Law 1.0 standpoint, seem to be the core, or real, crimes; and, we see a risk management mentality taking shape. In relation to the latter, as new technologies that might assist with the deterrence and detection of crime come on stream, we find new tools being co-opted into the criminal justice system. However, more radical rethinking follows the pattern of civil justice in seeking both to automate the ex post process as well as to apply technological management ex ante with a view to preventing the commission of crimes.

While automation streamlines the process, we might harbour the thought that it would be so much better if crimes were not committed in the first place. This encourages the deployment of technologies in a preventive capacity. Whether or not such deployment works, or has unintended effects, is important; but it is also important to scrutinise the justice of these new preventive measures and to ask whether they conform to the ideals of due process and respect for human rights that we demand in relation to punitive practices.[27] It might be tempting to rethink criminal law and criminal justice as simply an exercise in risk management; but, we should at least pause to ask whether this is the way that we should frame our thinking.[28] Rethinking, as we will from time to time emphasise, is not an unqualified good: it can take us in many directions, not all of which are desirable.

Crucially, in all areas of legal practice, we will need to rethink the relationships between humans and machines—the relationship between consumers of legal services who will interface with machines as well as the relationship between providers and officials who work with machines. We cannot assume that these relationships will be unproblematic. There are likely to be questions about the acceptability to consumers of legal services that are provided by machines rather than by human professionals; and, there are likely to be questions about humans over-relying on their machines (even if the paper rules provide that no decision having legal effects should be made solely by automated machines); and there will be some scepticism about the sensitivity of machines to context and particularity.[29] There is more to rethinking our

---

[27] See, the important critique in Bernard E. Harcourt, *Against Prediction* (Chicago: University of Chicago Press, 2007).

[28] Generally, see Andrew Ashworth and Lucia Zedner, *Preventive Justice* (Oxford: Oxford University Press, 2014); and, specifically on technology, see Deryck Beyleveld and Roger Brownsword, 'Punitive and Preventive Justice in an Era of Profiling, Smart Prediction and Practical Preclusion' (2019) 15 *International Journal of Law in Context* 198.

[29] See, e.g., Christopher Markou and Simon Deakin, '*Ex Machina Lex*: Exploring the Limits of Legal Computability' in Christopher Markou and Simon Deakin (eds), *Is*

1.5 RETHINKING LEGAL AND REGULATORY INSTITUTIONS

In Part IV of the book, we turn to rethinking legal and regulatory institutions. The questions here are specifically about designing institutions that are fit for purpose in their engagement with new technologies, this applying to institutional fitness at all levels, within and beyond nation-states.[30]

Broadly speaking, while more than one design might be fit for purpose, it is suggested that no design will be fit unless it is clear both where the responsibility for engaging with new technologies lies and how that responsibility is to be discharged; and, unless there are mechanisms for developing and disseminating an intelligence about best regulatory and governance practice when dealing with new technologies. Relative to these desiderata, we fall short in the UK. Here, there is neither an institutional hub with the responsibility to monitor technological developments and to gather up the lessons to be taken from regulatory experience with emerging technologies, nor is there a clear understanding about which body or group should act as first responders to emerging technologies. All in all, there is a conspicuous lack of consistency or coordination. If we, or others, get it right, we do not know why; and if we, or others, get it wrong, we do not know why or what lessons we should take from this. No doubt, the UK is not alone in this respect. Indeed, more generally, in Europe, despite engaging with emerging technologies for many decades, the Commission is still looking for authoritative guidance on how to undertake governance of today's emerging technologies.

As an exercise in rethinking our institutional design, let us suppose that a community resolves to do things in a more organised, coordinated, and systematic way. To this end, the community establishes a central intelligent hub whose responsibility is to gather and synthesise all that we learn from our experience of engaging with new technologies as well as to liaise with and coordinate the activities of a set of nodes charged with the lead responsibili-

---

Law Computable? (Oxford: Hart, 2020) 31. Similarly, see Rebecca Crootof, '"Cyborg Justice" and the Risk of Technological-Legal Lock-In' (2019) 119 *Columbia Law Review* 1; and John Morison and Adam Harkens, 'Re-engineering justice? Robot judges, computerised courts and (semi) automated legal decision-making' (2019) 39 *Legal Studies* 618, 619, declaring 'an initial and strong scepticism that the essentially social nature of law can be reproduced by machines, no matter how sophisticated'.

[30] See Roger Brownsword, 'Law Disrupted, Law Re-imagined, Law Re-invented' (n 5).

Introduction to rethinking law, regulation, and technology 15

ties for, respectively: (i) foresight and horizon-scanning; (ii) making the first response to an emerging technology; (iii) making the initial formal intervention (whether a legal and regulatory response or a 'soft law' approach); and (iv) monitoring how the response operates in practice. The community also charges a body with the appropriate auditing responsibilities.

There are many practical questions to be resolved about how such a network would interact with whatever existing bodies and institutions, both public (like legislatures and courts) and civil society, undertake these functions; and, an important part of the rethinking would be to reorientate the courts' (Law 1.0) understanding of 'coherence'. Traditionally, this is about doctrinal coherence, about the integrity of doctrine; but, in the landscape of Law 3.0, a key role for the courts would be to review governance to ensure that the conditions of the triple licence are met where the legality and legitimacy of technologies and their applications are questioned. With a growing use of alternative methods for resolving disputes, the flow of litigation into the courts might slow but there would be important new work in putting the spotlight on the legality of technologies relative to, in particular, the community and social licence.

As we look beyond the design and mission of local institutions, one of the key points in rethinking law, regulation, and technology is that all applications of technology should meet the terms of a (global) commons' licence. The commons is not confined to particular nation-states. Whether in relation to the conditions for human existence[31] or for the enjoyment of human agency,[32] there can be cross-border spill-over effects. Accordingly, if the essential infrastructure for human social existence is to be secured, this implies that there needs to be a considerable degree of international coordination and shared responsibility.[33]

Although the international regulatory architecture is already extensive, regulatory stewardship of the kind that is contemplated requires a distinctive and dedicated approach. It might be, therefore, that we need to have bespoke international laws and new international agencies to take this project forward.[34]

---

[31] See Roger Brownsword, 'Migrants, State Responsibilities, and Human Dignity' (2021) 34 *Ratio Juris* 6.

[32] See, e.g., the critique of our 'information societies' in Shoshana Zuboff, *The Age of Surveillance Capitalism* (London: Profile Books, 2019).

[33] See David A. Wirth, 'Engineering the Climate: Geoengineering as a Challenge to International Governance' (2013) 40 *Boston College Environmental Affairs Law Review* 413, esp. at 430–436.

[34] Compare, e.g., Seth D. Baum and Grant S. Wilson, 'The Ethics of Global Catastrophic Risk from Dual Use Bioengineering' (2013) 4 *Ethics in Biology, Engineering and Medicine* 59; Grant Wilson, 'Minimizing global catastrophic and existential risks from emerging technologies through international law' (2013) 31 *Virginia Environmental Law Journal* 307; and Dennis Pamlin and Stuart Armstrong, 'Twelve

However, rethinking international agencies has to take into account two particular challenges. First, the effectiveness of such agencies tends to be compromised by the self-serving instincts and influence of powerful nation-states; sadly, international relations is not a model of consistent and constructive cooperation. Second, nation-states will be quick to contest the legitimacy of agencies that intrude on what is seen as a matter for the particular community. To the extent that the agency acts as a global hub spreading intelligence about smart governance in the face of emerging technologies, that should be acceptable. However, to charge the agency with the responsibilities of stewardship for the global commons would be a very different matter and it would need to be handled very carefully. In particular, it would be important to emphasise that the stewardship relates only to the global commons, a critical infrastructure in which all humans have a shared interest.

1.6   RETHINKING THE INSTITUTION OF LAW

In Part V of the book, we begin to rethink fundamental questions about the authority of law and about why we should respect the law (just because it is 'the law'). To some degree, the de-centring of the state (as in the pluralist and transnational law literature, as well as in the accompanying practice of governance) makes it problematic to conceive of the authority of law in the traditional way. When orders of rules are overlapping and competing with one another, questions about who to recognise as having authority and about whose law should be respected are provoked.[35] However, what we are facing here is not so much a conflict of laws problem about identifying the applicable legal rules but a challenge to the institution of law itself. Quite simply, why should we respect any rules other than our own?

Traditionally, the case for recognising the authority of law and respecting its rules is made on prudential or moral grounds. The case is either that it is in our interests to defer to law because the alternative (a lawless and disordered Wild West) is worse; or that law aspires to instate a *just* order which, again, is better than the alternatives. However, with the development of cyberspace, some will contend that these arguments miss the point; quite simply, the point is that the relevant and preferable alternative to law (which represents governance by other humans) is self-governance. While this is a head-on challenge to the

---

risks that threaten human civilisation: The case for a new risk category' (Oxford: Global Challenges Foundation, 2015) 182 (mooting the possibility of establishing a Global Risk Organisation, initially only with monitoring powers).

[35]   See, e.g., Roger Cotterrell and Maksymilian Del Mar (eds), *Authority in Transnational Legal Theory* (Cheltenham: Edward Elgar, 2016); and, in the context of cyberspace, Chris Reed and Andrew Murray (n 3).

Introduction to rethinking law, regulation, and technology   17

authority of Westphalian Law, it still presupposes that what we should respect are the *rules* of law and governance by *humans*.

The radical shift in our thinking comes when we entertain the prospect of governance by machines and by technological management. Might such technological governance be better than the traditional alternative? Quite rightly, the jury is still out. Nevertheless, if we allow that smart machines and technological management might outperform governance by humans who rely on rules, why should we then recognise the authority of the latter, why should we respect the rules? This prompts a rethink about what it is that we might distinctively value about law as a human rule-based enterprise. If we make the perhaps optimistic assumption that governance by machines will take care of the welfare of humans, why should we value a version of law that performs less well in that respect? Might it be that, rather like the cyberlibertarians, what we value is self-governance (in this case, self-governance by humans rather than governance by machines)?[36] When we insist that the applications of AI should be 'human-centric', is it the promotion of human welfare or the preservation of self-governance that is at issue? When we say that autonomous systems should be 'trustworthy', is it human welfare or human control that is at issue?

We also need to consider the implications of governance by machines if we treat this not as a better-performing model of law, but as a fundamentally different mode of governance. The question then is whether it makes sense to ask whether we should recognise the 'authority' of the machines or 'respect' this mode of governance. Are these questions and concepts predicated on law being a human enterprise that operates through rules? Furthermore, this last question invites a more general rethink about the meaningfulness of a whole raft of concepts associated with law where the context is no longer one of governance by humans who promulgate rules.[37]

So, when we bring technology into our thinking about law and regulation, some familiar questions about the authority of, and respect for, the law are amplified. However, there is more to it than that. Arguably, what we ultimately make of the idea of the authority of law and respect for legal measures will hinge on whether we favour a mode of governance that maintains the central role for humans, that allows for both the best expressions of humanity but also

---

[36]   We might note a certain irony in this train of thinking. Cybertechnologies prompt a rebellious human instinct of self-governance, an instinct that we find antithetical to the sovereignty of nation-states and the rule of law. However, as cyber and other technologies subsequently encroach on governance by humans, that rebellious instinct becomes our last stand against the machines.

[37]   Compare the general thesis in Alasdair MacIntyre, *After Virtue* (London: Duckworth, 1981). Concepts that are meaningful in a particular context might lose their meaning (even though the linguistic references remain) once that context has changed.

the worst, or a mode of governance that relies on technological management at the front end to reduce the incidence of those worst expressions of humanity and expert machines at the back end to do better than humans in responding to such expressions.

1.7   RETHINKING THE LAW SCHOOL

In the final part (Part VI) of the book, we re-assess both the teaching and research philosophies and practices of our law schools in the United Kingdom. Given the rather different philosophies and practices in other parts of the world, the rethinking sketched here might not be applicable in all places. Nevertheless, and bearing in mind the current interest in 'digital law', some elements of the rethinking of how and what we teach and of what we research are surely applicable beyond our island.[38]

Starting with how we teach, the obvious thought is that consumers of legal education, just like users of dispute-resolution services, will value convenience, efficiency, and expertise. Accordingly, taking our lead from online dispute resolution, we can imagine technologically enabled legal education being delivered in ways that mean that students do not need to be in a particular physical place at a particular time, that they do not need to have access to hard-copy collections of source material in bricks-and-mortar law libraries, and that they can be instructed in virtual environments or by AI-enabled avatars, and so on. Indeed, following the recent experience of the university law schools in maintaining their programmes through Covid-19, this is all very easy to imagine. This is not to say that humans will play no role as legal educators, but, in all likelihood, the extent of their involvement will turn on students' willingness to pay for whatever added value the human touch is thought to have.

The curriculum, too, will be fundamentally rethought. We can take it that the curriculum will continue to reflect the law school mission to teach students 'to think like a lawyer'. However, what the law schools currently teach in their undergraduate programmes is largely from the Law 1.0 playbook and, correspondingly, reflects the Law 1.0 vision of what it is to think like a lawyer. Such a narrow vision does not do justice to the breadth and variety of the legal

---

[38]   To give just one example: in July 2021, the annual Conclave held by the School of Law at the BML Munjal University, India, was designed precisely to bring together members of academia and industry to discuss the need for teaching law from the perspective of technology and to suggest relevant changes to be made to the law curriculum. See, https://www.facebook.com/BMLMunjalUniversity/videos/the-law-conclave -2021-adapting-legal-education-to-digital-reality/326448019103239/?trk=public_post -content_share-embed-video_share-article_title (last accessed 1 July 2021).

landscape. The full sweep of the Law 3.0 landscape should be represented in the law programme, each mode of legal engagement with new technologies reflecting a different conception of what it is to think like a lawyer and, as a set, pointing to the need for lawyers to be fluent in more than one of the conversational languages and logics.[39]

As for legal scholarship, this is still dominated by Law 1.0 commentaries and analysis; and, while a more 'contextual' approach does take researchers into Law 2.0 and even Law 3.0 questions, we need a new research focus and agenda.[40] There is no shortage of questions. Pretty much every chapter in this book already suggests several lines of inquiry—about the relationship and interaction between Law 1.0, Law 2.0, and Law 3.0; about legality, the rule of law and legitimacy; about the 'triple licence' and 'new coherentism'; about how to bring technology to bear on the law jobs (about LawTech and RegTech); about institutional designs and missions; and about recognising the authority of, and respect for, the law. Arguably, it is implicit in several of these lines of inquiry that there is a need for new kinds of cross-disciplinary research collaborations. At all events, lawyers, it will be suggested, need to shake off their conservative instincts and recognise the urgency of engaging with such questions. Our legal futures are uncertain, but if rules are to be pushed into the background, if humans are to be de-centred, and if technology is to be in the foreground, our research needs to be critically engaged with these radical developments.

Of course, the de-centring of humans and rules might indicate a quite different future for the law schools. If governance is taken over by smart machines and technological management, society might need technicians more than it needs lawyers; to the extent that law survives as a university programme, it might find itself subsumed within the history department or as a niche interest in the technology departments. However, if the law schools are able to engage critically with the changing modalities of governance in our increasingly technological societies, they could become important hubs for the intellectual and practical life of their communities.

Stated shortly, the challenge for our law schools is to think outside the box of Law 1.0—and, to do so in both their teaching programmes and in their research. This will not be easy, but the opportunities for those law schools that can break free of their doctrinal chains will be enormous.

---

[39]   Compare Joshua A.T. Fairfield, *Runaway Technology* (New York: Cambridge University Press, 2021).

[40]   Compare Roger Brownsword and Han Somsen, 'Law, Innovation and Technology: Fast Forward to 2021' (2021) 13 *Law, Innovation and Technology* 1.

1.8 CONCLUDING REMARKS

After thousands of years of gradual technological development, technological innovation and application has gone into a different gear. The acceleration in technological development has disrupted societies, required considerable human adjustment, and brought with it a mixed bag of benefits and harms. Whether, as lawyers, we are technophiles or technophobes, we need to rethink law, regulation, and technology. Above all, we need to rethink the legal landscape and the regulatory environment in a way that reflects governance by an assemblage of laws, regulations, and technological measures.

Having engaged in this initial act of rethinking, a number of other major exercises in rethinking follow on. We need to rethink 'legality'; we have flagged up a five-pronged rethink of the rule of law; and we have also signalled that our thinking about legitimacy needs to be overhauled so that the depth of regulatory responsibilities (particularly responsibilities for, and risks in relation to, the global commons) is taken fully into account.

The transformation of legal and regulatory practice, aided and abetted by new technological tools, is already under way. Our rethinking of law, regulation, and technology will need to stay not only connected but also critically connected to the evolving landscape of LawTech and RegTech. Sadly, our legal and regulatory preparedness for emerging technologies is hopelessly inadequate, whether we assess it nationally, regionally, or internationally; and a radical reboot of our institutions is called for.

Further, if we do not already question the reasons that we might have for recognising the authority of law and for respecting it as an institution, the movement towards governance by machines and technological management will surely prompt a rethink about our attitude towards the law. Why should we respect machines that simply say 'no'? Why should we accept that our practical options have been foreclosed by technological management? How far are we prepared to see humans being de-centred from the legal and regulatory enterprise?

Finally, our rethinking of law, regulation, and technology points to some major changes in the philosophy and practice of our law schools. The philosophy of the law school, both in its teaching and research, needs to be aligned with the landscape of Law 3.0, and teaching practice needs to take advantage of the technological tools that are available to deliver more affordable, more convenient, more efficient, and more expert teaching.

In this book, the process of rethinking some very traditional and resilient ideas has begun. To some extent, we are catching up with events; but we also need to be thinking ahead. Technological development is unlikely to stop any time soon. Our tendency to default to technological solutions will intensify.

What we begin to see with both LawTech and RegTech is surely just the beginning. Rethinking law, regulation, and technology will not end with the last page of this book; this will be a continuing process of work in progress as communities decide whether, and, if so, how far, they are ready to rethink law and regulation as essentially human (human-centric) enterprises in favour of governance that is guided (on the most favourable assumption) by the best interests of humanity but which is left to technology. Do we want governance by humans or governance for humans? Or less starkly, when do we want governance by humans, when will we accept governance by humans who are working with smart machines, and when (if ever) will it be appropriate to leave governance to smart machines and technological management?

PART I

Rethinking law, regulation, and technology

2. Rethinking law, rethinking regulation, and rethinking technology

2.1 INTRODUCTION

In this chapter, and in this part of the book, we will focus on rethinking our understanding of law, regulation, and technology. The emphasis here is on our conceptual thinking, on our idea of law, of regulation, and of technology (and the relationships between them). It will be in subsequent parts that our rethinking will be more practical.

How should we set about 'rethinking' some matter of interest—some discipline, some practice, some project? Where do we start? In principle, we might start by rethinking the 'field' of our interest or inquiry; or, it might be that our thoughts turn to the way that we 'frame' our thinking within that field; or, it might be that it is neither the field nor the framing that we rethink so much as the particular 'focus' of our reflections. While the field signals no more than the general orientation of our interest, the framing of our inquiries is more particular and the focus is, of course, relatively specific.

Suppose, for example, that our interest is in 'medicine', and let us suppose that we confine our interest to the various preventive, diagnostic, and therapeutic activities and practices associated with doctors and nurses, hospitals and clinics. This represents, so to speak, our 'field' of interest and inquiry. It specifies for ourselves and indicates to others the kind of thing (the 'ball park') for our interest and inquiry. However, it might be suggested that the field so specified is too narrow and that we should rethink it. The argument might be that, if we broaden the field, we will be able to think about 'alternative' and 'traditional' medicine alongside modern mainstream medicine as well as procedures or drugs that are designed to be purely cosmetic or enhancing rather than therapeutic. Or, of course, it might be suggested that our field of interest should be broadened to 'health' more generally.[1]

---

[1]   Compare, Roger Brownsword, 'Health Law: New Field, New Frame, New Focus' in Jean McHale and Atina Krajewska (eds), *Reimagining Health Law* (Cheltenham: Elgar, 2022) (forthcoming).

23

That said, it might not be the field so much as our framing that is the object of the invitation to rethink medicine. Let us suppose that the way that we frame our thinking about medicine follows pretty closely the organisation of health care (primary and secondary) and of hospitals (with different departments for accident and emergency, cardiology, general surgery, paediatrics, and so on). There are many ways in which this might be rethought. For example, it might be suggested that our picture of medicine would be sharper if our framing started with the distinction between publicly funded and privately funded medical services, or between acute and chronic care, or between low-tech medicine and high-tech medicine, and so on. Having rethought our framing, we might find that new questions are highlighted and that this then leads to a change in our focus. For instance, if we frame our thinking in terms of low-tech and high-tech medicine, we might be drawn to focus on and to explore the ways in which the introduction of new technologies transforms the relationships between health care workers as well as between doctors and patients.[2]

Accordingly, as we discuss the rethinking of law, regulation, and technology, and then the relationship between law, regulation, and technology, it might be that we are rethinking the 'field' for our inquiries, or the way in which we 'frame' our inquiries, or the particular 'focus' for such inquiries.[3]

Of course, any exercise in rethinking presupposes that there is already some way of thinking about the matter in question. Let us call this our 'baseline' way of thinking; and, let us allow that such a way of thinking might be anything between intensely reflective and wholly unreflective, embedded in tradition or newly forged, sophisticated or simple, and so on. So, in what follows, we can start by outlining the characteristics of what we take to be the baseline way of thinking about, respectively, law, regulation, and technology, and then explore how we might rethink the respective fields, frames, or foci of our thinking.

---

[2] Compare, e.g., Robert Wachter, *The Digital Doctor: Hope, Hype and Harm at the Dawn of Medicine's Computer Age* (New York: McGraw-Hill Professional, 2015).

[3] See, Roger Brownsword, 'Field, Frame and Focus: Methodological Issues in the New Legal World' in Rob van Gestel, Hans Micklitz, and Ed Rubin (eds), *Rethinking Legal Scholarship* (Cambridge: Cambridge University Press, 2016) 112, and Roger Brownsword, Eloise Scotford, and Karen Yeung, 'Law, Regulation and Technology: the Field, Frame, and Focal Questions' in Roger Brownsword, Eloise Scotford, and Karen Yeung (eds), *The Oxford Handbook of Law, Regulation and Technology* (Oxford: Oxford University Press, 2017) 3.

2.2 BASELINE THINKING ABOUT LAW, REGULATION, AND TECHNOLOGY

To start with law, we can take the baseline thinking to be represented by the so-called Westphalian model, according to which we find law primarily in nation-state constitutions and codes, in the operations of legislatures and high-level courts, and in the formal agreements made between nation-states. Such is the baseline field for our legal inquiries.

Given this field of law, there are many ways in which lawyers might then frame their thinking. For example, in a famous generic framing, HLA Hart proposes that we should think of law as a practice (a legal system) that is structured by rules—by primary rules that are directed at citizens (imposing duties and conferring powers) and by secondary rules that empower legal officials to make the primary rules and to adjudicate disputes, all this being unified by a master rule of recognition specifying the approved sources of law in the system and providing the ultimate test of the legal validity of a particular rule.[4] However, for many lawyers, their framing will be guided by their more specific cognitive interests—for example, those with an interest in comparative law might frame law in a way that draws on a particular way of classifying different 'families' of law, and those with an interest in, say, the law relating to transactions might frame their interest by differentiating between public and private law, and possibly contract law, restitution and tort law.

As for the focus of interest and inquiry, whether at the level of particular areas of law (such as criminal law, public law, private law, and so on) or particular issues within an area of law, there are any number of possibilities within this field. As the many law reviews attest, contributors find a myriad of legal topics about which to write. For example, those who have an interest in contract law might (as they did at one time in the last century) become intensely focused on questions arising from the use of standard form contracts and various kinds of exclusionary or limitation clauses; or, they might focus, as many do nowadays, on the tension between textual and contextual approaches to the interpretation of commercial contracts, or the implication of obligations of good faith and fair dealing.[5] That said, from an almost infinite number of possible foci, baseline thinking about law does not take any interest at all in technology. Even for lawyers who, in a progressive way, want to locate their doctrinal thinking within a larger economic and social context, technology is simply not in the picture in any material way.

---

4   HLA Hart, *The Concept of Law* (Oxford: Clarendon Press, 1961).
5   See, e.g., Roger Brownsword (ed), *Smith and Thomas: A Casebook on Contract* 14th ed (London: Sweet and Maxwell, 2021) Chapter 28 ('Contract Law 2021').

Turning to regulation, as Christel Koop and Martin Lodge have demonstrated in their survey of the literature, it is not easy to formulate a baseline concept.[6] Usage of the key terms ('regulation', 'regulatory', and so on) cannot be neatly captured in a shared concept. For many, the starting point is Philip Selznick's notion of regulation as the 'sustained and focused control exercised by a public agency over activities that are valued by the community'.[7] However, while this can be related quite readily to the kind of oversight, control, and intentional intervention exercised by so-called regulatory agencies over domains such as the environment, or food and drugs, or the utilities, it invites further elaboration. This might be supplied by Julia Black's much-cited view of regulation as 'the sustained and focused attempt to alter the behaviour of others according to defined standards and purposes with the intention of producing a broadly identified outcome or outcomes, which may involve mechanisms of standard-setting, information gathering and behaviour modification'.[8] From what is a relatively heterogeneous usage of the idea, let us suppose that the baseline thinking about regulation is that it is about the public channelling of conduct, designed to advance some valued purpose, and involving standard-setting, monitoring for compliance, and responding to deviance (directing, detecting, and correcting).

If this is the field of regulation, a fairly natural framing will feature some broad distinctions between the kinds of strategies employed by regulators to achieve their purposes. For example, the headline distinctions in the framing might be between measures that aim to disincentivise certain conduct or that incentivise regulatees, or between command-and-control coercive approaches and approaches that seek to develop a cooperative relationship with regulatees, or between responsive and non-responsive enforcement, or between risk-based and non-risk-based approaches, and so on. Given this kind of framing, there are a number of potential foci, but they are nearly all concerned with ascertaining 'what works', that is to say, with the effectiveness of particular regulatory approaches in delivering on their purposes. In practice, there are all sorts of ways in which regulatory interventions might fall short, being less than fully effective and, indeed, manifestly counterproductive. The reasons for this are manifold, ranging from the corruption, capture, (lack of) competence, and (limited) capability of regulatory agencies and agents to the resistance pre-

---

[6]   Christel Koop and Martin Lodge, 'What is Regulation? An Interdisciplinary Concept Analysis' (2017) 11 *Regulation and Governance* 95.

[7]   Philip Selznick, 'Focusing Organizational Research on Regulation' in Roger Noll (ed), *Regulatory Policy and the Social Sciences* (Berkeley: University of California Press, 1985) 363, at 383.

[8]   Julia Black, 'Critical Reflections on Regulation' (2002) 27 *Australian Journal of Legal Philosophy* 1, at 26.

sented by regulatees and cultures of (non or token) compliance. Following one regulatory failure after another, one crisis or scandal after another, there is an open invitation to regulatory theorists to join the post-mortem.

So much for the baseline thinking in relation to law and in relation to regulation. What should we take to be the baseline thinking about technology? Here, we should differentiate between the following three questions:

(i)   What is the baseline view of technology within technological disciplines?
(ii) What is the baseline view of technology within traditional unreconstructed legal thinking?
(iii) What should count as technology from the perspective of law and regulation as rethought?

We will not attempt to answer the first question because we are not proposing that technologists should revise their thinking.[9]

We can make short shrift of the second question because the baseline position for lawyers and regulatory scholars is that technology (however specified) is not of any particular relevance to their interests and inquiries. To be sure, some lawyers, such as patent lawyers, might benefit from having a technical background because they need to have an understanding about the workings of the products or processes that are put forward for patenting; and, lawyers who work in regulatory agencies where an understanding of technical matters is relevant might also be sensitive to the technological state of the art. However, for present purposes, we can proceed on the basis that the baseline view is that technology, even if some part of the context for the operation of law and regulation, is not something about which lawyers or regulators need to have a view or spend time thinking about.

The third question is more difficult. Within legal and regulatory thinking that now recognises the potential relevance of technology, it is unclear what precisely lies within the field of interest.[10] No doubt, few would dissent from the proposition that we are thinking about 'tools' and 'instruments', about 'machines' and 'equipment', about 'methods' and 'techniques' which, in various ways, we find helpful in achieving our objectives. Technologies are

---

9   But, for the relatively recent history of the concept, see Leo Marx, 'Technology: The Emergence of a Hazardous Concept' (2010) 51 *Technology and Culture* 561.

10   Compare, Roger Brownsword, Eloise Scotford, and Karen Yeung (n 3) at 6, where 'technology' is taken as covering 'those entities and processes, both material and immaterial, which are created by the application of mental and/or physical effort in order to achieve some value or evolution in the state of relevant behaviour or practice'. This generic and somewhat abstract stipulation is treated as including 'tools, machines, products or processes that may be used to solve real-world problems or to improve the status quo' (ibid).

means to ends rather than ends in themselves. Conceptually speaking, there is clear water between humans who use such tools and the tools (things) that they use. However, as technologies get 'smarter' (like the devices on which we increasingly rely), even this clear water can become muddy, leading to some uncertainty in our thinking about where technology begins and where it ends.[11]

If the field is specified in this somewhat provisional way, we might frame our thinking about particular tools by placing them in categories such as biotechnologies, information and communication technologies, nanotechnologies, neurotechnologies, additive manufacturing technologies, and so on; and we could imagine many potential foci for our interest across these technologies or in relation to any particular one of them. However, what should and should not count as relevant technology (for the purposes of legal and regulatory inquiries) is a matter to which we will return later in this chapter.[12]

2.3   RETHINKING LAW

If we are to rethink law, we are likely to start by rethinking the baseline view of the field as we have specified it. Taking the Westphalian view, the field of law is restricted to the rules and practices of national legislatures and courts and to international agreements reached between and formalised by nation-states. However, we might wonder whether this specification is too narrow.

2.3.1   The Field

If we are looking for an opening to rethink the field of law, we might start with Lon Fuller's famous specification of the legal enterprise as being that of the subjection of human conduct to the governance of rules.[13] So specified, law is about the making of rules, the enforcement of rules, and the settlement of disputes relative to the rules. In modern societies, the making of legal rules and the settlement of disputes is associated with particular institutions (legislatures and courts) and the practice of law is undertaken by particular professional persons. If we are asked what we are talking about when we say that we are talking about the law, these are the kind of things that we might mention in response. However, while the baseline Westphalian view fits this specifica-

---

[11]   Compare, e.g., Mireille Hildebrandt, *Smart Technologies and the End(s) of Law* (Cheltenham: Edward Elgar, 2015); and Mireille Hildebrandt and Kieron O'Hara (eds), *Life and the Law in the Era of Data-Driven Agency* (Cheltenham: Edward Elgar, 2020).
[12]   See section 2.5 below.
[13]   Lon L. Fuller, *The Morality of Law* (New Haven: Yale University Press, 1969).

Rethinking law, rethinking regulation, and rethinking technology 29

tion, it does not exhaust it—both within and beyond the nation-state, there is a landscape of law to be explored and charted.[14]

First, as Fuller himself recognised, governance by rules can be undertaken at many levels below the commanding heights of the nation-state. This possibility is very clearly expressed by Karl Llewellyn, who, in his well-known 'law-jobs' theory, states that all groups must set out the basic ground rules for the group, agree upon processes for resolving disputes between members of the group, and also agree who shall have authority to make the rules and decide the disputes.[15] In this way, we can recognise that the rules of clubs and associations, or simply the 'house rules', are de facto the law within their limited sphere of application. While such rules and group practices might simply supplement national law, in other cases they might be oppositional (for example, where the group is a drug cartel or the Mafia).

From Eugen Ehrlich's 'living law'[16] found in the customs and practices of provincial Bukowina (then part of the Austro-Hungarian empire) to Robert Ellickson's study of the informal norms of 'neighbourliness' and 'live and let live' recognised by the close-knit group of ranchers and farmers of Shasta County, California,[17] there is a literature that charts the rules that actually guide human conduct—and, in each case, the rules that actually guide the group are not the rules of national law. In this vein, Orly Lobel, in her excellent discussion of the optimal regulatory conditions for innovation, takes into account not only several relevant strands of national law (especially intellectual property law, competition law, and contract law), but also a range of social norms that

---

[14] For a useful map of this landscape, see Marc Hertogh, 'What Is Non-State Law? Mapping the Other Hemisphere of the Legal World' in Hanneke van Schooten and Jonathan Verschuuren (eds), *International Governance and Law: State Regulation and Non-State Law* (Cheltenham: Edward Elgar, 2008) 11. Hertogh's map of non-state law highlights two distinctions: (i) between forms of non-state legal order that exist alongside or in the shadow of state law and those forms that exist entirely independently of state law; and (ii) between 'rules of conduct' (which are actually observed by the relevant persons) and 'norms for decisions' (which are recognised by legal institutions and officials).

[15] Karl N. Llewellyn, 'The Normative, the Legal, and the Law-Jobs: The Problem of Juristic Method' (1940) 49 *Yale Law Journal* 1355.

[16] Eugen Ehrlich, *Fundamental Principles of the Sociology of Law* (New Brunswick: Transaction Publishers, 2001 [1913]).

[17] Robert C. Ellickson, *Order Without Law* (Cambridge, Mass.: Harvard University Press, 1991). Although the rural group is close-knit, there are significant sub-groups— for example, there is a contrast between the 'traditionalists' who let their cattle roam, and the 'modernists' who 'keep their livestock behind fences at all times in order to increase their control over their herds' (at 24).

operate alongside (and interact with) the law.[18] In many spheres of competition and innovation, Lobel points out, it is the foreground social norms which impose informal restraints that are more important than the formal restraints (if any) found in the background laws. Accordingly, if we specify law too narrowly, we will miss out how the subjecting of human conduct to the governance of rules actually works in many sectors and scenarios.

Second, if we limit law to the rules of nation-states and international treaties and covenants, we will miss the many rules that arise from 'transnational' custom and practice or more formal articulation of the relevant rules.[19] Historically, merchants who crossed national borders carried with them codes that applied in marketplaces; and, transnationally, there are many examples of clubs and associations that are in effect like local clubs or associations except that their scaling-up involves going beyond the boundaries of nation-states. In the age of the Internet, we also have striking examples of private rule-making and dispute-settlement (notably at ICANN on domain names) that is not part of national law and which also crosses borders.[20] So, for example, the rules that apply to persons who use social media networks such as Facebook are subject to Silicon Valley 'law' whether they are in California or elsewhere in the United States or beyond the US borders;[21] and, as Natasha Tusikov has highlighted, online intermediaries can, and do, operate as rule-enforcers by denying facilities to those who are identified as rule-breakers, irrespective of their physical location.[22]

While some will already have adjusted their thinking about law so that these additional manifestations of the governance of rules are in their field of interest, others will stick to the traditional narrow field of interest. For them, it is not that they are unaware of the invitation to rethink law, it is that they decline to accept it. For those who decline, it is a worry that the proposed field of law

---

[18]   Orly Lobel, *Talent Wants to Be Free* (New Haven: Yale University Press, 2013). One of the critical variables here is whether regulators take a 'Californian' view of restraint of trade clauses or a 'Massachusetts' view, the former signalling a reluctance to keep employees out of the market, the latter being more supportive of the employer's interest in restraining ex-employees.

[19]   See, e.g., Roger Brownsword, 'Framers and Problematisers: Getting to Grips with Global Governance' (2010) 1 *Transnational Legal Theory* 287, and *Law, Technology and Society: Reimagining the Regulatory Environment* (Abingdon: Routledge, 2019) pp 20–22.

[20]   See, e.g., Chris Reed and Andrew Murray, *Rethinking the Jurisprudence of Cyberspace* (Cheltenham: Edward Elgar, 2018) Ch 2.

[21]   See, e.g., Tomer Shadmy, 'The New Social Contract: Facebook's Community and Our Rights' (2019) 37 *Boston University International Law Journal* 307.

[22]   See, e.g., Natasha Tusikov, *Chokepoints: Global Private Regulation on the Internet* (Oakland: University of California Press, 2017).

becomes over-inclusive, that law is everywhere.[23] Whether these invitations have been accepted or declined, there is yet a further invitation to rethink the field of law.

This further invitation proposes that we should extend our field of interest so that the field of law also includes technical or technological measures that are employed in support of rules or in place of rules that would otherwise be relied on. In this vein, inspiration should be taken from Lawrence Lessig's well-known identification of four regulatory modalities that bear in on the governance of human conduct.[24] Each of these modalities—the rules and standards of the law; social norms; pricing and other market signals; and the coding of hardware and software—and combinations of these modalities can govern human conduct. Although we might want to differentiate between, on the one hand, the coding of hardware and software and, on the other, rules (like rules of law or social norms) that govern human conduct by signalling what ought or ought not to be done, the point here is simply that we might rethink the field of law so that technological instruments are included within our field of interest and inquiry. Indeed, as I have argued in other books, we might rethink law so that our field of interest includes not only rules and standards that prescribe what we ought or ought not to do, but also technologies in a very broad sense (including the architecture of places and spaces, and the design of products and processes) that shape the environments in which humans act and which determine which actions are practically available and which are not.[25]

2.3.2   The Framing

If we rethink the field of law in the ways just indicated, there are two major revisions to the baseline view: first, the inclusion of rules and norms that are sub-national and transnational; and, second, the inclusion of technologies and technical measures. Both these revisions are likely to be reflected in our framing.

First, our framing is likely to reflect the contrast between the characteristics of Westphalian rules and those of less formal rules. So, for example, our framing might contrast formal top–down rules with less formal bottom–up governance, the law-in-the-books with the law-in-action, or with the living

---

[23]   Simon Roberts, 'After Government? On Representing Law Without the State' (2005) 68 MLR 1.

[24]   Lawrence Lessig, *Code and Other Laws of Cyberspace* (New York: Basic Books, 1999).

[25]   See, especially, Roger Brownsword, *Law, Technology and Society—Reimagining the Regulatory Environment* (n 18), and *Law 3.0* (Abingdon: Routledge, 2020).

law; state-centric rules with governance that lies beyond the nation-states; centralised governance with distributed governance, and so on.[26]

Second, given our inclusion of technological measures, our framing will probably contrast normative measures (which speak the language of what ought and ought not to be done) with non-normative technological measures (which guide humans by fixing what can and cannot be done in practice). To repeat, by extending our field of interest, we do not imply that informal rule-based governance is the same as formal rule-based governance or that computer 'code' or codes of law are the same. In fact, quite to the contrary, it is the sense that these are different phenomena that shapes and sharpens the framing of our inquiries in relation to the expanded range of phenomena that are now in our field of interest; and the thought is that we will better understand the similarities and differences between these phenomena if we have them all on our radar.

2.3.3   The Focus

With the field of law revised and extended, none of the baseline foci for inquiry are lost. Legal scholars will continue to ask the questions that they have asked where the baseline view prevails. However, they will now have an agenda of new questions and the focus of 'responsive' legal scholarship will shift towards new lines of inquiry.[27] In particular, questions are likely to be provoked about both the title and authority of those who purport to govern human conduct and the legitimacy of the various measures that they rely on. This is not to say that the baseline view discourages questions being asked about the authority of national governments or about the rules that they prescribe; but, the new questions concern the title and authority of transnational and sub-national private governing bodies as well as the legitimacy of using new technologies and automated processes for the purposes of guiding and governing human conduct.

---

[26]   For example, in the editorial introduction to Hanneke van Schooten and Jonathan Verschuuren (eds) (n 14), the central question is said to be 'To what extent does non-state law currently influence state regulation, and what should be the consequences of non-state law for state regulation?' (at 2).

[27]   Compare, e.g., Roger Brownsword, '3D Printing, Transformative Technologies, and Responsive Legal Scholarship' in Dinusha Mendis, Mark Lemley, and Matthew Rimmer (eds), *3D Printing and Beyond: The Intellectual Property and Legal Implications Surrounding 3D Printing and Emerging Technology* (Cheltenham: Elgar, 2019) 137.

2.4 RETHINKING REGULATION

To the extent that regulatory scholars lack a settled baseline view, the lines of rethinking are less distinct than in the case of traditional legal scholarship.

2.4.1 The Field

Amongst regulatory scholars it seems that resistance is relatively low in relation to the idea that the field of regulatory scholarship should include both public and private regulators and should encompass the use of technological measures.[28] While the former opens the field to self-governance and transnational governance, the latter opens it to architecture, code, design, and so on. Accordingly, we would expect a proposal to reconceive the field of law in terms of a 'regulatory environment' comprising both rules (rules of Westphalian law and other rules) and non-rule regulatory measures to be seen as much less radical if viewed from a regulatory perspective than from the perspective of traditional legal scholarship.[29]

2.4.2 The Framing

The way in which we might reframe our inquiries within a field of regulation so conceived might track the ways in which legal framing might be rethought. For example, the contrast between regulation by rules and techno-regulation might be prominent; and, the contrast between techno-regulation that is initiated by private, as opposed to public, regulators might again be a feature of the reframing. However, for present purposes, a contrast that is of some importance in the evolution of the subject of 'law, regulation, and technology' is that between viewing technology as something to be regulated (as a regulatory target) and as an instrument to be used by regulators (as a regulatory tool). Thus, when Karen Yeung and I chose the title 'Regulating Technologies' for an edited collection on law, regulation, and technology, this signalled that, while one part of the collection was about how to regulate new technologies, the other part was about employing technologies as instruments in the regulatory repertoire.[30]

---

[28] In relation to public and private regulators, compare the analysis in Koop and Lodge (n 6).

[29] See, e.g., the range of measures included in Bronwen Morgan and Karen Yeung, *An Introduction to Law and Regulation: Text and Materials* (Cambridge: Cambridge University Press, 2007).

[30] Roger Brownsword and Karen Yeung (eds), *Regulating Technologies* (Oxford: Hart, 2008).

Where the field is framed in terms of getting the regulatory environment right for emerging technologies, the baseline emphasis would tend to be on economic considerations, on maintaining competitive markets, on consumer welfare, and the like; and, with this emphasis, the framing would tend to highlight questions about regulatory effectiveness, economy, and efficiency. However, much of this can be, and already has been, rethought.[31] The framing is no longer simply of an economic nature and, as technology comes onto the radar (whether as a regulatory target or as a regulatory tool), there are questions that go beyond the effectiveness of regulatory action. For example, there are questions about how best to maintain the connection between emerging technologies and covering regulatory frameworks, about the legitimacy of regulatory positions taken up in relation to controversial technologies or applications, about the legitimacy of the technological tools now being employed by regulators, and of course about the accountability and responsibility of powerful privately managed technological enterprises.

2.4.3   The Focus

Given a rethought, non-economic, framing, any particular emerging technology, any particular domain of application, and any particular application might be the focus of inquiry. For example, Alison McLennan, focusing on the regulation of synthetic biology,[32] frames her inquiry in terms of the 'legitimacy of the regulatory regime, its effectiveness, its "prudence" or response to risk, its "connection" or ability to keep up with the science, and its "cosmopolitanism" or ability to deal with differing values and approaches internationally'.[33] Viewed through this frame, the focus is particularly on the approach of, and the recommendations made by, the US Presidential Commission, which was one of the first to assess the benefits and risks of synthetic biology and how it should be governed.[34] Relative to the various regulatory challenges, McLennan concludes that the Commission under-rated the novelty of synthetic biology and, in consequence, fell short on the prudential criterion in advocating a less precautionary approach than would be appropriate. In short, while the

---

[31]   See, e.g., Tony Prosser, *The Regulatory Enterprise* (Oxford: Oxford University Press, 2010).

[32]   Alison McLennan, *Regulation of Synthetic Biology* (Cheltenham: Edward Elgar, 2018).

[33]   McLennan (n 32) at 7.

[34]   The Presidential Commission for the Study of Bioethical Issues, 'New Directions: The Ethics of Synthetic Biology and Emerging Technologies' (December 2010), available at https://bioethicsarchive.georgetown.edu/pcsbi/sites/default/files/PCSBI -Synthetic-Biology-Report-12.16.10_0.pdf (last accessed 8 February 2021).

Commission's advocacy of responsible stewardship and prudent vigilance 'emphasised what was *similar* about the risk profile of synthetic biology and recombinant DNA technology…the *differences* in the regulatory challenges posed were not explored'.[35]

2.5   RETHINKING TECHNOLOGY

As we have said, there is more than one question concerning the baseline view of technology.[36] However, so long as our interest in technology derives from our legal and regulatory inquiries, we do not need to agonise about this. Quite simply, the unreconstructed baseline view is that technology is of little or no interest or relevance to those whose fields of interest are law and regulation; and the fundamental change in our thinking is that technology—or, if not technology per se, then particular technologies in particular social contexts having particular applications—actually is relevant and needs to be received within the field of interest.

That said, what precisely is it that, in the name of 'technology', we are bringing on to our legal and regulatory radar? If we start with the idea that technology comprises various kinds of tools and techniques that we humans find useful, we could further specify this in ways that are unhelpful because they are either too narrow or too broad. Hence, if we think of technology exclusively in terms of machines and physical equipment, this is likely to be too narrow. Conversely, if we take a much broader view so that technology is conceived of as various kinds of skills or methods or processes that are used to achieve some goal, this threatens to collapse the distinction between the legal enterprise of subjecting human conduct to governance by rules and subjecting it to governance by technology (because rules can be characterised as a method used to achieve a goal). Nevertheless, some might follow Joshua Fairfield in biting this particular bullet.[37] Rejecting the familiar claim that law will not be able to keep up with the rapid pace of technological developments, Fairfield says:

> But the kind of law that can keep up will be something that is barely recognizable to us now as law. Once we shift our frame of reference for thinking about law, we can see something fairly simple. Law can keep up with technology because law *is* technology: social technology, but technology nonetheless.[38]

---

[35]   McLennan (n 32) at 125, emphasis in original; and, see also 350–353.

[36]   See 2.2 above.

[37]   Joshua A.T. Fairfield, *Runaway Technology* (New York: Cambridge University Press, 2021).

[38]   Fairfield (n 37) at 11.

With this framing, we have a contrast between two kinds of technology: law as a social technology conceived of as 'the practical implementation of rules and norms through human social systems'[39] and those technologies that law has problems in keeping up with. If this reframing does not make the desired practical difference,[40] there is another bullet that we might be invited to bite: namely, that we should hand over governance to the machines and give up on our rules and norms.[41]

Arguably, too, we might want to avoid views that lack discrimination, lumping together technologies that are of interest with those that are unremarkable. On what basis, though, are we to classify a technology or tool as one of interest or as one that is unremarkable? One of the stock examples of the latter is the microwave oven; but, if health and safety or environmental concerns came to be voiced about 'over-exposure' to microwave ovens, this unremarkable technology might become a technology of interest. Indeed, even if the concerns were dismissed by the scientific establishment, some consumers and environmentalists might remain unconvinced; in which case, microwave ovens might become a technology that also attracts the interest of some lawyers and regulatory scholars.[42]

Generally speaking, as Lyria Bennett Moses rightly remarks, 'most discussion is in fact confined to technologies that are relatively "new" or evolving.'[43] In the literature, the questions typically concern 'how to regulate nanotechnology, the internet or biotechnology, not how to regulate cars, boilers or building construction',[44] the latter already being subject to regulation and not raising fresh regulatory questions. So, perhaps we should simply accept that, while our rethinking recognises that technology counts, what actually counts

---

[39] Fairfield (n 37) at 13.

[40] Fairfield (n 37) says that we need to focus on law as change, on 'the principles of guiding that change, of managing change and the speed of change, of figuring out how to create communities of people who generate life-giving rules more quickly and responsively to changes in their environment' (p 48). More specifically, Fairfield declares that his interest is 'in viewing law as the discipline of developing social technological tools to help humans coordinate in the face of hard technological change' (ibid.).

[41] Fairfield (n 37) thinks that it is unlikely that we will do this, see his discussion at 45–46.

[42] Compare Adam Burgess, *Cellular Phones, Public Fears, and a Culture of Precaution* (Cambridge: Cambridge University Press, 2004) (concerning the 'risk shadows' associated with concerns, not about microwaves, but mobile phones and cell towers).

[43] Lyria Bennett Moses, 'How to Think About Law, Regulation, and Technology: Problems with "Technology" as a Regulatory Target' (2013) 5 *Law, Innovation and Technology* 1, at 9.

[44] Ibid.

as (significant) technology is relative to our particular interests, and, in practice, our interests (reflecting particular lines of inquiry that we have in mind) tend to home in on new and emerging technologies and their applications.[45] Accordingly, for some legal and regulatory scholars, it might be the challenges that emerging technologies present as regulatory targets that is of interest, whether because of their rapid development, or their widespread adoption, or the contested nature of their utility or compatibility with the community's values; but, for others, it might be those technologies that can be utilised as regulatory instruments that is of interest. In other words, for some scholars, it will be technologies that present regulatory problems that are of interest; but, for others, it will be technologies that offer regulatory solutions that are of interest. Either way, microwaves might or might not be salient; and what is salient will change as technologies emerge and mature.

2.6 THE RELATIONSHIP BETWEEN LAW, REGULATION, AND TECHNOLOGY

Having discussed how we might rethink, respectively, law, regulation, and technology, we turn now to the question of how we might rethink the relationship between law, regulation, and technology. To undertake a comprehensive analysis of this question, we would need to analyse the relationships between law and regulation, between law and technology, and between regulation and technology, and we would need to undertake the analysis from both the side of law and regulation and the side of technology. However, we will discuss only the relationship between, on the one side, law and regulation and, on the other, technology; and we will largely approach the matter from the former side.

The starting point, as we have said, is that we treat law and regulation as one thing and technology as something separate, altogether different, and, crucially, of little or no interest to lawyers and regulatory scholars. However, as emergent technologies have captured the interest of legal and regulatory communities, this picture has changed.

First, we find a number of threads of interest being spun out from particular areas of law and regulation to particular developments in technology. For example, medical lawyers become interested in articulating a new legal framework for the technologies of assisted conception and embryology; environmental lawyers become interested in regulating the research and development as well as the commercial exploitation of genetically modified crops; and intellectual property lawyers become interested in the application of patent

---

[45] Compare Michael Guihot, 'Coherence in Technology Law' (2019) 11 *Law, Innovation and Technology* 311.

law to innovative processes and products in human genetics. Similarly, we find tort lawyers asking questions about the liability rules for harms brought about in novel online environments, contract lawyers taking an interest in the facilitation of e-commerce, and criminal lawyers engaging with 'cybercrime'.

Second, these discrete threads begin to form a tapestry of interests often in a particular stream of technology (such as biotechnologies or nanotechnology), but also there might be a convergence of threads as they come to focus on the application of a particular technological feature (as happened when lawyers coming from different areas of law came together to focus on the implications of developments in human genetics for their particular legal specialities)[46] or they focus on a particular type of application (as is the case with the interest in human enhancement where a variety of technologies might be implicated).[47] In the examples given in the previous paragraph, the first group of threads come together to represent an interest in law, regulation, and biotechnology; and the threads of the second group come together to represent an interest in law, regulation, and information and communication technologies. In short order, these groups are joined by legal and regulatory interests in nanotechnologies, in neurotechnologies, in convergent technologies, and so on. However, we have still not reached the stage at which lawyers and regulatory scholars take a more generic interest in technology and its application.

Third, at much the same time, a thread of interest in criminal justice and a range of new technologies takes shape. This is not an interest in the criminalisation of conduct around new technologies so much as an interest in deploying new technologies for the more effective achievement of crime control. Here, it is the use of DNA profiling, of surveillance and identification technologies (such as CCTV and facial recognition), of geo-locating technologies, and of automated vehicle recognition, and the like, that attracts attention.

Fourth, consolidating these changes to the baseline view, we reach a point where we can say that our thinking about the relationship between law, reg-

---

[46] As with the essays in Roger Brownsword, W.R. Cornish, and Margaret Llewellyn (eds) *Law and Human Genetics: Regulating a Revolution* (Oxford, Hart Publishing, in conjunction with the *Modern Law Review*, 1998).

[47] At the time that the regulation of nanotechnologies was particularly in the spotlight, there was a burst of interest in questions of (nano) human enhancement: see, e.g., Bert Gordijn, 'Converging NBIC Technologies for Improving Human Performance: A Critical Assessment of the Novelty and Prospects of the Project' (2006) 34 *Journal of Law, Medicine and Ethics* 726. However, in principle, the positions taken were relevant regardless of the technology applied for enhancing purposes. See, e.g., John Harris, *Enhancing Evolution* (Princeton: Princeton University Press, 2007); and Michael Sandel, *The Case Against Perfection* (Cambridge, Mass.: Harvard University Press, 2007). Generally, see Roger Brownsword, 'Regulating Human Enhancement: Things Can Only Get Better?' (2009) 1 *Law, Innovation and Technology* 125.

ulation, and technology is that there are two dimensions of technology—one a dimension of challenge, the other a dimension of opportunity—that are of interest to legal and regulatory scholars. The dimension of challenge presents technology as a problem, as an object to be controlled by laws and regulations. One of the challenges here is to figure out how to apply older laws, legal principles, classifications, and templates to these newly emergent technologies; and the other challenge is to articulate regulatory frameworks that are sustainable and appropriate in relation to such technologies. In both cases, the aim is to connect law, old or new, to these technologies.[48] By contrast, the dimension of opportunity presents technology as a potential solution, as a tool to be used for the more effective performance of legal and regulatory functions.[49]

Fifth, this view of law, regulation, and technology is fortified by a stream of new technologies (including additive manufacturing, augmented reality, cloud computing, blockchain, quantum computing, robotics, artificial intelligence, and machine learning) which add further challenges and opportunities for lawyers and regulatory scholars to ponder. Not only that, we might refine our thinking in relation to technologies that are not quite so new. For example, in *Rethinking Cyberlaw*, Jacqueline Lipton argues that 'it is important to move the debate away from questions about *whether* cyberlaw is a distinct field toward what the field actually comprises.'[50] More specifically, Lipton proposes that we should reconceptualise cyberlaw as the 'law of the global intermediated information exchange'.[51] From this it follows that 'the central focus of a reconceptualized cyberlaw field should be on issues involving regulation of information, and on the role of these intermediaries within information exchanges.'[52]

This takes us pretty much to where we are with our current thinking about law, regulation, and technology…but not quite. What we now need to add to this picture is a layer of 'jurisprudential' thinking about what we should make of all this. One set of thoughts and questions here is analogous to the threads of connection that we described above. These are thoughts and questions that are formulated by jurists whose theoretical views about the rule of law,

---

[48] For a sophisticated discussion, see Hin-Yan Liu, Matthias Maas, John Danaher, Luisa Scarcella, Michaela Lexer, and Leonard Van Rompaey, 'Artificial Intelligence and Legal Disruption: A New Model for Analysis' (2020) 12 *Law, Innovation and Technology* 205.

[49] For an extended introduction to both dimensions, see Roger Brownsword and Morag Goodwin, *Law and the Technologies of the Twenty-First Century* (Cambridge: Cambridge University Press, 2012).

[50] Jacqueline Lipton, *Rethinking Cyberlaw* (Cheltenham: Edward Elgar, 2015) at 13.

[51] Ibid., at 70.

[52] Ibid., at 3–4.

the authority of law, respect for the law, and so on, now need to be revisited and re-imagined in a context where technology has a role to play in the performance of legal and regulatory functions. The other set of thoughts and questions derives from the appreciation that technology is not only disruptive of society and economy, but also of law. With this insight, we can look afresh at law and regulation as practices that have been, are, and will continue to be disrupted by technological developments.[53]

Finally, having approached the question from the perspective of lawyers and regulatory scholars, it should be said that there also seems to have been some rethinking on the side of scientists and technologists. Of course, scientists and technologists have long understood that their research and development takes place subject to various legal and regulatory provisions; regulatory compliance has to be taken seriously. However, there might be some movement away from viewing regulation and governance as the (ab extra) imposition of prohibitions or requirements on scientists and technologists to seeing also that regulation can be facilitative and that scientists and technologists can play a key role in setting the terms of governance. In line with this latter approach, scientific and technological communities have often taken the initiative in establishing codes of best practice, promoting the idea of 'responsible innovation',[54] and proposing moratoria and the like in relation to the development of new technologies—for example, as when, in 1975, the relevant research community famously met

---

[53] See, e.g., Roger Brownsword, Law Disrupted, Law Re-imagined, Law Re-invented' (2019) 1 *Technology and Regulation* 10, 'Law, Technology, and Society: Responding to the Disruption, Disconnection, and Displacement of Law' (2020) 121 *Revista Interesse Público* 167–197 (Brazil, in Portuguese, translated by Rodrigo Scopel), and 'Law, Technology, and Society: In a State of Delicate Tension' (2020) XXXVI *Politeia* 137, 26.

[54] On which, see René von Schomberg and Jonathan Hankins (eds), *International Handbook on Responsible Innovation* (Cheltenham: Edward Elgar, 2019). While there are a number of ways of defining or characterising 'responsible innovation', one of the starting points highlighted by von Schomberg and Hankins (in the editorial introduction to the Handbook) is to see it as marking 'the shift from an exclusive focus on the development of technologies and their technological potential, to the outcomes and management of an innovation process with a view to aligning innovation with broadly shared public values and expectations. In the context of responsible innovation, the setting of social objectives takes precedence over the maximisation of the technological potential' (p 19). Or, as Dirk Stemerding has put it, in the context of research and innovation in synthetic biology, the shift from technology assessment to responsible research and innovation is from 'a technological options-orientated approach to a societal objectives-orientated approach as two different modes of sociotechnical integration', see Dirk Stemerding, 'From Technology Assessment to Responsible Research and Innovation in Synthetic Biology' in von Schomberg and Hankins (above) 339, at 351.

at the Asilomar Conference on Recombinant DNA[55] and, again, at the same venue in 2017, when they agreed a set of precautionary guidelines for the use of AI.[56] Moreover, to the extent that lawyers and regulators seek out technical solutions to their problems, the interactions between the legal/regulatory and technological development communities will surely intensify.[57]

2.7   CONCLUDING REMARKS

The Westphalian model of law has exerted a considerable grip on the legal imagination. However, the rethinking of law places it within a larger field of regulation and governance and presents technology as salient for legal and regulatory scholarship. From thinking that regulation is marginal to the law and treating technology as having no particular legal significance, we now come to view regulation as critical and technology as an important feature of the regulatory space, whether as an object to be regulated or as a tool to be applied for regulatory purposes. Moreover, 'law, regulation, and technology' as a field of interest and inquiry now attracts an increasing number of lawyers. Of course, the field and its components continue to evolve; 'law, regulation, and technology' is not the finished article, it is work in progress. Nevertheless, it is possible to sketch the legal landscape as it now looks, and this is our task in the next chapter.

---

[55]   https://en.wikipedia.org/wiki/Asilomar_Conference_on_Recombinant_DNA (last accessed 25 January 2021).

[56]   Available at https://futureoflife.org/ai-principles/ (last accessed 18 March 2019).

[57]   See, further, Part VI (on rethinking legal research).

3. The new landscape of law, regulation, and governance

3.1 INTRODUCTION

To a large extent, the rethinking of (Westphalian) law has already happened. As we have said, neither the idea of transnational law nor that of code as law is new.[1] However, if we synthesise these various individual exercises in de-centring and rethinking, we see a radically different landscape of law. In that landscape, three paradigms (which we will term, respectively, Law 1.0, Law 2.0, and Law 3.0) co-exist. Each paradigm has its own way of engaging with new technologies, each has its own conception of what it is to think like a lawyer, each has its own critical reference points, and each has its own distinctive headline questions.[2]

The distinctive headline question in Law 1.0 is the traditional one of how legal precedents, principles, and concepts apply to a situation in which some technology or its application is implicated. In Law 2.0, the question, as first formulated, is whether the law, represented by historic principles and concepts as well as by legislative schemes, is fit for purpose. This question then becomes whether the regulatory environment in relation to some technology or its application is fit for purpose. In Law 3.0, the question is whether technological or technical measures might prove more fit for regulatory purpose than whatever rules are currently relied on. In other words, the question is whether technology or technical measures might be part of the solution to a regulatory problem—which then generates the question of whether emerging technologies might be employed in ways that improve the performance of legal and regulatory tasks.

To introduce these three ways of legal engagement with new technologies, each with its own distinctive framing and focal questions, we can start with two of the most influential law review articles of all time: Samuel Warren and

---

[1] See section 1.2.2 above.
[2] As elaborated in Roger Brownsword, *Law 3.0: Rules, Regulation and Technology* (Abingdon: Routledge, 2020).

The new landscape of law, regulation, and governance 43

Louis Brandeis' 'The Right to Privacy',[3] and Oliver Wendell Holmes' 'The Path of the Law'.[4]

3.2 THREE PATHS FOR THE LAW

In an article that is particularly well known to lawyers who reflect on the relationship between law and technology, Samuel Warren and Louis Brandeis posed a textbook Law 1.0 question to which they responded by arguing for recognition of a right to privacy.[5] The question, in their own words, was 'whether the existing law affords a principle which can be properly invoked to protect the privacy of the individual; and, if it does, what the nature and extent of such protection is'; and, their response was that, thanks to 'the beautiful capacity for growth which characterizes the common law', such a principle could be found and, moreover, it could be relied on 'to afford the requisite protection, without the interposition of the legislature'.[6] The reason why the question needed to be asked was (as the authors judged it) the unacceptable use of 'mechanical devices' associated with the camera and photography which had led to the 'unauthorized circulation of portraits of private persons'.[7] In some contexts, it was not practical to take photographs without the consent of the parties who would sit for the photographer; here, the interest of the individual in their privacy could be protected either by contract law or by the law of confidentiality. However, because 'the latest advances in photographic art [had] rendered it possible to take pictures surreptitiously',[8] the answer needed to be based in tort law. Even though the unauthorised taking and circulation of photographs did not cause any injury or damage to a person or their property, Warren and Brandeis argued that a right to privacy was already implicit in the general principles of law relating to the protection of the interest in personality and the right to be let alone. The precise way in which the jurisprudence of the privacy right was to be developed would be left to the courts,[9] but the enduring message of the article is that the common law is flexible and has the capacity

---

[3]   Samuel D. Warren and Louis D Brandeis, 'The Right to Privacy' (1890) 5 *Harvard Law Review* 193.

[4]   Oliver Wendell Holmes, 'The Path of the Law' (1897) 10 *Harvard Law Review* 457.

[5]   Samuel D. Warren and Louis D Brandeis (n 3).

[6]   Ibid., at 195.

[7]   Ibid., at 195.

[8]   Ibid., at 211.

[9]   For that multi-pronged development in the jurisprudence, see William L. Prosser. 'Privacy' (1960) 48 *California Law Review* 383.

to be applied in ways that respond appropriately to technological applications that are unacceptable.

A few years after the publication of Warren and Brandeis' article, we have the publication, in the same law review, of Oliver Wendell Holmes' equally famous (or, should we say, notorious) article. Holmes' article is in no sense a response to Warren and Brandeis. It is entirely unrelated; it has nothing to say about privacy; and we might wonder what it has to say about law and technology, because its principal claim to fame is the insistence that we should conceive of the law simply as 'prophecies of what the courts will do in fact'[10]—an insistence that, quite predictably, jurists in the twentieth century lined up to dismiss as absurd.[11] However, readers might equally well wonder what any of this has to do with Holmes' title; and, it is only when we focus on Holmes' critique of the claim that 'the only force at work in the development of the law is logic'[12] that we can link his remarks to path(s) for the law and begin to appreciate the significance of much of what he says for our understanding of the legal landscape.

According to Holmes, there is what we would now term a certain 'path dependency' in the law. Lawyers, reasoning in what we would call a Law 1.0, way, look back at the precedents, sometimes apply principles imaginatively in order to respond to what they see as the justice of the case, but they are not sensitised to the policy implications of their applications of the law or to what ends are served by the law. Thus, speaking of tort law, Holmes says:

> Our law of torts comes from the old days of isolated, ungeneralized wrongs, assaults, slanders, and the like, where the damages might be taken to lie where they fell by legal judgment. But the torts with which our courts are kept busy today are mainly the incidents of certain well known businesses. They are injuries to person or property by railroads, factories, and the like. The liability for them is estimated, and sooner or later goes into the price paid by the public. The public really pays the damages, and the question of liability, if pressed far enough, is really the question of how far it is desirable that the public should insure the safety of those whose work it uses....
>
> I think that the judges themselves have failed adequately to recognize their duty of weighing considerations of social advantage. The duty is inevitable, and the result of the often proclaimed judicial aversion to deal with such considerations is simply to leave the very ground and foundation of judgments inarticulate, and often unconscious....[13]

---

[10]   (n 4), at p. 461.

[11]   See, e.g., William Twining, 'Bad Man Revisited' (1973) 58 *Cornell Law Review* 275.

[12]   (n 4), at p. 465.

[13]   Ibid., at p. 467.

In other words, the context of 'the old days' has changed. In a context of industrialisation and new transport technologies, there are decisions to be made about the collective good and about the distribution of risk and liability. To make decisions which are rational, lawyers need to be clear about what goods or ends are to be pursued and how. Thus, according to Holmes, 'a body of law is more rational and more civilized when every rule it contains is referred articulately and definitely to an end which it subserves, and when the grounds for desiring that end are stated or are ready to be stated in words.'[14]

Such remarks suggest that there is more than one path for the law. One path (akin to Law 1.0) is traditional and historical, largely dogmatic and doctrinal. The other path is more instrumentally rational (akin to Law 2.0). The latter, Holmes wishes, is the path that law will take, ushering in

> a time when the part played by history in the explanation of dogma shall be very small, and instead of ingenious research we shall spend our energy on a study of the ends sought to be attained and the reasons for desiring them…[a time when we have learned] that for everything we have we give up something else, and we are taught to set the advantage we gain against the other advantage we lose, and to know what we are doing when we elect.[15]

So, while Warren and Brandeis celebrate the organic capacity of the common law to find solutions without the 'interposition of the legislature', Holmes anticipates that new technologies will present problems the solution to which will require a quite different mindset and, unless we mandate judges to operate in a more rational and regulatory-instrumental way, there will be a need for the interposition of the legislature.

Not surprisingly, neither Warren and Brandeis, nor Holmes, foresaw that cameras and other technologies of the time might be deployed for regulatory purposes, let alone the possibility of securing privacy 'by design'; and so a further path for the law is not indicated. However, to the extent that Law 3.0 presents communities with a choice between the advantages of governance by rules and the advantages of governance by technology, we can probably take it that it would be Holmes who would be pressing for an open and informed election and who would, quite possibly, be advocating that we should embrace the opportunities presented by technology.[16]

---

[14] Ibid., at p 469.
[15] Ibid., at p 474.
[16] Compare the concluding (uncomplimentary) assessment of Holmes in Mathias Reiman, 'Horrible Holmes' (2002) 100 *Michigan Law Review* 1676, 1689.

3.3 LAW 1.0

In what we can term Law 1.0, the focal question is the one that lawyers traditionally ask when confronted by new technologies or by novel situations. In common law jurisdictions, that question is how the precedents and the historic principles of the law apply to, or fit with, the technology or situation. For example, we might ask how the general principles of tort law apply to defamatory content that is hosted online; or how the principles of contract law might be applied to those platforms in which the relationship between the roles and the responsibilities of the parties are not clear or, again, how those principles might be applied to so-called 'smart contracts'; or we might ask how copyright law maps onto creative works generated by AI or by those who engage in remixing; or we might ask how traditional concepts of property, assignment, and novation map onto transfers of tokenised assets.[17] The list of potential questions is not endless, but it is long and it gets longer with each new technology and its applications.

Often, this kind of question will be asked (and answered) by lawyers who are advising clients on their best reading of the legal position. However, where such questions are referred to courts, the flexibility of the law notwithstanding, there is a tendency towards conservative rulings coupled with no more than incremental development of the law. So, for example, although patent offices were able to adjust their understanding of patentability and disclosure to accommodate new products and processes in biotechnology,[18] the courts were not so quick to recognise body parts, embryos, and gametes as property in order to ground tort claims.[19]

---

[17] For just a handful of examples, see Law Commission of Ontario, 'Defamation Law in the Internet Age' (Final Report, March 2020); Christian Twigg-Flesner, 'The EU's Proposals for Regulating B2B Relationships on Online Platforms—Transparency, Fairness and Beyond' (2018) 7 *Journal of European Consumer and Market Law* 222; Kevin Werbach and Nicolas Cornell, 'Contracts *Ex Machina*' (2017) 67 *Duke Law Journal* 313; Primavera De Filippi and Aaron Wright, *Blockchain and the Law* (Cambridge, Mass.: Harvard University Press, 2018); Saleh Al-Sharieh, 'The intellectual property road to the knowledge economy: remarks on the readiness of the UAE Copyright Act to drive AI innovation' (2021) 13 *Law, Innovation and Technology* 141; Yahong Li, 'The age of remix and copyright law reform' (2020) 12 *Law, Innovation and Technology* 113; David Fox, 'Tokenised Assets in Private Law' paper given at the conference on 'Law, Technology, and Disruption' held at City University Hong Kong, 19–21 March 2021.

[18] Alain Pottage and Brad Sherman, *Figures of Invention: A History of Modern Patent Law* (Oxford: Oxford University Press, 2010).

[19] Leading examples of the reluctance to recognise detached body parts as either a property object or as the property of the source, include *Moore v Regents of University of California* 51 Cal. 3d 120, 793 P.2d 479, 271 Cal. Rptr. 146 (Cal. 1990),

The new landscape of law, regulation, and governance 47

This is not to say that practitioners of Law 1.0 are uncritical of the state of the law. To the contrary, the 'coherence' of the body of legal doctrine is a matter of intense and enduring concern.[20] Contradictions and inconsistencies in the body of doctrine are not to be tolerated; precedents and principles should not simply be ignored; legal doctrine should not be distorted; law should be applied in a way that respects its integrity—all of this being regarded as desirable in itself. Given this culture, there is a good deal of nervousness about stretching legal principles, or creating ad hoc exceptions, in order to accommodate a hard case, all of which merits modern study in its own right.[21] Similarly, at times of rapid economic, social, and technological development, the concern for doctrinal coherence can inhibit major development of the law. While critics will say that the law should move with the times, judges will tend to exercise restraint and be mindful of being accused of assuming an unauthorised legislative role. Accordingly, while the courts will give an answer to the question that is put to them, they do not have either the resources or the mandate for expansive lawmaking or for setting new policies. This means that the burden of responding to questions that invite a serious overhaul of the regulatory environment moves elsewhere.

3.4   LAW 2.0

The paradigmatic question in Law 2.0, the kind of question that regulatory scholars and various kinds of regulatory agencies typically ask, is whether

---

and *Greenberg v Miami Children's Hospital Research Institute* 264 F. Supp. 2d 1064 (S.D. Fla. 2003). For general critique of judicial conservatism in the context of claims arising from the reproductive applications of modern biotechnologies, see Dov Fox, *Birth Rights and Wrongs* (New York: Oxford University Press, 2019). On the other hand, compare Joshua A.T. Fairfield, *Runaway Technology* (New York: Cambridge University Press, 2021) at 54–59, where Fairfield's presentation of judicial development of the old idea of 'trespass' to apply in cyberspaces suggests that traditional legal concepts are flexible enough if only the members of the judiciary are imaginative enough. Compare, too, the thrust of the analysis in Simon Chesterman, *We the Robots? Regulating Artificial Intelligence and the Limits of the* Law (Cambridge: Cambridge University Press, 2021).

[20]   For discussion of coherentist thinking (as per Law 1.0), see Roger Brownsword, *Law, Technology and Society: Re-imagining the Regulatory Environment* (Abingdon: Routledge, 2019) 192–194, and *Law 3.0* (Abingdon: Routledge, 2020) Ch 8.

[21]   For classic studies in the last century, see Benjamin N. Cardozo, *The Nature of the Judicial Process* (New Haven, Yale University Press, 1921) and Karl N. Llewellyn, *The Common Law Tradition* (Boston: Little, Brown and Co., 1960). For commentary linking both books, see C.E. Clark and D.M. Trubek, 'The Creative Role of the Judge: Restraint and Freedom in the Common Law Tradition' (1961) 71 *Yale Law Journal* 255.

existing rules are fit for purpose, whether the rules are effective and appropriate in serving regulatory policies, and whether perhaps new rules are required. In short, the question is whether the regulatory environment is fit for purpose. This is an exercise in setting and serving policy and the reasoning (with its focus on effectiveness) is one of instrumental rationality. In practice, the engagement with this question will be in the political and public arena.

The answers given to the headline questions in Law 2.0 are not constrained in the way that we find in the courts. It is not a matter of finding an answer from within a limited set of materials; there is no pressure for consistency and nor for doctrinal coherence. Regulation can make a fresh start and regulators can develop bespoke responses to particular questions in a way that would offend doctrinal coherentism. So, for example, regulators can adopt any number of absolute or strict liability offences (relating to health and safety, the environment, and so on) that would offend the classical code of criminal law in which it is axiomatic that proof of mens rea is required.[22] Or, if the protection of the investment in databases does not fit well with standard IPRs, a bespoke regulatory regime can be put in place;[23] and, if innovation policy is not well served by limiting patents to *human* inventors (thereby excluding AI invention), the limitation should be removed.[24] In Law 2.0 circles, there is no need to justify a departure from an historic legal principle or classificatory scheme; in Law 2.0, regulators operate with a new brush which, if they so wish, they can use to sweep the law clean.

Although much regulatory discourse is focused on finding what works, modern scholarship in law, regulation, and technology undertakes a much broader critique. It is not simply a matter of regulation being effective in serving its purposes; those purposes and the means employed must be legitimate, and there needs to be a sustainable connection between regulatory interventions and rapidly changing technologies and their applications.[25] It follows that this invites a much more complex critical appraisal of the fitness of the regulatory environment. As Anne Cheung and Rolf Weber rightly remark

---

[22] Seminally, see Francis Sayre, 'Public Welfare Offences' (1933) 33 *Columbia Law Review* 55.

[23] As in Directive 96/9/EC (on the legal protection of databases).

[24] Compare the discussion in Ryan Abbott, *The Reasonable Robot* (Cambridge: Cambridge University Press, 2020) Chs 4 and 5.

[25] See, e.g., Roger Brownsword, *Rights, Regulation and the Technological Revolution* (Oxford: Oxford University Press, 2008); Roger Brownsword, Eloise Scotford, and Karen Yeung (eds), *The Oxford Handbook of Law, Regulation and Technology* (Oxford: Oxford University Press, 2017); Tony Prosser, *The Regulatory Enterprise* (Oxford: Oxford University Press, 2010).

when introducing their collection on the regulation of the rapidly evolving ecosystem of cloud computing services:

> Containing the forces of technology within the existing legal landscape has long constituted an uphill battle. Computer scientists are always one step ahead of the barely imaginable and thinking ahead to the next generation of tools and gadgets that will change the world...Whilst the law does not wish to act so quickly that it stifles innovation, it also does not want to lag so far behind as to be useless.[26]

So, the law needs to make its regulatory moves at the right time; and, even if regulation seems 'to work', there might be questions about the acceptability of the position that has been taken up in relation to a new technology.

With regard to this question of acceptability, the test is whether the regulatory environment strikes the optimal balance between providing regulatory support for beneficial innovation and providing adequate protection against the risks of harm that might be caused by an emerging technology. Recalling Jacqueline Lipton's proposal that cyberlaw should focus on the role of online intermediaries, she frames the regulatory challenge very much in these terms:

> When considering the role of online intermediaries, a careful balance must be struck between the promotion of innovation by these entities and the need to protect existing legal rights (including intellectual property rights, rights to privacy and protection of reputation). The field of cyberlaw must be geared to strike this balance by ensuring that online intermediaries do what is reasonable to prevent cyber-wrongdoing while at the same time avoiding the placement of costly and impossible burdens on these entities that would chill innovative practices.[27]

While not all legal scholars would follow Lipton's proposal for narrowing the field of interest—and, obviously not, where their field of technological interest does not have 'intermediaries' playing the role that they play in online environments—many scholars do focus (just like Lipton) on finding the right balance between over-regulating (and stifling innovation) or under-regulating (and exposing consumers and others to unacceptable risks).[28]

---

[26] Anne S.Y. Cheung and Rolf H. Weber, 'Introduction: A Walk in the Clouds' in Anne S.Y. Cheung and Rolf H. Weber (eds), *Privacy and Legal Issues in Cloud Computing* (Cheltenham: Edward Elgar, 2015) 1, at 2.

[27] Jacqueline Lipton, *Rethinking Cyberlaw* (Cheltenham: Edward Elgar, 2015) at 156.

[28] See, e.g., Roger Brownsword, 'Legal Regulation of Technology: Supporting Innovation, Managing Risk and Respecting Values' in Todd Pittinsky (ed), *Handbook of Science, Technology and Society* (New York: Cambridge University Press, 2019) 109.

50 *Rethinking law, regulation, and technology*

3.5   LAW 3.0

With the emergence of Law 3.0, the questions are whether technical measures might be used in support of the rules relied on to serve regulatory policies, whether technologies might be used to assist those who are undertaking legal and regulatory functions, and whether the technologies and technical measures might actually supplant the rules and the humans who make, administer, and enforce them.[29]

Sometimes, where the technologies at issue have already been developed, the question is whether and how they might be given useful regulatory application. For example, blockchain technology and smart contracts might be considered as a way of supporting the principle of sanctity of contracts (by automating payments), and various kinds of upcoming technologies (such as facial recognition and AI) might be considered as tools to support policies of crime prevention and reduction, security, or immigration control, and the like. At other times, the technologies have not yet been developed but we already have an idea about how they might be given regulatory application. For example, as Jack Stilgoe says of geoengineering: 'The technological sublime of the geoengineering imaginary has had almost no connection with the technological mundanity of everyday engineering. Nevertheless, geoengineering has risen rapidly up scientific and policy agendas, driven by the potency of its promise.'[30] As in all human thinking, our rethinking in Law 3.0 can get ahead of itself.

Beyond such technological support and assistance for governance by rules, there is a vision of governance by machines in which rules are no longer directed at citizens, humans are out of the loop, expert systems do the work, and environments are fully managed by the technology. Typically, in such environments, the intent and effect of 'technological management' is either to design in one or more acceptable actions or to design out those actions that are treated as unacceptable. That said, technological management might also be employed in a less restrictive way to remove the cause of conflict (for example, overcoming scarcity of resources by digitizing materials or by using nanotechnologies).[31]

It is not altogether clear who should respond to the questions that are on the agenda in Law 3.0, nor who should be parties to the conversation. Because

---

[29]   See, e.g., Simon Deakin and Christopher Markou (eds), *Is Law Computable?* (Oxford: Hart, 2020).

[30]   Jack Stilgoe, 'Shared Space and Slow Science in Geoengineering Research' in René von Schomberg and Jonathan Hankins (eds), *International Handbook on Responsible Innovation* (Cheltenham: Edward Elgar, 2019) 259, 260.

[31]   See Chapter 1, 1.3 (for three articulations of Law 3.0).

the technological solutions will often be developed in the private sector, there seems to be a need for a public/private partnership or some form of co-regulation where public bodies set the desired regulatory objectives but leave it to industry to develop the best technological means. However, there also needs to be urgent and intensive public engagement when proposals are made that contemplate humans being taken out of the loops of law and regulation (as with governance by machines) or rules being replaced by technological management. For humans at least, any of this is likely to be a big deal.[32]

Scholars who take an interest in governance by technology will, of course, ask whether it works, whether it is robust and resilient, whether it has unintended negative effects, and the like. However, they will also ask whether it is legitimate.[33] For example, if digital rights management technologies over-reach on their protection of IP rights, this is clearly incompatible with the rule of law;[34] and, similarly, where the criminal justice agencies rely on AI tools to make decisions about where to police or whom to bail or remand in custody, and so on, this needs to be compatible with due process and human rights.[35] Moreover, there are also recurring deeper questions about whether technological measures (that do the regulatory work) change the complexion of the regulatory environment in ways that crowd out human autonomy, human dignity, and moral development.[36]

In short, Law 3.0 offers a wide spectrum of regulatory deployment—with technologies being deployed both in support of rules and in place of rules, to assist human decision-makers and to replace human decision-makers, to interface with both regulatees and with regulators, to support legal officials and to supplant them, and to supervise both regulatees and legal officials, and so on—as a result of which, in various ways, the needle shifts from governance by rules to governance by machines and technological management.[37]

---

[32] See Roger Brownsword, 'Artificial Intelligence and Legal Singularity: The Thin End of the Wedge, the Thick End of the Wedge, and the Rule of Law' in Simon Deakin and Christopher Markou (n 29) 135.

[33] See, e.g., Alain Supiot, *Governance By Numbers* (trans by Saskia Brown) (Oxford: Hart, 2017).

[34] Seminally, see Lawrence Lessig, *Code and Other Laws of Cyberspace* (New York: Basic Books, 1999).

[35] See Roger Brownsword and Alon Harel, 'Law, Liberty and Technology—Criminal Justice in the Context of Smart Machines' (2019) 15 *International Journal of Law in Context* 107.

[36] See, e.g., Roger Brownsword, 'Lost in Translation: Legality, Regulatory Margins, and Technological Management' (2011) 26 *Berkeley Technology Law Journal* 1321.

[37] For interesting case studies, see Alexandra Molitorisova and Pavel Šístek, 'Reimagining Electronic Communications Regulatory Environment with AI: Self-Regulation Embedded in "Techno-Regulation"' (2021) 12 *European Journal of*

3.6 THREE CO-EXISTING CONVERSATIONS

In the new legal landscape, we find three conversations, three modes of engagement. These conversations are discrete and different, but it needs to be emphasised that, at any rate at this stage of the evolution of the regulatory environment, they are co-existent. Law 2.0 might have overtaken Law 1.0, and Law 3.0 might overtake both Law 1.0 and Law 2.0, but neither Law 1.0 nor Law 2.0 has been fully eclipsed. Indeed, far from it: Law 1.0 remains the default conversation for lawyers; and, Law 2.0 is probably the default conversation still in law and technology circles. Moreover, it is in the co-existence of Law 1.0 and Law 2.0 that we can begin to unlock long-standing puzzles about both principles and policies and law and politics. Quite simply, while Law 1.0 sustains the idea that legal reasoning is based on principle rather than policy, and that there is a clear distinction between law and politics, Law 2.0 challenges these notions by highlighting the role of policy in regulatory reasoning (which often is articulated in a legislative form) and by changing the setting to the conspicuously political arenas in which regulation is conducted.

While there might be instances where there is a constructive synergy or complementarity between the three legal conversations, there is no guarantee that they will always be in a state of smooth, unproblematic, and peaceful co-existence.[38] For, the conversations reflect different inputs into the regulatory environment and different modes of governance. Consider, for example, the conversations that might be under way about the governance of new unmanned and autonomous transport technologies, whether vehicles, vessels, or drones.

First, in the Law 1.0 conversation, the questions will be about the application of precedents and legal principles to these new forms of transportation. In some cases, the application might be unproblematic. For example, the cornerstone principles of freedom and sanctity of contract will be applicable to much commercial dealing around these technologies. The allocation of risks and responsibilities will, as usual, be governed by the terms and conditions on which the parties have agreed for the supply, repair, or servicing of such

---

Law and Technology (available at http://ejlt.org/index.php/ejlt/article/view/819/1031) (understanding radio spectrum management as a precursor of technologically managed environments more generally); and Lachlan Robb, Felicity Deane, and Kieran Tranter, 'The Blockchain Conundrum: Humans, Community, Regulation and Chains' (2021) 13 *Law, Innovation and Technology* (forthcoming) (analysing blockchain applications in securing trust and confidence in cross-border supplies of beef).

[38] See, e.g., Karen Yeung, 'Regulation by Blockchain: The Emerging Battle for Supremacy Between the Code of Law and Code as Law' (2019) 82 *Modern Law Review* 207.

vehicles, vessels, or drones. However, there will be more difficult cases such as the application of the principle of fault-based liability where accidents involving these technologies cause death or personal injury, or damage to property. Famously, in the nineteenth century, it was the shortcomings of the traditional legal principles in relation to railway accidents that led to a more regulatory approach being taken.[39] Accordingly, in such cases, it might already be accepted that we have reached the limits of Law 1.0.

Second, in a Law 2.0 conversation, the central questions are about the fitness of the regulatory environment. Given that much of the law on transportation will have been written on the assumption that human operators will be in control of vehicles and vessels, and will have been explicitly addressed to drivers and masters, and the like, there will be questions about how best to reconnect the law to those forms of transport where humans are no longer in control or, in the case of remotely controlled vessels, on board.[40] There will also be questions about the arrangements for compensation where there are accidents involving these new modalities. If fault-based liability has not already been replaced by strict liability or by no-fault compensation schemes, this will surely be an item on the Law 2.0 agenda.[41]

That said, as Mark Chinen has argued, we should not underestimate the influence of 'the paradigm of the blameworthy individual', where responsibility is fixed by reference to culpable individuals.[42] If a Law 2.0 conversation is to avoid being constrained by the predicates of Law 1.0 thinking, we need 'to change the way we understand responsibility or the way we understand the responsible agent'.[43] The problem is that the former is impeded by the thinking that underlies Law 1.0 and the latter involves a quantum change in our thinking even though, as Chinen remarks, autonomous machines might develop to a point at which 'it becomes just as plausible to say that the machine itself is responsible for a harm as it is to say that the responsibility lies with its human owners and users'.[44]

---

[39] See, Roger Brownsword, *Law, Technology and Society* (n 20).

[40] On autonomous road vehicles, see Nynke E. Vellinga, 'Automated driving and its challenges to international traffic law: which way to go?' (2019) 11 *Law, Innovation and Technology* 257; and, on autonomous vessels, see Robert Veal, Michael Tsimplis, and Andrew Serdy, 'The Legal Status and Operation of Unmanned Maritime Vehicles' (2019) 50 *Ocean Development and International Law* 23.

[41] Compare Maurice Schellekens, 'No-fault compensation schemes for self-driving cars' (2018) 10 *Law, Innovation and Technology* 314; and Abbott (n 24) Ch. 3.

[42] Mark Chinen, *Law and Autonomous Machines* (Cheltenham: Edward Elgar, 2019) 127.

[43] Ibid., at 103.

[44] Ibid., at 224.

Third, there might also be a Law 3.0 conversation in which the questions are again about the fitness of the regulatory environment but now asking whether there might be any technical measures that might act in support of the rules or even supplant them—that is, questions that ask whether, as Chinen puts it, it might be possible 'to reduce harm by designing autonomous technologies that "obey" the law'.[45] Recall, for example, the conversations at the time of the disruption at London Gatwick airport shortly before Christmas 2018, when an unauthorised drone was sighted in the vicinity of the airfield. Much of the focus then was on the possibility of finding a technological solution, ideally one that rendered it impossible in practice for a drone to be flown near an airport (or, failing that, a technology for disabling and safely bringing down unauthorised drones). In other words, rather than relying on rules to manage the risks associated with air travel, the conversation was about finding a solution by improving the design and safety-specification of drones and/or airfields.

In principle, each of these conversations could find its own place and make its own contribution to the governance regime. For example, if a regulatory body with a Law 2.0 mindset coordinates the conversations, a particular question might be referred for Law 1.0 inquiry;[46] and, a group, including technical experts, might be set up to explore the Law 3.0 options. However, if it is not clear who is coordinating the conversations, it could lead to some confusion, some inefficiency, and possibly some friction. In this context, we should note Chinen's insightful remarks about the likely scenario where it is the courts that happen to be asked to make the early decisions in laying down the ground rules for responsibility and liability:

> The overarching question is whether these early decisions will be perceived as achieving satisfactory outcomes when harms are caused by autonomous technologies. If not, we are likely to see a tug of war between the expansion of responsibility and who can be held responsible and efforts against such expansion, with both sides

---

[45] Ibid., at 147.

[46] Compare, e.g., the Law Commission's consultation on smart contracts (available at https://www.lawcom.gov.uk/project/smart-contracts/). At para 1.5 of the Call for Evidence, we read the following:

> To ensure that the jurisdiction of England and Wales remains a competitive choice for business, there is a compelling case for reviewing the current legal framework…to ensure that it supports and facilitates the use of smart contracts. While the technology and use cases are still developing, it may not be appropriate to suggest legal reforms which could stifle innovation or risk becoming outdated almost immediately…. [W]e are therefore starting with a scoping study to identify the current law and any potential issues.

In other words, the background conversation and thinking are Law 2.0, but the foreground inquiry (as the document confirms) is largely of a Law 1.0 nature.

using arguments based on fairness and economics. All the while, this tug of war will be an impetus for designing safer and in many cases more sophisticated machines and systems.[47]

In other words, if the opening shots are fired by Law 1.0, and if they are not judged to be acceptable, the battle will move to a Law 2.0 arena, and while the regulatory regime is contested there will be, in Law 3.0 quarters, attempts to design out the wrinkles that are causing the friction.

3.7   CONCLUSION

Summing up, in the landscape of Law 3.0, we find three distinct modes of engagement with emerging technologies. Each mode has its own particular framing, its own range of focal concerns, and each relates to a particular input into the regulatory environment as we should now conceive of it. Whereas the principle-based thinking in Law 1.0 and the policy-focused thinking in Law 2.0 are both articulations of governance by rules, in Law 3.0 we are contemplating more technical and technological forms of governance. This represents a sea-change in how societies are to be ordered. Arguably, code is not just law by another name; it is a radically different regulatory modality and form of governance. If governance is no longer based on rules, and if humans are to be taken out of the legal and regulatory loop, this prompts questions about the adequacy of our rule-based notions of legality and the rule of law as well as our ideas about legitimacy. Some major rethinking looks as though it will be required here; and this is what we now undertake in the next part of the book.

---

[47]   Chinen (n 42) at 233.

PART II

Rethinking legality, the rule of law, and legitimacy

4. Rethinking legality

4.1 INTRODUCTION

According to the baseline view of law, the closely related ideals of legality and the rule of law connote governance by rules as opposed to arbitrary and unpredictable governance by 'men'. Putting this in Hartian terms, from the perspective of citizens, legality signifies governance by primary rules that are made and administered by bodies and 'officials' whose title and actions are duly authorised by the constitutional secondary rules. Such a scheme of governance represents the template for the rule of law and all questions about the legitimacy of particular legal acts are to be answered internally within and by the system of rules.

Having rethought law, regulation, and technology so that we now view the rules of such a Hartian model of a legal system as just one element of the regulatory environment, and having brought technical measures and technologies into that environment, we need to rethink our ideas about legality, the rule of law, and legitimacy. In particular, we need to rethink these ideas alongside the possibility of technologies being increasingly employed to assist governance by rules (governance by rules in conjunction with technical measures) and, eventually, to supersede rules (technological management) and to displace humans (governance by machines).

In this chapter, we will focus on the rethinking of legality, and we will deal with the rule of law and then legitimacy in the following two chapters.

4.2 THE BASELINE VIEW OF LEGALITY

In a classic discussion of the ideal of 'legalism', understood as a set of procedural requirements, Lon Fuller proposed that the rules and standards set should be general, promulgated, prospective, clear, non-contradictory, (reasonably) constant, and not impossible to comply with.[1] He also suggested that it was

---

[1] Lon L. Fuller, *The Morality of Law* (New Haven: Yale University Press, 1969). For an application of the Fullerian principles to particular instances of cyberlaw, see Chris Reed, 'How to Make Bad Law: Lessons from Cyberspace' (2010) 73 MLR 903, esp at 914–916. As Reed summarises it (at 927): 'Complexity makes laws hard to

of the essence of the rule of law that enforcement should be congruent with the rules and standards so promulgated. Where the rules are not promulgated, prospective, clear, non-contradictory, and (reasonably) constant, regulatees will simply not know where they stand; even if they wish to comply with the regulatory standard, they will not know what it is. If the standard set requires impossible acts, then ex hypothesi regulatees cannot comply. Reliance on highly specific regulations will drain most regulatory resource and, again, it will leave many regulatees unclear about their position. And, if there is a disconnect between the rules set and the enforcement practice, not only will regulatees be unclear about their position, but they will lose respect for the regulatory regime.

For many years, jurists have debated whether the Fullerian principles speak only to the conditions for effective governance or whether, as Fuller insists, they go to the heart of the distinctively *legal* (and reciprocal) form of governance.[2] Although, in the context of debates concerning the essential nature (or concept) of law, there is a fundamental choice between a moralised idea of law (evincing a necessary connection between law and morals) and an idea of law as a by and large effective institution for the ordering and direction of social life, in the larger regulatory picture other distinctions loom large.[3] In particular, there is the choice between normative and non-normative ordering, between rules, principles, and standards (signalling ought and ought not) and the management of practical options (signalling can and cannot).[4] For Fuller, as for his critics, law and morals alike operate with normative signals; but, what are we to make of legality in regulatory environments where non-normative signals (speaking only to what is practicable or possible) predominate?

Rather than dismissing out of hand the relevance of the Fullerian principles—on the ground that they relate only to normative regulatory strategies and not at all to governance by non-normative strategies—we can consider the principles, trying to capture their spirit and intent, with a view to understanding what they

---

understand, contradictory rules make compliance impossible and frequent change compounds these difficulties.'

[2]   See, e.g., HLA Hart's review of *The Morality of Law*, at (1964–65) 78 *Harvard Law Review* 1281.

[3]   For discussion, see Roger Brownsword, '*Law as a Moral Judgment*, the Domain of Jurisprudence, and Technological Management' in Patrick Capps and Shaun D. Pattinson (eds), *Ethical Rationalism and the Law* (Oxford: Hart, 2016) 109.

[4]   Relative to this distinction, pricing or other financial measures that are intended to incentivise or disincentivise the doing or not doing of x are likely to fit with normative signalling; however, where financial measures make it practically impossible to do x, such measures will fit with non-normative signalling.

might signify for the acceptable use of technical measures and technological management.[5]

4.3 EXTENDING THE FULLERIAN PRINCIPLES OF LEGALITY

When Fuller characterises law as the human enterprise of governance by rules, this is more than a description of a distinctive mode of governance. What Fuller invites readers to do is to reflect on the significance of a public commitment to governance by rules. To commit to governance by rules is to generate the expectation that there will be rules, that there will be a reasonable opportunity both to know what the rules specify and to comply with them, that legal officials will be guided by the rules, that disputes will be settled in accordance with the rules, and so on. Converting these expectations into principles of legality, our question is whether they might be applied in relation to modes of governance that rely on technical measures or technologies in support of the rules and, beyond that, technological management that replaces rules.

Rather than working through the Fullerian principles one-by-one, we can reorganise them so that they express the background expectations to which they relate in the following way. The expectations are:

1. that citizens will know, or could reasonably have known, that there were rules, and they will know, or could reasonably have known, what the rules required. Accordingly, if a sanction for rule-breaking is to be applied where citizens were not given a fair warning and a fair opportunity to comply with the rules, this will defeat the relevant expectations and prompt a grievance. Anticipating this grievance, we have the epistemic requirements that the rules should be promulgated, that the rules should be clear, that the rules should not involve any contradiction, and that the rules should be relatively constant (lest citizens were unaware that the rules had changed);

2. that it will be practically possible for citizens to comply with the rules. In line with this expectation, we have the injunctions against requirements

---

[5] Compare Lodewijk Asscher, "Code" as Law. Using Fuller to Assess Code Rules' in E. Dommering and L. Asscher (eds), *Coding Regulation: Essays on the Normative Role of Information Technology* (The Hague: TMC Asser, 2006) 61, at 86:
> Code can present constraints on human behaviour that can be compared with constraints by traditional laws. We have argued that even though code is not law, in some instances it can be useful to ask the same questions about code regulation as we do about traditional regulation. Code as law must be assessed by looking at the results of regulation in terms of freedom and individual autonomy and compared to the balance struck in traditional law.

with which compliance is impossible as well as against the retrospective operation of the rules. We might also treat the principle of relative constancy as speaking to practical possibility where, although what the rules require is not in itself problematic, too frequent changes in the requirements of the rules militate against both knowing what the rules now require and being in a position to comply;

3. that the rules should be administered in accordance with their published terms. This requirement of accurate administration is expressed through the principle of congruence; and

4. that no citizen should be singled out by a rule or targeted personally. This expectation, and its corresponding grievance, is anticipated by the principle of generality.

We can now work through these four categories (the epistemic principles, the practical possibility principles, the principle of accurate administration, and the principle of generality) to explore how the organising ideas might be applied to the use of technical measures in support of the rules or to technological management and governance by machines.

4.3.1 The Epistemic Principles

The relevant principles here are promulgation, clarity, avoidance of contradictory directives, and constancy; and, as we have suggested, they address potential grievances about penalties being applied for rule-breaking where the existence of, or the particular requirements of, the rules could not reasonably be known.

One of the first implications of a commitment to governance by rules is that the rules and their requirements should be promulgated and should be clear. Regulatees need to know, and expect to know, where they stand; and, particularly where there are penalties for non-compliance, regulatees expect to be given a fair warning if they are at risk. This implies that transparency is an important aspect of legality, and the question is whether this continues to be the case where we have governance either by rules assisted by technologies or governance by machines.

Where technologies are deployed in support of the rules—for example, where surveillance and identification technologies are deployed in support of the rules of the criminal law—it continues to be imperative that citizens know that there are rules and know what the rules require. However, is it implicit in a regime of governance by rules supported by technologies that citizens should also know that technologies (and even which technologies) are being employed? To the extent that we are trying to anticipate the grievance that there was no fair warning about the rules and no fair opportunity to comply, it does not seem to follow that there should also be transparency about the supporting technologies.

That said, in some communities, there might already be an expectation that where surveillance or identification technologies are employed, there should be reasonable notice that this is the case; and, in some communities, there might even be a constitutional requirement that reasonable notice is given—indeed, even that there should be transparency about how the technology operates (otherwise there might be difficulties in challenging decisions made by the technology). To be sure, the question of transparency and the right to an explanation are becoming major debating points in relation to the leading-edge developments in AI and machine learning.[6] However, unless we thicken up our idea of legality, such requirements for a fair warning are extraneous to what is implicit in the enterprise of governance by rules.

Where technological management is in operation, citizens are no longer guided directly by rules. In technologically managed zones, there are only so many practical options available (those options that regulators treat as acceptable), and citizens should not find themselves in situations that are judged to be 'non-compliant'. If, through no fault of their own, citizens do act in ways that are non-compliant (but, because the technology permits the action, they believe in good faith to be compliant), they should certainly not be penalised. Arguably, regulators should warn citizens that a zone is technologically managed. For example, in the smart cities and places of the future, where the available options are heavily technologically managed, there probably needs to be clear signalling to regulatees that they are entering or acting in such a zone. To this extent, clarity of transmission is still something that matters. However, the reason that it matters seems to be because it is insisted upon as a condition of governance by technologies rather than being implicit in the enterprise of governance by rules.[7]

---

[6]   See, e.g., Nathalie A. Smuha, 'From a "race to AI" to a "race to AI regulation": regulatory competition for artificial intelligence' (2021) 13 *Law, Innovation and Technology* 57; House of Lords Select Committee on Artificial Intelligence, Report on *AI in the UK; ready, willing and able?* (Report of Session 2017-19, published 16 April 2017, HL Paper 100) at para 105: available at https://publications.parliament.uk/pa/ld201719/ldselect/ldai/100/10007.htm#_idTextAnchor025 (last accessed 11 August 2018); and, the European Commission's proposal for a Regulation on AI, COM(2021) 206 final (Brussels, 21.4.2021), Article 13 of which provides for 'transparency' in relation to high-risk AI systems and Title IV of which puts in place 'transparency' obligations for AI systems that (i) interact with humans, (ii) are used to detect emotions or determine association with (social) categories based on biometric data, or (iii) generate or manipulate content ('deep fakes').

[7]   Compare Colin Gavaghan, '*Lex Machina*: Techno-regulatory Mechanisms and "Rules by Design"' (2017) 15 *Otago Law Review* 123, 145, concluding that

In a regime of governance by rules, the paradigmatic case of contradiction is where one rule prohibits the doing of x while another permits or requires the doing of x. Where technologies are employed in support of rules, the same applies: contradictory rules, now reinforced by technologies that push in one direction and pull in another, are incompatible with governance by rules, and this invites citizens to be aggrieved in the way that adherence to legality seeks to avoid. However, what does non-contradiction imply in a context of technological management? Perhaps the obvious implication is that, in a particular situation, the relevant technologies should be consistent in allowing or disallowing a certain 'act'. Where the technologies are simply talking to one another, some inconsistency might be inconvenient. However, if humans are misled by the inconsistency, and if there are penalties for doing some act that should have been prevented, but where the technology has failed, it would seem to be unfair to apply the penalty—or, at any rate, it would be unfair if the agent acted in the good faith belief that, because the signal was set to 'possible', this implied that the act was permitted. Again, though, this seems to be a condition for acceptable governance by machines rather than implicit in governance by rules.

While laws need to be revised from time to time, there is a problem if they are changed so frequently that regulatees are uncertain of their legal position. Just as a lack of clarity in the law breaches the fair warning principle, the same applies to a lack of constancy. Where technologies are employed in support of rules, especially where they are used to communicate rule changes, the problem of a lack of constancy might be exacerbated. Frequent changes in the technological signals (as on some stretches of motorway) might be confusing. In technologically managed environments—for example, in consumer markets where dynamic pricing is employed—the available options might be changing all the time;[8] but, this is not going to lead to situations in which citizens are

---

techno-regulatory mechanisms 'are already widespread and, likely to become more so as our lives become more urbanized and technologized.' At 135, Gavaghan suggests that, in addition to asking the general question about whether a measure is 'likely to be effective, what we think of the values it embodies, whether the likely benefit is worth the cost, and so forth', we should ask whether *technological* measures are (i) visible, (ii) flexible, (iii) simply enforcing rules already agreed upon by democratic means, and (iv) employing unusually intrusive or inflexible means of enforcement. At 135–137, specifically on the matter of visibility, Gavaghan suggests that we should ask whether we know that technological measures are employed, whether we know that they are in operation in a particular place or at a particular time, and whether we know the precise details or limits of such measures.

[8] For discussion, see Ariel Ezrachi and Maurice E. Stucke, *Virtual Competition* (Cambridge, Mass.: Harvard University Press, 2016).

non-compliant so much as surprised (if the changes are out of line with their expectations).

There is one other point. While it might seem self-evident that clarity in the drafting of legal instruments is desirable both in itself and for the sake of legality, there are contexts in which clarity can obstruct consensus and willingness to sign off on a law. This is the context, familiar in international law, where stakeholders need some leeway in the interpretation of the document. Indeed, in the EU, member states have a systematic opportunity to put down a marker for their concerns in the Recitals to a Directive (which, technically, are not legally binding) rather than qualify the Articles. Such constructive ambiguity or vagueness in the law might or might not be defensible, but its prevalence is likely to inhibit the translation of such provisions into code. It could be, therefore, that the pragmatic acceptance of, and need for, some leeway in the law (this, strictly speaking, being a departure from the ideals of legality) is one of the things that slows down the shift to governance by machines and technological management.[9]

4.3.2 The Practical Possibility Principles

The relevant principles here concern possibility, prospectivity, and constancy; and the grievance that these principles address is that citizens did not have a reasonable opportunity to comply with the rules and their requirements.

The injunction against requiring the impossible responds not only to the irrationality of requiring persons to defy the law of gravity or to be in two places at one and the same time, but also to the unfairness of penalising persons for failing to comply with rules that require the literally impossible or that impose penalties on persons who, through no fault of their own, find themselves in circumstances where compliance is simply not possible. Equally, this would apply to court orders for specific performance or the like where the act in question is no longer possible—for example, an order to rectify an error in a blockchain register. What should we make of this where technologies support rules in ways that reduce the chances of non-compliance or where transactions and interactions are technologically managed so that it is non-compliance rather than compliance that is impossible?

On the face of it, because technological management operates in a mode that redefines what is possible and what is impossible within a particular regulatory space, it should not fall foul of requiring the impossible. To be sure, in some

---

[9] For the tension between the virtue of legality/the rule of law and the prevalence of discretionary leeways in rules, see further Joseph Raz, 'The Law's Own Virtue' (2019) 39 *Oxford Journal of Legal Studies* 1.

dystopian world, regulators might introduce a rule that requires regulatees to defy the restrictions imposed by technological management and penalises those who fail to succeed; but we can discount this bizarre possibility.

Rather, if the injunction against requiring the impossible has any continuing relevance, its thrust will be to avoid unfairly penalising regulatees in their various encounters with technological management. For example, would it be unfair to penalise an agent who attempts (but fails) to perform an act which that agent knows is impossible because it is prevented by technological management? For example, would a one-time and now frustrated vandal be fairly punished for persistently throwing stones at bus shelters equipped with shatterproof glass? Would it be unfair if the defendant responded, not by pleading the Fullerian principle that he should not be punished for failing to satisfy an impossible 'legal' requirement, but by arguing that his act was innocuous and that he should not be penalised for failing to do something that, because of technological measures, was no longer possible to do? Conversely, suppose that, some measure of technological management is prone to malfunction from time to time, such that an agent might in some circumstances be unclear whether a particular act is or is not possible (and by implication permissible). Should it be open to such an agent to plead that, where technological management is in place, 'can implies may'?

So far, we have assumed that rules requiring the impossible are prospective; if they are actually retroactive, that simply compounds the impossibility. However, what about rules that do not require the impossible as such but which cannot be complied with because they are retroactive? No one surely would gainsay Fuller's remark that a regime 'composed exclusively of retrospective rules could exist only as a grotesque conceit worthy of Lewis Carroll or Franz Kafka'.[10] Certainly, where penalties are applied for breach of rules that have retrospective effect, this is contrary to the reasonable expectations of regulatees who have been led to believe that governance by rules will apply; regulatees not only do not know where they stand, but they are denied a fair warning that they are non-compliant and that they are liable to be penalised. Even if the rules are themselves extremely unfair or difficult to justify, it is an independent requirement that they should be applied only with prospective effect. This is a basic requirement of due process and it is implicit in governance by rules.

In a non-normative context, it is very difficult to imagine how technological management could itself operate retrospectively (although, no doubt, digital records can be wiped clean and amended). Quite simply, where technological management is introduced to make a particular act impossible, or to remove what was previously a practical option, it takes effect as of then. No doubt, as

---

[10]   Fuller (n 1) at 74.

in the Fullerian world of rules, it would be good practice to give regulatees fair warning that such technological measures are to be introduced; and, if regulatees operate on the assumption that what is possible in technologically managed environments is permissible, it would be unfair to penalise by retrospective rule or decree those regulatees who, in good faith, have acted on that assumption. However, on the face of it, neither technological management nor governance by machines in themselves introduce new risks of unfair retrospective penalisation of conduct.

4.3.3 The Principle of Accurate Administration

As is well known, Fuller attaches a very high importance to the principle of congruence, to officials administering the rules in accordance with their terms as declared. If officials operate with a secret rulebook, this clearly violates the idea of legality. However, judges will sometimes be faced with applying rules that are open to more than one interpretation or with rules that lead to results that seem unjust in the particular case. Here, it is not so easy to apply the rules as declared—and, in some of these kinds of cases, there will be a challenge if there is an ambition to convert the rule into computable code.[11]

Where rules are administered by automated systems, congruence demands that the technology should faithfully follow the rules as intended. As we have said, this presents a considerable challenge to the coding of rules.[12] However, this is still recognisably an issue of legality within a Fullerian universe of rules. Arguably, it is also within the spirit of congruence that the use of technical measures in support of rules should not reduce the accuracy of the application of the rules. For example, where a rule empowers officials to act on 'reasonable suspicion', we accept that there will be some false positives. Where guidance is given by a supportive technology, an extension of the principle of accurate administration would limit the rate of false positives and false negatives to whatever band of tolerance is accepted.

In a context of technological management, there are no rules to be administered as such. The regulatory spaces are designed in ways that eliminate both the option of unacceptable (non-compliant) conduct and the need for human interventions to enforce compliance. To be sure, there might still be issues with false positives or false negatives, but the margins of acceptability would be set

---

[11] See, e.g., Kevin D. Ashley, *Artificial Intelligence and Legal Analytics* (Cambridge: Cambridge University Press, 2017).

[12] See Danielle Keats Citron, 'Technological Due Process' (2008) 85 *Washington University Law Review* 1249.

by background debates and agreement. The relevant standards would not flow from legality as such.

A further thought is that, because technological management promises to close the normative gap (the possible gap between the standard as declared and as administered), congruence takes on a different significance. The spirit of congruence is that regulators and their enforcement agents should operate in a way that accords with the expectations of regulatees as reasonably formed on the basis of the regulatory signals. In a context of technological management, as we have remarked already, regulatees might reasonably expect that where an act is possible, regulators treat it as optional and no negative regulatory reaction should ensue where the act is done—at least, this is so unless regulatees clearly know that there has been a malfunction or something of that kind (analogous to regulatees looting shops during a police strike or bringing in excess tobacco and alcohol during a strike by the customs and excise officers). So, congruence, along with clarity, constancy, and the like, demands that regulators and their agents do not penalise regulatees who, in good faith, have misunderstood the regulatory position.

4.3.4   The Principle of Generality

Fuller, recalling the historic abuse of prerogative power, also identifies ad hominem 'rules' as contrary to the very idea of legality. Of course, courts hand down rulings that apply only to the particular parties, but legislative acts should be of general application. By contrast, some articulations of technological management might be specific to particular individuals—for example, as profiling becomes more fine-grained and the management of access is more personalised, the targeting of particular individuals will be even more pronounced.[13] Instead of focusing on dangerous acts or dangerous classes, precision profiling is likely to identify and isolate dangerous individuals. Whereas the idea of governance by rules implies a degree of generality (governance is not a succession of bespoke one-off directions to individuals), this is not the case with forms of governance that rely on technologies that are capable of precisely this specificity of direction and decision. If this latter form of governance offends a community's ideas of fairness or legality but is more accurate than more general profiling and targeting strategies, some hard choices will need to be made.

---

[13]   Compare, too, the possibility of tailored guidance by 'micro-directives': see, Anthony Casey and Anthony Niblett, 'Self-Driving Laws' (2016) 66 *University of Toronto Law Journal* 429 and 'The Death of Rules and Standards' (2017) 92 *Indiana Law Journal* 1401.

Picking up this last point, consider the hypothetical case (proposed by Bert-Jaap Koops) of a street food seller who is denied a licence to operate in a zone that security services require to be risk-free.[14] The seller does not understand why he is judged to be a security risk; and, if there is to be due process, he needs to know on what basis the automated decision was made. Responding to the seller's question, it might simply be said that the decision-making process (the algorithm employed) has been approved and authorised for the particular purpose. If the seller presses for further and better particulars, it might be said that a broad range of factors were taken into consideration in the process—including, for example, the seller's credit rating, his address, his contacts with the police, and a conviction many years ago for being in possession of cannabis. None of these factors might strike the seller as indicating that he is a security risk but, if he presses further, he is again met with the response that the algorithm is approved and authorised. Nevertheless, the seller is left unable to understand why he has been classified as a risk, and he is aggrieved that he has been singled out.

What the hypothetical highlights is not so much the inscrutability and seeming irrationality of some algorithmic decisions, but the potential tension between the community's acceptance of this mode of governance and the perceptions of individuals who are singled out. Accordingly, we might argue that, where technological measures or automated decisions are widely used, particular attention should be paid to the need for openness, or transparency—in authorising the use of, as well as in operationalising, such measures or technological modes of governance. While such requirements might not follow from a commitment to governance by rules (from legality), they are supported by ideals of fairness and due process, and they continue to be key principles of legitimate governance.[15] So far as public regulators are concerned, there needs to be an authorising rule framework setting out the process for adopting automated decisions or measures of technological management, with particular proposed uses being openly debated (for example, in the legislative assembly

---

[14]   Bert-Jaap Koops, 'On Decision Transparency, or How to Enhance Data Protection after the Computational Turn' in Mireille Hildebrandt and Katja de Vries (eds), *Privacy, Due Process and the Computational Turn* (Abingdon: Routledge, 2013) 196, at 212–213.

[15]   Compare Ian Kerr, 'Prediction, Pre-emption, Presumption' in Hildebrandt and de Vries (n 14) 91 at 109:

At its core—whether in the public or private sector, online or off—the due process concept requires that individuals have an ability to observe, understand, participate in and respond to important decisions or actions that implicate them.

or by administrative notice and comment procedure). As Danielle Keats Citron Fuller's most evocative observation has recommended:[16]

> [A]gencies should explore ways to allow the public to participate in the building of automated decision systems....
> In the same vein, agencies could establish information technology review boards that would provide opportunities for stakeholders and the public at large to comment on a system's design and testing. Although finding the ideal makeup and duties of such boards would require some experimentation, they would secure opportunities for interested groups to comment on the construction of automated systems that would have an enormous impact on their communities once operational.

Moreover, as we will argue in the next chapter, private use of technological management should be permitted only within publicly agreed limits and, if new uses are proposed, they should be approved by open special procedures (possibly akin to applications for planning permission). In all cases, ideals of fairness should support the process by insisting that tricks or traps should be avoided.

4.4 LEGALITY AND RECIPROCITY

In our discussion of legality, we have assumed a degree of reciprocity between rule-makers and those to whom the rules apply. This is in line with Fuller's attempts to trace his differences with his legal positivist critics. This led him to identify the following two key assumptions made by the legal positivists:

> The *first* of these is a belief that the existence or non-existence of law is, from a moral point of view, a matter of indifference. The *second* is an assumption…that law should be viewed not as the product of an interplay of purposive orientations between the citizen and his government but as a one-way projection of authority, originating with government and imposing itself upon the citizen.[17]

The second of these assumptions is elaborated in a crucial contrast that Fuller draws between a legal form of order and simple managerial direction. He sketches the distinction between the two forms of order in the following terms:

> The directives issued in a managerial context are applied by the subordinate in order to serve a purpose set by his superior. The law-abiding citizen, on the other hand, does not apply legal rules to serve specific ends set by the lawgiver, but rather follows them in the conduct of his own affairs, the interests he is presumed to serve in following legal rules being those of society generally. The directives of a manage-

---

[16] Danielle Keats Citron (n 12), at 1312.
[17] Fuller (n 1), at 204.

rial system regulate primarily the relations between the subordinate and his superior and only collaterally the relations of the subordinate with third persons. The rules of the legal system, on the other hand, normally serve the primary purpose of setting the citizen's relations with other citizens and only in a collateral manner his relations with the seat of authority from which the rules proceed. (Though we sometimes think of the criminal law as defining the citizen's duties towards his government, its primary function is to provide a sound and stable framework for the interactions of citizens with one another.)[18]

As Fuller concedes, these remarks need 'much expansion and qualification';[19] and he tries to give more substance to them by characterising the relationship, in a legal order, between government and citizens in terms of 'reciprocity' and 'intendment'.[20] Perhaps Fuller's most evocative observation is that 'the functioning of a legal system depends upon a cooperative effort—an effective and responsible interaction—between lawgiver and subject'.[21]

From this clutch of ideas, it is the association of legal ordering with an open and two-way reciprocal process that is most fruitful. For, in the larger context of the regulatory environment, it implies that the legal approach—an approach to be valued—is one that embeds participation, transparency, due process, and the like. Hence, if we take our lead from Fuller, we will reason that, whether we are dealing with a regulatory enterprise that subjects human conduct to the governance of rules (in the way that both Fuller and his critics agreed was the pre-theoretical nature of law) or that relies on technological control to design-in or design-out conduct, we should hold on to the idea that what we value is a reciprocal enterprise, not just a case of management, let alone technological management, by some regulatory elite.

In line with this reading of Fuller, Mireille Hildebrandt's conception of legality might be interpreted as implicating a reciprocal relationship between the makers of legal rules and their subjects. According to Hildebrandt, we should distinguish between 'legality' (roughly, due process and justice) and mere 'legalism' (mechanical application of the rules). For Hildebrandt, it is governance by rules with a commitment to legality, not mere legalism, that is to be valued against rule by technologies.[22] Where legality is respected, legal texts are open to interpretation and contestation (in courts) before their application in individual cases; and, in this way law is able to serve more than the

---

[18] Fuller (n 1), at 207–208.
[19] Fuller (n 1), at 208.
[20] Fuller (n 1), at 209 et seq.
[21] Fuller (n 1), at 219.
[22] Mireille Hildebrandt, *Smart Technologies and the End(s) of Law* (Cheltenham: Edward Elgar, 2015).

demand for certainty by responding to the demand for individual justice and for legitimate purposes.[23]

While this kind of rethinking of legality might well appeal, we should ask whether it goes beyond what is strictly entailed by the enterprise of governance by rules to the more substantive terms and conditions of rule-making authority that we find in particular constitutional settlements and that lead us to the rule of law. No doubt, our thinking about legitimate governance can be expressed in more than one way—by packing it all into our conception of legality, or into our conception of the rule of law, or into both legality and the rule of law. Having rethought legality in a way that does not fully cover our legitimacy concerns, there is more work to be done; and this is where the rule of law comes into play.

4.5   CONCLUDING REMARKS

In this chapter we have tried to apply the spirit and intent of the Fullerian idea of legality to governance by machines and technological management. Underlying Fuller's analysis is the thought that a commitment to governance by rules already commits rule-makers and rule-appliers to respect the constraints of that mode of governance. The content of the rules is left open but a commitment to governance by rules does imply that the reasonable expectations of the subjects of the rules—that is to say, the expectations reasonably encouraged by the declared commitment to governance by rules—will be respected. To this extent, rule-makers and rule-appliers are precluded from deviating from the terms that are implicit in the declared mode of governance; and, in this sense, there is a reciprocity in the relationship between rule-makers and their subjects.

Nevertheless, we might still feel that, if not quite a fresh start, some supplementation of this relatively thin notion of legality needs to be made. To be sure, the Fullerian ideals continue to be applicable to the normative dimensions of the regulatory environment; but, once governance by machines and technological management are employed, these ideals as specified no longer apply in an entirely adequate way. However, if supplying that supplementation becomes too substantive, we are in danger of encroaching on the rule of law and clouding whatever distinction we might want to maintain between legality and the rule of law.

Last but not least, it should be said that we might judge that it is a mistake to try to rethink legality. Instead, it is governance by rules and Fullerian legality that we need to hold on to. Rather than trying to rework legality to cover

---

[23]   Ibid., at e.g., 154–155.

governance by machines, we should be resisting governance by machines and holding on to governance by rules. The importance of this caveat should not be understated. Just because we have the technological capacity to instate governance by machines or technological management, it does not follow that we should do so. Between technological development and its application, there needs to be deliberation; and even if the direction of travel is away from governance by rules and legality as we have known it, reversal or redirection should not be ruled out. Implicit in these remarks is the recurrent concern about the role played by humans in the legal enterprise. For Fuller, there is more to legality than governance by rules; legality presupposes a context in which there is a reciprocal interaction between those who subject human conduct to the governance of rules and those who are so subjected. It might seem unnecessary to emphasise that law is an essentially human enterprise; but, when governance by technology emerges as a practical option, this might actually be the most important thing to underline about law.

5. Rethinking the rule of law

5.1 INTRODUCTION

Westphalian thinking about the rule of law starts with the idea that the legal enterprise is committed to governance by rules, the rules being published and then faithfully administered. The rule of law marks the end of arbitrary governance. Debates are largely between those who advocate sticking with a 'thin' and 'formal' (or 'procedural') version of the rule of law and those who argue for a 'thicker', more 'substantive' version.[1] Needless to say, even as traditional debates are revisited and played out in the present century, technology does not figure in them.[2]

Recognising that in these debates there are many versions of the rule of law,[3] the ideal should be understood as reflecting a bilateral compact: on the one side, rulers demand that citizens respect the rules; on the other side, citizens demand that rulers act in accordance with the rules. Thus, from a citizen's viewpoint, the distinctive focus of the rule of law, in contrast with legality, is on the authorising rules, on the constitutive (or secondary) rules that set the terms and conditions to be observed by the rulers.

---

[1] See, e.g., Paul P. Craig, 'Formal and Substantive Conceptions of the Rule of Law: An Analytical Framework' [1997] *Public Law* 467. At 467, Craig explains that whilst formal conceptions 'address the manner in which the law was promulgated (was it by a properly authorised person, in a properly authorised manner, etc.); the clarity of the ensuing norm (was it sufficiently clear to guide an individual's conduct so as to enable a person to plan his or her life, etc.); and the temporal dimension of the enacted norm (was it prospective or retrospective, etc.)', they do not 'seek to pass judgment upon the actual content of the law itself'. By contrast, substantive conceptions 'wish to take the doctrine further. Certain substantive rights are said to be based on, or derived from, the rule of law. The concept is used as the foundation for these rights, which are then used to distinguish between "good" laws, which comply with such rights, and "bad" laws which do not.'

[2] See, e.g., Joseph Raz's recent defence of a restricted and rethought conception of the rule of law in 'The Law's Own Virtue' (2019) 39 OJLS 1, where the core idea is that governance is manifestly intended to serve the interests of the governed.

[3] Generally, see Joseph Raz, 'The Rule of Law and its Virtues' (1977) 93 LQR 195; and David Dyzenhaus, 'Recrafting the Rule of Law' in David Dyzenhaus (ed), *Recrafting the Rule of Law* (Oxford: Hart, 1999) 1.

Rethinking the rule of law 73

If, in the spirit of Fullerian thinking, the relationship between citizens and their rulers is to be reciprocal, this implies that there has to be some input by the citizenry into both the primary rules and the secondary authorising rules.[4] In other words, if we are not already thinking about the rule of law as a compact in which processes for citizen participation in making the primary rules are established and in which citizens also have a say in expressing substantive constraints in the authorising rules, we have reason to rethink the rule of law along these lines. So, for example, we might argue that the rule of law should require rulers (as a matter of process) to respect the principles of deliberative democracy or the like;[5] and, we might also argue that, because our community aspires to respect human rights, this should be reflected (as a matter of substance) in the authorising rules. Accordingly, if it were proposed that the police should make use of CCTV surveillance, or DNA profiling, or AI and so on, this might be a matter on which public consultation was required[6] and, in any case, the measures authorising the use of such technologies would need to be compatible with the community's commitment to respect human rights.[7]

It is in the nature of our rethinking of law, regulation, and technology, however, that a more radical rethink about the rule of law is called for.[8] Given that the regulatory environment is now viewed as including technical measures and technologies, and given that the latter have been developed and applied by both private and public regulators, some more fundamental rethinking is needed. We need to rethink where the rule of law applies, to whom it applies, to what it applies, and how it applies. This is the nature of the rethink that is presented in the following section of the chapter. After that, an indication is given of what the rule of law might provide for the authorised use of technological management or the use of machines for governance purposes.

---

[4] On Fullerian reciprocity, see section 4.4 above.

[5] As argued for in Norman Lewis and Ian Harden, *The Noble Lie: British Constitution and the Rule of Law* (London: Harper Collins, 1986).

[6] See, e.g., the House of Lords Justice and Home Affairs Committee's call for evidence in relation to its inquiry into new technologies in law enforcement (July 22, 2021), available at: https://committees.parliament.uk/committee/519/justice-and-home -affairs-committee/news/156778/call-for-evidence-launched-on-new-technologies-in -law-enforcement/ (last accessed 30 July 2021).

[7] See, e.g., the human rights challenge to the legislative framework for DNA profiling in the *Case of S. and Marper v The United Kingdom* (2009) 48 EHRR 50. For discussion, see Roger Brownsword and Morag Goodwin, *Law and the Technologies of the Twenty-First Century* (Cambridge: Cambridge University Press, 2012) 75–108.

[8] Compare Emre Bayamlıoğlu and Ronald Leenes, 'The "Rule of Law" Implications of Data-Driven Decision-Making: A Techno-Regulatory Perspective' (2018) 10 *Law, Innovation and Technology* 295, esp 303–311 (on the implications of techno-regulation for the rule of law).

5.2 RETHINKING THE RULE OF LAW

There are five prongs to our proposed rethinking of the rule of law. First, the rule of law, although developed to apply to governance by rules in offline analogue environments, must apply equally to those who assume governance responsibilities in online environments and to those who interact and transact in those environments. Second, the rule of law must apply equally to both public and private regulators. Third, it must cover both rules and technical measures. Fourth, the rule of law (echoing the idea of legality) must secure inclusive procedures and integrity of process. Finally, in line with those who argue for thicker versions, the rule of law must also include substantive elements that underwrite the law's claim to legitimacy.

5.2.1   Online as Well as Offline

One of the virtues of Westphalian nation-states was that their borders were fixed; within the nation-state and its borders, its laws applied; beyond its borders, its laws did not apply. However, in the twenty-first century, matters are somewhat different. In order to respond to large-scale migration (by refugees and asylum seekers), borders are no longer fixed: de facto border controls are applied in zones both within the state and beyond its historic borders. As Ayelet Shachar puts it in her critique of these shifting borders, we need to adjust our thinking: instead of 'studying the *movement of people across borders* [we should] critically investigate the *movement of borders to regulate the mobility of people*'.[9] Not only that: Westphalian states are also re-imagining, in a characteristic Law 3.0 way, how they might deploy new technologies to regulate the mobility of people—for example, in the European Union thoughts have been turning to 'futuristic iBorder control strategies that "re-engineer" the system of border crossing and migration control'.[10] Clearly, the rule of law and, as Shachar argues, human rights, must move with these borders.

With one controlling thought leading to another technological application, this might be scaled up to roll out global ID systems. According to Shachar, such systems

> [which] have long been the dream of law enforcers…are now closer to becoming a reality. Even the United Nations has teamed up with leading technology firms to explore plans for creating a digital ID network running on blockchain technology to

---

[9]   Ayelet Shachar, *The Shifting Border: Legal Cartographies of Migration and Mobility* (Manchester: Manchester University Press, 2020) at 7 (emphasis in original).
[10]   Ibid., at 36.

provide tamper-resistant legal documents for refugees and other displaced persons who lack them, creating a '"stamp"—a unique identifier between the refugee and the data on the servers—that proves they have been authenticated for each service they receive' at refugee camps or from official aid organizations.[11]

In post-pandemic conditions, it is not difficult to anticipate how public health considerations might converge with migration and security concerns to add weight to the arguments in support of the development and deployment of such ID and 'passporting' systems.

However, two decades before any of this, it was apparent that the development of cybertechnologies and cyberspaces was going to introduce a quite new legal cartography. Thus, opening their seminal paper on the regulation of online communications, David Johnson and David Post[12] wrote:

> Global computer-based communications cut across territorial borders, creating a new realm of human activity and undermining the feasibility – and legitimacy – of laws based on geographic boundaries. While these electronic communications play havoc with geographic boundaries, a new boundary, made up of the screens and passwords that separate the virtual world from the 'real world' of atoms, emerges. This new boundary defines a distinct Cyberspace that needs and can create its own law and legal institutions. Territorially based law-makers and law-enforcers find this new environment deeply threatening.[13]

Generally speaking, as we have said, Westphalian legal systems map onto geographical territories with clear boundaries.[14] We know when and where we cross from one legal system to another; within each legal system the authorities enjoy a measure of control and legitimacy. However, as Johnson and Post highlight, cyberspace—or, as we now know it, the burgeoning global population of online suppliers of goods and services, online content, cybercriminals, and so on—challenges the effectiveness of local legal rules as well as raising questions about their legitimacy. According to Johnson and Post, the remedy is to treat cyberspace as a place in its own right, with its own self-regulating codes. This would overcome jurisdictional competition with regard to defamation, professional qualifications, IP, and so on, as well as facilitating the creation of bespoke online law. This would not signal the

---

[11]   Ibid., at 38.

[12]   David R. Johnson and David Post, 'Law and Borders – Rise of Law in Cyberspace' (1996) 48 *Stanford Law Review* 1367.

[13]   Ibid., at 1367.

[14]   Subject, that is, to the increasingly prevalent, but still controversial, effects doctrine in theories of jurisdiction, whereby a state claims jurisdiction in relation to events that have effects on its territory but that neither begin nor end on its territory, nor involve one of its nationals.

end of law, but the relationship between traditional top–down lawmakers and subjects would have to change. As Johnson and Post conclude, 'Law, defined as a thoughtful group conversation about core values, will persist. But it will not, could not, and should not be the same law as that applicable to physical, geographically-defined territories.'[15]

Clearly cyberspace raises its own regulatory challenges. However, we have to push back against the idea that the rule of law simply does not apply to activities and actors in cyberspace. The 'Internet separatists', as Joel Reidenberg calls them,[16] seem to think that the rule of law and national rules of law simply do not apply to their online activities. This seems to be the case, for example, when millions of youngsters engage in unlawful file-sharing, when thousands of users of Twitter conspire to disclose the identity of persons in defiance of protective court orders,[17] and when trolling and online racial abuse is rampant. Hence, as Reidenberg says:

> The defenses for hate, lies, drugs, sex, gambling, and stolen music are in essence that technology justifies the denial of personal jurisdiction, the rejection of an assertion of applicable law by a sovereign state, and the denial of the enforcement of decisions…. In the face of these claims, legal systems engage in a rather conventional struggle to adapt existing regulatory standards to new technologies and the Internet. Yet, the underlying fight is a profound struggle against the very right of sovereign states to establish rules for online activity.[18]

The upshot of all this is very clear. We cannot give people a free pass on the rule of law simply because they are acting, whether as regulators or as regulatees, in online environments.

5.2.2 Private as Well as Public

It is already implicit in the first prong of our rethinking that the rule of law must apply to both public and private regulators (whether the latter are officially identified as such or simply exercise de facto regulatory control). To be sure, we might pause at the suggestion that the rule of law must also be applied

---

[15] Ibid., at 1402.

[16] Joel R. Reidenberg, 'Technology and Internet Jurisdiction' (2005) 153 *University of Pennsylvania Law Review* 1951.

[17] See, e.g., Frances Gibb, Anushka Asthana, and Alexi Mostrous, 'Paper Faces Legal Threat over Picture of Footballer' *The Times*, May 23, 2011, p1 (the Ryan Giggs case).

[18] Reidenberg (n 16), at 1953–1954.

to private parties. For example, in assessing Philip Selznick's proposal that the rule of law should be extended to industry, Martin Krygier asks:

> What should that be taken to mean? Perhaps that protective legislation should be applied to factories? That it should be clearly drafted, publicly promulgated, free of contradiction, stable? Perhaps, more adventurously, that it should provide workers in industry with particular legal rights?[19]

Already, in these suggestions, we can hear echoes of a Fullerian idea of legality; but, if we are more adventurous, we might apply the idea that the rule of law demands, as Selznick put it, the 'progressive reduction of arbitrariness' and even the restraint of power by 'rational principles of civic order'.[20]

More recently, Julie Cohen has argued that it is self-evident that 'institutions for recognising and enforcing fundamental rights should work to counterbalance private economic power rather than reinforcing it. Obligations to protect fundamental rights must extend—enforceably—to private, for-profit entities if they are to be effective at all.'[21] The point is that, even if public regulators respect the conditions set by the community, it will not suffice if private regulators are left free to use technological management in ways that compromise the community's moral aspirations, or violate its constitutive principles, or exceed the agreed and authorised limits for its use. Accordingly, it should be a condition of the rule of law (the Rule of Law 2.0, as Cohen terms it)[22] that the *private* use of technical measures, machines, and technological management should be compatible with the general principles for their (public) use. This applies whether the private regulators are operating at a distance from public regulators or, as is increasingly the case in some contexts (such as the development of 'smart' cities) in partnership with them.[23]

This need for an extended application of the rule of law is reinforced by Shoshana Zuboff's critique of the surveillance capitalism that thrives in

---

[19] Martin Krygier, 'Philip Selznick: Incipient Law, State Law, and the Rule of Law' in Hanneke van Schooten and Jonathan Verschuuren (eds), *International Governance and Law: State Regulation and Non-State Law* (Cheltenham: Edward Elgar, 2008) 31, at 32.

[20] As highlighted by Krygier (n 19) at 41, drawing on Philip Selznick, *Law, Society, and Industrial Justice* (New York: Russell Sage, 1969).

[21] Julie E. Cohen, *Between Truth and Power* (Oxford: Oxford University Press, 2019) at 267.

[22] Cohen (n 21) at 237 and 266–268, arguing for a Rule of Law 2.0 that reflects the need to entrench respect for fundamental human rights in a networked digital (information) era.

[23] For some of the problems to which this can give rise, see Teresa Scassa, 'Designing Data Governance for Data Sharing: Lessons from Sidewalk Toronto' (2020) *Technology and Regulation* 44.

our connected and networked societies.[24] The fact of the matter is that our information societies are wired for connection and designed to be 'smart'. Increasingly, human interactions and transactions—whether in commerce or communication, in transport or health— are mediated by these technologies; increasingly, the smooth running of our societies depends on the integrity of its technological infrastructures. Without doubt, these technologies are hugely enabling. Nevertheless, as Zuboff observes, while we 'celebrate the networked world for the many ways in which it enriches our capabilities and prospects', 'being connected' is by no means an unqualified good.[25] In particular, Zuboff argues, we should not assume that 'the networked form has some kind of indigenous moral content, that being "connected" is somehow intrinsically pro-social, innately inclusive, or naturally tending towards the democratization of knowledge'.[26]

To be sure, making it clear that the rule of law applies to private regulators will not necessarily bring those parties into line. For example, where the rule of law specifies the consent of users as the required authorisation for the terms and conditions set by private proprietors of platforms or other online environments, this might translate into a licence for the proprietors rather than protection for the users. Moreover, as Zuboff notes, experience thus far suggests that lawmakers, regulators, and courts—despite there being very large penalties on paper and the occasional hefty fine in practice[27]—are relatively powerless to control the prospective surveillance capitalists who are adept at responding to both social resistance and regulatory interventions.[28] Still, to concede that the rule of law does not apply to parties who act with regulatory intent in their civil society dealings is to give up the ghost. Applying the rule of law to private regulators might not be sufficient, but it is certainly necessary.

We should also mention one other consideration. If we exempt private regulators from the discipline of the rule of law, this can give rise to difficult legal questions about whether a party is acting in a public or private regulatory capacity (or carrying out public or private regulatory functions).[29] In the bigger

---

[24]   Shoshana Zuboff, *The Age of Surveillance Capitalism* (London: Profile Books, 2019).

[25]   Shoshana Zuboff (n 24) at 4. Compare, too, Brett Frischmann and Evan Selinger, *Re-Engineering Humanity* (Cambridge: Cambridge University Press, 2018).

[26]   Zuboff (n 24) at 9.

[27]   Mathieu Rosemain, 'France fines Google $57 million for European privacy rule breach' Reuters, *Technology News*, 21 January 2019: available at https://www.reuters .com/article/us-google-privacy-france/france-fines-google-57-million-for-european -privacy-rule-breach-idUSKCN1PF208 (last accessed 19 April 2020).

[28]   Zuboff (n 24), Ch 5.

[29]   As exemplified in the British case law on whether, for the purposes of the Human Rights Act 1998, a body is a public authority. For discussion, see Roger Brownsword,

picture, this is a much less important consideration. Nevertheless, it makes no sense to create such doctrinal distinctions that present opportunities for private enterprises (often in the vanguard of technological development) to argue for exemption.[30]

5.2.3 Both Rules and Technical Measures

Again, it is implicit in the first prong of our rethinking that the discipline of the rule of law must apply to both rules and technical measures. Regulators, whether in online or offline environments, should not be able to bypass the rule of law simply by relying on technical measures or new technologies either in support of rules or in place of governance by rules. For example, it makes no sense to insist that end-user licences or terms and conditions imposed by contract must be compatible with the rule of law but then exempt the designed-in protection of the identical interests (as with digital rights management) from the scrutiny of the rule of law.

In a different context, Bernard Harcourt has cautioned that criminal justice thinking is increasingly driven by our realisation that we can make use of new technologies to prevent crime but without attention being paid to whether we should so utilise these tools and, in particular, whether such use is compatible with an independent theory of just punishment.[31] Harcourt expresses his concern as follows:

> The perceived success of predictive instruments has made theories of punishment that function more smoothly with prediction seem more natural. It favors theories of selective incapacitation and sentencing enhancements for offenders who are more likely to be dangerous in the future. Yet these actuarial instruments represent nothing more than fortuitous advances in technical knowledge from disciplines, such as sociology and psychology, that have no normative stake in the criminal law. These technological advances are, in effect, exogenous shocks to our legal system, and this raises very troubling questions about what theory of just punishment we would independently embrace and how it is, exactly, that we have allowed technical knowledge, somewhat arbitrarily, to dictate the path of justice.[32]

'General Considerations' in Michael Furmston (ed), *The Law of Contract* 6th ed (London: LexisNexis, 2017) paras 1.245–1.253.

[30]   Indeed, we might think that public bodies should be taking up the opportunities they have (through privatisation and contracting) to spread public law values: see, e.g., Jody Freeman, 'Extending Public Law Norms Through Privatization' (2003) 116 *Harvard Law Review* 1285.

[31]   Bernard E. Harcourt, *Against Prediction* (Chicago: University of Chicago Press, 2007).

[32]   Harcourt (n 31) at 3.

When Harcourt refers to theories of just punishment that have a normative stake in the criminal law, we can, as he rightly says, draw on a 'long history of Anglo-Saxon jurisprudence—[on] centuries of debate over the penal sanction, utilitarianism, or philosophical theories of retribution'.[33] However, the general point is that, whichever of the candidate theories we 'independently embrace', we will have a view about the justification for an actuarial approach that turns on considerations other than whether the technical knowledge that we have 'works' in preventing and controlling crime.

Putting all this in other words, although emerging technologies might be attractive to those who undertake public policing functions or private security, or who seek to secure compliance with their background legal rights, their application needs to be explicitly authorised; and this means that the rule of law must apply.[34]

5.2.4 Processual Inclusivity and Procedural Integrity

In the next chapter, we will elaborate on the idea that there should be a 'social licence' for new technologies and their applications. The test for the acceptability of new technologies and their applications is not simply whether they can survive in the market. Pre-market, and pre-circulation, there needs to be public engagement, debate, and approval. Exactly how this is operationalised might vary from one community to another. However, anticipating the idea of a social licence, we can say at this stage that the rule of law should put down a marker for processual inclusivity and procedural integrity where the ground rules for the application of a new technology are being debated, or where there is a material change in the use of technological instruments, and particularly where it is proposed to introduce some element of governance by technology (so that rules and humans are taken out of the loop).

That said, it is one thing to make a commitment to inclusive and deliberative public engagement, and it is quite another to deliver it. Famously, reflecting on the public debate on GM foods in the UK, Sheila Jasanoff identifies a number of difficulties and dilemmas:

> It was conducted, to start with, under severe resource and time constraints by the government's dubiously legitimate and competent public relations unit, the Central

---

[33] Harcourt (n 31) at 188. For a succinct overview, see Ted Honderich, *Punishment: The Supposed Justifications* (London: Hutchinson, 1969).

[34] For a similar argument see Benjamin Bowling, Amber Marks, and Cian Murphy, 'Crime Control Technologies: Towards an Analytical Framework and Research Agenda' in Roger Brownsword and Karen Yeung (eds), *Regulating Technologies* (Oxford: Hart, 2008) 51.

Office of Information. As a result, many regional meetings drew those already knowledgeable about the issues, who were least likely to contribute fresh perspectives to the exchanges. Coordination with the other two strands of the process [the first strand was a cost/benefit study undertaken by the Strategy Unit, and the second was a Science Review led by the government's chief scientific adviser] proved difficult. Even the website, organized around bland questions and oversimplified answers, seemed ill suited to arousing the interest of persons not already involved in the debate. In sum, the effort underscored a dilemma confronting state efforts to democratise the politics of new and emerging technologies: on the one hand, interacting only with identifiable stakeholders may simply strengthen the traditionally cosy relations between business and government; on the other hand, the public that needs to be engaged in broader debates about the pros and cons of technology is elusive and, in the absence of reliable precedents, hard to engage in deliberations whose very authenticity and purpose are widely questioned.[35]

How might these obstacles be overcome? Clearly, dialogue and engagement should begin well before decisions about a particular technology or its applications have become locked in;[36] parties have to act in good faith; it will not do to treat the consultation as an exercise in persuading the public rather than genuinely engaging with the public—consultation should not be viewed by governments or sponsors as an exercise in 'getting the message across'; there should be a commitment to take fully into account the outcome of the process (not just the outcomes that suit the interests of the sponsors); the dialogue should be properly integrated with other processes of technology assessment; it should be properly resourced and professionally undertaken;[37] and, unlike the flawed process around the care.data initiative, communication should be accurate and mixed messages should be avoided.[38]

---

[35]   Sheila Jasanoff, *Designs on Nature* (Princeton: Princeton University Press, 2005) 129.

[36]   See, the Royal Society and the Royal Academy of Engineering, *Nanoscience and Nanotechnologies: Opportunities and Uncertainties* (RS Policy document 19/04) (London, July 2004); and the Nuffield Council on Bioethics, *Emerging Biotechnologies* (London, December 2012).

[37]   The Royal Society and the Royal Academy of Engineering (n 36) at para 38.

[38]   Compare Policy Exchange, 'What's wrong with care.data?' (28 February 2014), available at https://policyexchange.org.uk/whats-wrong-with-care-data/ (last accessed 20 February 2021). See, too, Scassa (n 23) for the lessons that might be drawn from the failed data governance scheme for the Sidewalk Toronto development.

5.2.5 Substantive as Well as Procedural

According to Brian Tamanaha,[39] the pathology of instrumentalism arises where the use of legislatures and courts in pursuit of (partisan) ends together with the acts of officials within those institutions is no longer constrained by the rule of law. It follows, argues Tamanaha, that 'legislators must be genuinely oriented toward enacting laws that are in the *common* good or *public* interest'; that 'government officials must see it as their solemn duty to abide by the law in good faith; this duty is not satisfied by the manipulation of law and legal processes to achieve objectives'; and 'that judges, when rendering their decisions, must be committed to searching for the strongest, most *correct* legal answer; they must resist the temptation to succumb to the power they have to exploit the inherent indeterminacy of law to produce results they desire.'[40]

Following Tamanaha in insisting that laws are oriented towards the common good or the public interest, our rethinking of the rule of law focuses on more substantive matters. In some respects, the community's substantive thinking might be 'defensive' and 'precautionary': power tends to corrupt; power enabled by new technologies could be abused; and the rule of law needs to put in place appropriate protective provisions. In other respects, though, the substance of the rule of law is aspirational, expressing a vision of what the community wants to be—especially a vision of how it sees governance that might displace both rules and human directors. This will take us, in the next section of this chapter and in the following chapter, to the idea of a 'community licence' for new technologies. It is not enough that new technologies and their applications are socially acceptable (meeting the standard for a social licence); they also need to be compatible with the community's fundamental values. While there might be a considerable jurisprudence about the compatibility of new technologies and their applications with, say, human rights to privacy and human dignity, more work will need to be done in articulating substantive authorising provisions for governance by machines and technological management.

If we rethink the rule of law in this way, it goes beyond the procedural requirements of legality, it stretches right across the regulatory environment, and it goes a long way towards assuring the legitimacy of Law. However, there is still more work to be done in rethinking legitimacy.

---

[39] Brian Z. Tamanaha, *Law as a Means to an End* (Cambridge: Cambridge University Press, 2006).

[40] Ibid., at 250 (emphases in original).

5.3 GOVERNANCE BY MACHINES, TECHNOLOGICAL MANAGEMENT, AND THE RULE OF LAW

The rule of law, rethought as indicated, covers all proposed applications of emerging technologies, including applications for legal and regulatory purposes. How might a rethought version of the rule of law be articulated in relation to a proposed scheme of governance that either takes humans out of the loop (governance by machines) or employs technological management?

As we have said, in the next chapter, we will elaborate the ideas of a social licence and a community licence, both of which are vital building blocks in our revised understanding of the rule of law. We will also elaborate there an overarching idea of a global licence (for the protection and maintenance of the global commons on which all human communities rely). In the present discussion, however, it is the social and community licences that are focal.

5.3.1 The Rule of Law and the Community Licence

Where the aspiration of a particular community is not simply to be a moral community (a community committed to the primacy of moral reason) but a particular kind of moral community, then it will be a condition of the rule of law that reliance on governance by machines or the use of technological management (just as with rules and standards) should be consistent with its particular constitutive features—whether those features are, for instance, liberal or communitarian in nature, rights-based or utilitarian, and so on.

One recurrent thought in this book is that a community might attach particular value to preserving both human officials (rather than machines) and rules (rather than technological measures) in the administration of the law or in some particular areas or for particular legal functions (perhaps that the members of the final court of appeal should always be humans). For example, it might be suggested that core crime should be ring-fenced against technological management. However, while this proposal might appeal to liberals who fear that technological management will impede due process and to those moralists who hold that it is always important to have the opportunity freely to do the right thing, it is likely to be opposed by those who fear that such a strategy is a hostage to fortune.

Whatever its thinking, whatever the outcome of debates about such matters, the community has the opportunity to declare its position—indeed, to enshrine in its constitution, as part of its fundamental and distinctive values, its particular take on the relationship between humans, machines, and governance.

84 *Rethinking law, regulation, and technology*

When this is done, the community's position will be incorporated as one of the elements in the rule of law, as one of the tests for its community licence.

5.3.2 The Rule of Law and the Social Licence

Where the use of technological management is proposed as part of a risk management package, so long as the community is committed to the ideals of deliberative democracy, it will be a condition of the rule of law that there needs to be a transparent and inclusive public debate about the terms of the package. It will be a condition that all views should be heard with regard to whether the package amounts to both an acceptable balance of benefit and risk as well as representing a fair distribution of such risk and benefit (including adequate compensatory provisions). Before the particular package can command respect, it needs to be somewhere on the spectrum of reasonableness. This is not to suggest that all regulatees must agree that the package is optimal; but it must at least be reasonable in the weak sense that it is not a package that is so unreasonable that no rational regulator could, in good faith, adopt it.

For example, where technologically managed places or products operate dynamically, making decisions case-by-case or situation-by-situation, then one of the outcomes of the public debate might be that the possibility of a human override is reserved. In the case of driverless cars, for instance, we might want to give agents the opportunity to take control of the vehicle in order to deal with some hard moral choice (whether of a 'trolley' or a 'tunnel' nature) or to respond to an emergency (perhaps involving a 'rescue' of some kind).[41] Beyond this, we might want to reserve the possibility of an appeal to humans against a decision that triggers an application of technological management that forces or precludes a particular act or that excludes a particular person or class of persons. Indeed, the concern for last-resort human intervention might be such a pervasive feature of the community's thinking that it is explicitly embedded as a default condition in the rule of law—in the way, for example, that we might interpret Article 22 of the GDPR (which we discuss below in 5.3.3).

Similarly, there might be a condition that interventions involving technological management should be reversible—a condition that might be particularly important if measures of this kind are designed not only into products and places but also into people, as might be the case if regulators contemplate

---

[41] For discussion, see Roger Brownsword, *Law, Technology and Society: Re-imagining the Regulatory Environment* (Abingdon: Routledge, 2019) Ch 10.

making interventions in not only the coding of product software but also the genomic coding of particular individuals.[42]

The community might want to be satisfied that the use of technological measures is accompanied by proper mechanisms for accountability. When there are problems, or when things go wrong, there need to be clear, accessible, and intelligible lines of accountability. It needs to be clear who is to be held to account as well as how they are to be held to account; and, the accounting itself must be meaningful.[43] There might also be a concern that the use of technological management will encourage some mission creep. If so, it might stipulate that the restrictive scope of measures of technological management or their forcing range should be no greater than would be the case were a rule to be used for the particular purpose. In this sense, the restrictive sweep of technological management should be, at most, co-extensive with that of the equivalent (shadow) rule.

Recalling our discussion of legality, the community might also be mindful that regulators should not try to trick or trap regulatees; and this is a principle that is applicable whether the instrument of regulation is the use of rules or the use of technological management. Accordingly, it should be a condition of the rule of law that technological management should not be used in ways that trick or trap regulatees and that, in this sense, the administration of a regime of technological management should be in line with the reasonable expectations of regulatees. Crucially, if the default position in a technologically managed regulatory environment is that, where an act is found to be available, it should be treated as permissible, then regulatees should not be penalised for doing the act on the good faith basis that, because it is available, it is a lawful option.

5.3.3 Article 22 GDPR

Article 22 of the General Data Protection Regulation (GDPR),[44] like its predecessor Directive 95/46/EC, is an interesting example of a regulatory measure that is designed to keep humans in the loop where automated decision-making threatens significant human interests. However, this provision poses more questions than it answers.[45] We can start with the doctrinal points that have

---

[42] See, further, section 9.4 below (on possible red lines).

[43] See Joshua A. Kroll, Joanna Huey, Solon Barocas, Edward W. Felten, Joel R. Reidenberg, David G. Robinson, and Harlan Yu, 'Accountable Algorithms' (2017) 165 *University of Pennsylvania Law Review* 633, 702–704.

[44] Regulation (EU) 2016/679.

[45] For discussion, see, e.g., Roger Brownsword and Alon Harel, 'Law, Liberty and Technology—Criminal Justice in the Context of Smart Machines' (2019) 15 *International Journal of Law in Context* 107; and Orla Lynskey, 'Criminal Justice

already attracted attention; but, beyond such points, there is a more fundamental question about the status of Article 22: namely, does it speak to the social licence for automated decisions or to the community licence?

In order to claim the protection of Article 22, the data subject must show (1) that there has been a decision based solely on automated processing (2) which has produced adverse legal effects or (3) which has significantly affected him or her. Lawyers will detect several nice points of interpretation here.

First, how should we read the threshold condition of a decision that is based 'solely' on automated processing? For example, would we say that the processing of offences by body-worn video cameras (BWVs) is solely automated? How relevant is it that the camera has to be switched on by, as well as being worn by, a human police officer?[46] If we say that this is not solely automated, is it going to be too easy for data controllers to avoid this provision by introducing a degree of token human involvement? To counter such an avoidance of the law, we might treat 'solely' as meaning 'without significant human involvement', in which case the interpretive question becomes one of distinguishing between 'significant' and 'non-significant' human involvement. So, once again, is the involvement of police officers with BWVs 'significant' human involvement?

Second, while it is easy enough to think of examples of adverse legal effects (such as a denial of bail or a denial of parole), what might count as 'significant' effects? According to the guidance issued by the UK ICO:

> A legal effect is something that adversely affects someone's legal rights. Similarly significant effects are more difficult to define but would include, for example, automatic refusal of an online credit application, and e-recruiting practices without human intervention.[47]

To take an example from the European Commission, let us assume that 'a flaw in the [fully and solely automated] appointment scheduling system in a hospital will not normally pose risks of such significance as to justify legislative

---

Profiling and EU Data Protection Law: Precarious Protection from Predictive Policing' (2019) 15 *International Journal of Law in Context* 162; and, for the vexed question of whether there is 'a right to an explanation', see Sandra Wachter, Brent Mittelstadt, and Luciano Floridi, 'Why a Right to Explanation of Automated Decision-Making Does Not Exist in the General Data Protection Regulation' (2017) 7 *International Data Privacy Law* 76.

[46] For discussion, see Ben Bowling and Shruti Iyer, 'Automated Policing: The Case of Body-Worn Video' (2019) 15 *International Journal of Law in Context* 140.

[47] For guidance, see, https://ico.org.uk/for-organisations/guide-to-the-general-data -protection-regulation-gdpr/individual-rights/rights-related-to-automated-decision -making-including-profiling/ (last accessed 29 October 2018).

intervention.'[48] Presumably, this would contrast with, say, the use of AI in surgical procedures where a patient's life might be at stake if 'something goes wrong' as well as with the use of AI to make decisions about which Covid-19 patients should be prioritised for access to the limited resources of ICUs. But, then, what should we say about the use of AI in undertaking an initial triage of persons arriving at the hospital accident and emergency department? While we might agree with the Commission when it says that '[t]he objective of trustworthy, ethical and human-centric AI can only be achieved by ensuring an appropriate involvement by human beings in relation to high-risk applications',[49] the devil is in the detail. Until there is a jurisprudence to sharpen our thinking about where the lines of (significant or high) risk are to be drawn, about how we are to understand 'human-centric' applications of technologies, and about precisely what level and kind of involvement by humans is 'appropriate', to some extent at least, we are in the dark.

Third, what counts as a 'decision'? This is not a new question. However, if the smart cities of the future run on automated processes and if 'code/ spaces' are ubiquitous,[50] what does it take for a 'decision' to stand out from the background 'noise'? Given that the Data Protection Directive was already out of touch on the date of enactment[51]—this being because it was predicated on a world of large mainframe computers, highly visible data controllers, and data processing as the exception rather than the highly distributed rule—could it be that history is about to repeat itself? Could it be that the GDPR is predicated on a world in which automated decisions are the exceptions rather than the rule?

This leaves us with the question of whether we should understand Article 22 as a legislative compromise that speaks to the social licence or as a constitutional commitment that speaks to the community licence. In much EU jurisprudence, where rights are recognised, it is unclear whether these rights stand at the social licence level or at the community licence level. For example, in the *Google Spain* case,[52] the balancing exercise undertaken by the court mixes

---

[48]   European Commission, *White Paper: On Artificial Intelligence—A European Approach to Excellence and Trust*, COM(2020) 65 final, Brussels, 19.2.2020, p. 17.

[49]   Ibid. at 21. On 'high risk' applications, see the European Commission's proposal for a Regulation on AI, COM(2021) 206 final (Brussels, 21.4.2021).

[50]   See, James Bridle, *New Dark Age: Technology and the End of the Future* (Verso, 2018) 37–38.

[51]   Peter P. Swire and Robert E. Litan, *None of Your Business* (Washington: Brookings Institution Press, 1998).

[52]   Case C-131/12, *Google Spain SL, Google Inc v Agencia Española de Protection de Datos (AEPD), Mario Costeja González* [2014] available at http://curia.europa.eu/ juris/document/document_print.jsf?doclang=EN&docid=152065.

88 *Rethinking law, regulation, and technology*

fundamental rights with non-fundamental rights or legitimate interests.[53] In other words, it runs together questions about the community licence with those relating to the social licence. Although the GDPR gestures in the direction of the right to be forgotten in Article 17, where it elaborates the data subject's right to erasure, we are no nearer to settling the status, scope, and strength of this right.[54] Similarly, although Article 22 of the GDPR recognises a right, in certain circumstances, not to be subject to solely automated decisions, the status, scope, and strength of this right remain to be clarified.

5.4 CONCLUDING REMARKS

According to Mireille Hildebrandt, the 'challenge facing modern law is to reinvent itself in an environment of pre-emptive computing without giving up on the core achievements of the rule of law'.[55] Hildebrandt does not understate the seriousness of the consequences if we fail to meet this challenge:

> If we do not learn how to uphold and extend the legality that protects individual persons against arbitrary or unfair state interventions, the law will lose its hold on our imagination. It may fold back into a tool to train, discipline or influence people whose behaviours are measured and calculated to be nudged into compliance, or, the law will be replaced by techno-regulation, whether or not that is labelled as law.[56]

In other words, it is the ideal of legality together with the rule of law that stands between us and a disempowering techno-managed future.

Having argued in the previous chapter that a concept of legality fashioned for governance by rules can only go so far in protecting citizens against a techno-managed future, we have argued in the present chapter that the rule of law now needs to be rethought so that it does extend the required protection. By developing the rule of law along five key prongs that ensure that private

---

[53] On which, see Eleni Frantziou, 'Further Developments in the Right to be Forgotten: The European Court of Justice's Judgment in Case C-131/12, *Google Spain SL, Google Inc v Agencia Española de Proteccion de Datos*' (2014) 14 *Human Rights Law Review* 761, esp at 768–769.

[54] For insightful commentary, see Orla Lynskey, 'Control over Personal Data in a Digital Age: *Google Spain v AEPD and Mario Costeja Gonzalez*' (2015) 78 *Modern Law Review* 522 (arguing, inter alia, that the labelling of the right as a 'right to be forgotten' is misleading).

[55] Mireille Hildebrandt, *Smart Technologies and the End(s) of Law* (Cheltenham: Edward Elgar, 2015) at 17.

[56] Hildebrandt (n 55) at xiii; and at 226, Hildebrandt concludes by emphasising that it is for lawyers to involve themselves with such matters as 'legal protection by design'. See, too, Mireille Hildebrandt and Bert-Jaap Koops, 'The Challenges of Ambient Law and Legal Protection in the Profiling Era' (2010) 73 MLR 428.

reliance on techno-regulation is not given a free pass, we can at least take some necessary steps to avoid a disempowering techno-managed future. However, as we have indicated, we also need to rethink our idea of legitimacy—so that we have a clear basis for judging whether governance by machines and technological management can be treated as acceptable and justified. It is to this rethinking that we turn in the next chapter.

6. Rethinking legitimacy

6.1 INTRODUCTION

Because new technologies present novel regulatory opportunities but also, particularly in communities where there is a plurality of preferences and priorities, represent a major challenge for both regulators and their regulatee communities, there needs to be some rethinking of legitimacy.[1] When humans and prescriptive rules are de-centred by the automation of processes and reliance on smart machines, there are likely to be some pressing concerns about the legitimacy of both the process and the outputs of this mode of governance.[2]

If we build on a reworked understanding of the rule of law, as indicated in the previous chapter, then two legitimacy concerns have been addressed. First, the processual requirements should ensure that those who have conflicting and competing preferences and priorities in relation to some proposed measure will have a fair hearing. There is no guarantee that the ensuing best accommodation of interests will satisfy all parties, but it will at least be defensible. It is not as though the views of some group are being ignored. Second, the substantive provisions in the authorising rules should ensure that the fundamental values of the community are respected by the rulers. There is nevertheless a further concern which goes deeper and beyond each community. This is the concern that no community should act in ways that might compromise the basic preconditions for human existence, human agency, and human community itself. These preconditions are applicable in all places at all times. Accordingly, it is suggested that we should rethink the legitimacy of law and regulation by drawing on the idea of a 'triple licence'.[3]

The triple licence cross-checks the legitimacy of a technological application at three levels. First, for the social licence, the application has to be 'socially

---

[1] Nb the discussion in Chris Reed and Andrew Murray, *Rethinking the Jurisprudence of Cyberspace* (Cheltenham: Edward Elgar, 2018) Chs 7 and 8.

[2] Compare the discussion in Karen Yeung, 'Why Worry about Decision-Making by Machine?' in Karen Yeung and Martin Lodge (eds), *Algorithmic Regulation* (Oxford: Oxford University Press, 2019) 21.

[3] This is elaborated in Roger Brownsword, 'Law, Technology, and Society: In a State of Delicate Tension' (2020) XXXVI *Politeia* 137, 26.

90

acceptable'.[4] At this level, the licence signals that there has been a process of consultation and deliberation about the application of a technology and that the position taken up by regulators is not unreasonable and is broadly acceptable to members of the community. Second, for the community licence, the application has to be compatible with the fundamental values of the particular community in which it is being proposed. As we keep saying in Europe, the applications of AI and other technologies must be compatible with our commitment to human rights. Third, and most importantly, for the global licence, the application of a technology must be compatible with respect for the essential conditions for human social existence—that is, the protective and facilitative conditions that make it possible for humans to co-exist, to construct their own community orders, and to settle their conflicts and disputes. If an application fails in relation to any one of these licensing conditions, it will be lacking in legitimacy—and the seriousness of the failure will escalate as we move up from the social to the community level and then to the global level.

This exercise in rethinking has many implications, including a clearer appreciation of the line between what are matters of cosmopolitan concern and what are matters for local jurisdictions (namely the line between the global and the community/social) as well as of where and to what extent pluralism is permissible (within and between particular communities);[5] it invites the opening of a conversation about the use of technical solutions (such as geo-engineering or gene drives) to fix the global commons;[6] and, last but by no means least, it facilitates a more focused appreciation of where precautionary reasoning has particular salience (at the level of the global commons).[7]

We can start by sketching two baseline views of legitimacy, neither of which is adequate; and, then, we can elaborate on our proposed rethinking of this critical aspect of any regulatory environment.

---

[4]   See, Legal Services Board, *Striking the Balance: How Legal Services Regulation Can Foster Responsible Technological Innovation* (London, April 2021) esp. at para 4 and paras 91–99.

[5]   See, further, section 6.3 below.

[6]   See, e.g., Roger Brownsword and Han Somsen, 'Law, Innovation and Technology: Fast Forward to 2021' (2021) 13 *Law, Innovation and Technology* 1.

[7]   For discussion, see Roger Brownsword, *Law Technology and Society: Re-imagining the Regulatory Environment* (Abingdon: Routledge, 2019) 84–87; and, see further, Deryck Beyleveld and Roger Brownsword, 'Complex Technology, Complex Calculations: Uses and Abuses of Precautionary Reasoning in Law' in Marcus Duwell and Paul Sollie (eds), *Evaluating New Technologies: Methodological Problems for the Ethical Assessment of Technological Developments* (Dordrecht: Springer, 2009) 175, and 'Emerging Technologies, Extreme Uncertainty, and the Principle of Rational Precautionary Reasoning' (2012) 4 *Law, Innovation and Technology* 35.

6.2 TWO BASELINE VIEWS

There are two baseline views of legitimacy that are relevant to our discussion. The first is the traditional baseline associated with the Westphalian law view which refers questions about the legitimacy of rules or actions to the legal system's own internal tests. The second view is the baseline that is characteristic of much regulatory thinking. Here, the idea is that the legitimacy of regulatory actions follows from certain kinds of deliberative processes in which the various competing and conflicting interests are balanced and accommodated. Neither of these views is adequate.

6.2.1 Internal Test

In the Westphalian view of law, legitimacy is treated as internal to the legal system. Acts by citizens are legitimate provided that they are in accordance with the primary rules; acts by legal officials are legitimate provided that they are authorised by the secondary rules; the primary rules are legitimate because they are validated by the secondary rules; and the secondary rules, the apex rule apart, are valid because they are authorised by the apex rule. This is such an attenuated account of legitimacy that some might be inclined to reject such a manifestly self-serving view as no more than 'legitimating'.

There is one further point to make about this view. In some legal systems, the authorisation will need to be explicit. There needs to be a rule explicitly declaring that the act in question is lawful or authorised. In other legal systems, implicit authorisation is accepted as sufficient. Here, it is enough that no rule explicitly declares that the act in question is unlawful or not authorised. In practice, this is quite important because the particular application of an emerging technology might not have been anticipated, such that on the former view the application is not yet lawful (because it lacks explicit authorisation) while, on the latter view, it will be lawful in the absence of any contrary explicit provision. Given this difference, it might be argued that the former view takes legitimacy more seriously than the latter; but, even the former view suffers from a weak account of legitimacy.

To put the point shortly, if we are to take legitimacy seriously, in the way that we are taking both legality and the rule of law seriously, we have to do better. We have to rethink legitimacy.

6.2.2 Simple Balancing

As new technologies emerge, regulators will often be confronted with a plurality of views for and against the technologies and their proposed applications.

Rethinking legitimacy

While some will push for a permissive regulatory environment that is facilitative of beneficial innovation, others will push back against research that gives rise to concerns about the safety and reliability of particular technologies as well as their compatibility with respect for fundamental values. Yet, how are the interests in pushing forward with potentially beneficial technologies to be reconciled with the heterogeneous interests of the concerned who seek to push back against them?

A stock answer to this question is that regulators, neither over-regulating nor under-regulating, should seek an accommodation or a balance of interests that is broadly 'acceptable'. If the issue is about risks to human health and safety, regulators (having assessed the risk) should adopt a management strategy that confines risk to an acceptable level; and, if there is a tension between, say, the interest of researchers in accessing health data and the interest of patients in both their privacy and the fair processing of their personal data, regulators should accommodate these interests in a way that is reasonable—or, at any rate, not obviously unreasonable.

This baseline view of legitimacy is open to a number of objections. First, it is not clear on what basis it regards the particular interests that are pressed on regulators as legitimate or illegitimate, or indeed whether it differentiates between interests in this way. In order to distinguish between legitimate and illegitimate interests, a theory of legitimacy is required; and, this baseline view simply does not have any such theory. If, on the other hand, no distinction is drawn between legitimate and illegitimate interests, then illegitimate interests are allowed to shape an accommodation of interests that will be claimed to be 'legitimate'. Second, all interests (whether legitimate only or legitimate and illegitimate) are flattened in the balancing process. No distinction is drawn between 'higher order' and 'lower order' interests. Indeed, there is no ranking of interests (whether higher order or lower order). To do this, a theory of value would be needed and, again, this baseline view simply does not have any such theory. Third, a proposed balance of interests will be presented as legitimate if it is 'reasonable' or 'not unreasonable' relative to the interests put forward for consideration. Not only is this a weak view of legitimacy, but it allows for more than one accommodation to be legitimate; and, it has no resource to explain or justify why one reasonable accommodation was preferred to another. Finally, it is unclear whether the burden of justification is on those who argue for permission or those who argue for prohibition or restriction; and, nor is it clear whether, at any stage, the burden is transferred from one side to the other.

While there might be a place for a balancing of competing and conflicting interests, this baseline view lacks depth, not only depth in relation to the fundamental values of a particular community, but depth that goes beyond that.[8] Some further rethinking is required.

6.3 RETHINKING LEGITIMACY

In what follows, we will rethink legitimacy in a way that brings out dimensions of both breadth and depth. This rethink takes the form of a three-tiered lexically ordered scheme of regulatory responsibilities. However, before detailing these responsibilities, let me make five preliminary remarks.

First, there are two key lines drawn by this scheme. One of these lines is drawn between, on the one side, the first tier of responsibility and, on the other, the second and third tiers of responsibility. This line divides those responsibilities that are governed by cosmopolitan considerations from those responsibilities that are governed by the values and interests of each particular community. In other words, this is the line that divides what is rightly cosmopolitan from what is rightly local. A second key line is that drawn between the second and third tiers of responsibility. This line is within the domain of national or local sovereignty where it is the values and interests of each particular community that count. What this line anticipates is that the community will declare its constitutive values which will then be privileged over whatever non-constitutive values and interests it recognises.[9] So, on one side of the line, we have the constitutive (or defining, or fundamental) values of the particular community and, on other side, we have all other interests that are recognised as legitimate.

Second, in principle, we might appeal to certain values, such as human dignity, at any one of these three tiers. In other words, we might claim that respect for human dignity is a cosmopolitan principle that takes priority over any national or local considerations; or, we might locate human dignity in the constitutive values of a particular community;[10] or, we might argue that, in

---

[8] For a critique that adopts this view, see Roger Brownsword and Jeffrey Wale, 'Testing Times Ahead: Non-Invasive Prenatal Testing and the Kind of Community that We Want to Be' (2018) 81 *Modern Law Review* 646.

[9] The form of this model is neutral between liberal communities that are constituted by respect for specified fundamental rights and communitarian groups that are constituted by respect for specified basic duties. In principle, though, a community might not restrict itself to a simple two-category distinction between constitutive and non-constitutive values; it might, for example, operate with a three-category model of constitutive values, non-constitutive higher-order values, and non-constitutive lower-order values. However, for the sake of simplicity, in this discussion, I will stick with the two-category approach and the three-tiered scheme of responsibilities.

[10] Compare, e.g., European Commission, *Ethics Guidelines for Trustworthy AI* (Brussels, 2019) 13, where, having accepted that some ethically acceptable trade-offs have to be made, it is said that there might nevertheless be cases where 'no ethically

Rethinking legitimacy 95

a particular community, there is a legitimate interest in human dignity (or in dignified treatment, or in not suffering an indignity) that needs to be taken into consideration when regulatory decisions are made.

Third, when I refer to a particular 'community', it is not my intention to reinstate Westphalian legal thinking. Certainly, nation-states are candidate communities. However, my conception of such a community—as a particular group of humans that identifies with a constitutive set of commitments—might be instantiated neither by *all* nation-states and nor *only* by nation-states. Rather, what a global map of particular communities might show is that some nation-states are indeed particular communities so conceived but that there are also such communities to be found within nation-states as well as transnationally between and beyond nation-states.[11]

Fourth, this scheme of regulatory responsibilities is to be contrasted with those many (baseline view) debates where there is no clear ranking of interests, and where there is scepticism about foundational values.[12] Most importantly, at the first tier of the scheme, the premise is that regulators have a stewardship responsibility in relation to the anterior conditions for *humans* to exist and for them to function as a *community of agents* (inter alia by making various demands of their regulators). We should certainly say that any claimed third-tier interest or proposed accommodation of interests that is incompatible with the maintenance of these conditions (the 'commons') is totally 'unacceptable'—but it is more than that.[13] Unlike the second-tier constitutive values to which a particular community commits itself—distinctive values which may legitimately vary from one community to another—the essential preconditions are not contingent or negotiable. For human agents, to compromise the commons' conditions is simply unthinkable.

---

acceptable trade-offs can be identified. Certain fundamental rights and correlated principles are absolute and cannot be subject to a balancing exercise (e.g. human dignity).'

[11] I am indebted to Marcus Düwell's comments for this clarification: see https://www.youtube.com/watch?v=o9ejqNoUF8o (last accessed 19 March 2020).

[12] For a particularly clear adoption of this kind of balancing approach, see Public Health Agency of Canada, *Framework for Ethical Deliberation and Decision-Making in Public Health* (Ottawa, 2017). For general critique of this kind of approach, see Sarah Franklin, 'Ethical Research—the Long and Bumpy Road from Shirked to Shared' (2019) 574 *Nature* 627 (remarking on a 'sense of ethical bewilderment' in bioethical circles).

[13] Compare the AI practices that are prohibited (as 'unacceptable') by Title II of the European Commission's proposal for a Regulation on AI, COM(2021) 206 final (Brussels, 21.4.2021). Arguably, the intention here is to prohibit practices that compromise Union values, which is to say that they are 'unacceptable' relative to a community licence.

Fifth, in order to avoid any misunderstanding, let me say explicitly that there is a one-to-one correlation between the three tiers of regulatory responsibilities and the three strands of the triple licence. The first tier of regulatory responsibility correlates to the global licence; the second tier to the community licence; and the third tier to the social licence.

Accordingly, my proposal is that, when we are debating regulatory legitimacy, we should frame our thinking in the terms of this three-tiered scheme—where, to repeat, the first-tier responsibilities are cosmopolitan and non-negotiable; where the responsibilities at the second and third tiers are contingent, depending on the fundamental values and the interests recognised in each particular community; and, where vertical conflicts (between responsibilities and interests that are at different tiers) are to be resolved lexically by reference to the tiers of importance, responsibilities and interests that are engaged by a higher tier always outranking those in a lower tier.[14]

By way of elaboration, we can now speak to each of the three tiers of this proposed scheme of regulatory responsibilities, bearing in mind that each tier speaks to the conditions for meeting the correlative strand of the triple licence.

6.3.1   The First-Tier Stewardship Responsibility for the Commons

The first regulatory responsibility, a fundamental stewardship responsibility, is to protect and maintain the essential infrastructure for human social existence, the global commons. The commons has two dimensions: one relating to human existence; and the other relating to the human capacity for agency. These are the conditions, in Joshua Fairfield's terms, for the 'viability' of humans:[15] if the former conditions are compromised, human life is not viable and, if the latter conditions are compromised, human agency is not viable.

---

[14]   This scheme, it has to be conceded, does not resolve *horizontal* conflicts or tensions within any particular tier. Whether or not a strategy for resolving this kind of conflict or tension can be developed is a matter for further consideration, including (at the first tier) resolving any tension between the interests of the present generation of humans and the interests of future generations. On this latter point, see Marcus Düwell, https://www.youtube.com/watch?v=o9ejqNoUF8o (last accessed 19 March 2020).

[15]   Strikingly, see Joshua A.T. Fairfield, *Runaway Technology* (New York: Cambridge University Press) at 143:

Viability is simply this…. Each of us is the result of billions of years of organisms who *were*, and who passed on the capacity for being to their descendants. The only reason science, music, art, mathematics, comic books, and pizza exist is because living beings have conceived of them. The only reason answers exist is because of questions; and questions because of minds. If we think that thinking and wondering are any good at all, then we will wish to preserve wondering and thinking. And the only way to do that is to preserve our viability.

6.3.1.1 The existence conditions

The *human* species is defined by its biology; and the prospects for human life depend on whether the conditions are compatible with the biological characteristics and needs of the *human* species. Most planets will not support *human* life. The conditions on planet Earth are special for *humans*. However, the essential life-supporting conditions are not specially tailored to the needs of any particular human; these are the generic conditions for the existence of any member of the human species.

It follows that regulators should take steps to protect, preserve, and promote the natural ecosystem for human life.[16] At minimum, this entails that the physical well-being of humans must be secured; humans need oxygen, they need food and water, they need shelter, they need protection against contagious diseases, if they are sick they need whatever medical treatment is available, and they need to be protected against assaults by other humans or non-human beings.

6.3.1.2 The agency conditions

It is characteristic of human *agents* that they have the capacity to choose and to pursue various projects and plans whether as individuals, in partnerships, in groups, or in whole communities. Sometimes, the projects and plans that they pursue will be harmonious; but, often, human agents will find themselves in conflict or competition with one another. However, before we get to particular projects or plans, before we get to conflict or competition, there needs to be a context in which the exercise of agency is possible. This context is not one that privileges a particular articulation of agency; it is prior to, and entirely neutral between, the particular plans and projects that agents individually favour; the conditions that make up this context are generic to agency itself. It follows that regulators should take steps to instate, promote, and preserve the conditions for meaningful self-development and agency— or the 'conditions of personal self-determination' as Massimo Renzo[17] terms them.

---

[16]   Compare, J. Rockström et al, 'Planetary Boundaries: Exploring the Safe Operating Space for Humanity' (2009) 14 *Ecology and Society* 32 (http://www.ecologyandsociety.org/vol14/iss2/art32/) (last accessed 14 November 2016); and, Kate Raworth, *Doughnut Economics* (London: Random House Business Books, 2017) 43–53.

[17]   Massimo Renzo, 'Revolution and Intervention' (2020) 54 *Nous* 233, 243. Drawing on Joseph Raz, *The Morality of Freedom* (Oxford: Oxford University Press, 1986) 370–373, Renzo identifies these conditions with having the capacity to form and execute sufficiently complex intentions, having an adequate range of options from which to choose the sort of life that we want for ourselves, and being free from coercion and manipulation as we make such choices. Compare, too, Simon McCarthy-Jones, 'The Autonomous Mind: The Right to Freedom of Thought in the Twenty-First

These agency conditions start with a sense of the self, with a sense of one's own interests, one's own purposes, preferences, and priorities, and one's own identity. However, agency also implicates a sense of others, of their interests, and of what it is to give due consideration to agents other than oneself.[18] In short, the agency conditions are conducive to both self-development and the development of moral agency; and, it is important to repeat, these conditions are neutral between agents, not being designed to privilege any particular set of interests, any particular projects, or any particular view of what makes an action morally appropriate.

To elaborate on this latter point, the agency conditions, while being conducive to 'moral' development and 'moral' agency in a formal sense, must also remain impartial between competing moral visions, values, and ideals. So, for example, in her discussion of techno-moral virtues, (sous)surveillance, and moral nudges, Shannon Vallor is rightly concerned that any employment of digital technologies to foster prosocial behaviour should respect the importance of conduct remaining 'our *own conscious activity and achievement* rather than passive, unthinking submission'[19]—or, as I have argued on many occasions elsewhere, we should be concerned if technological management leaves agents with no practical option other than to do what those who manage the technology judge to be the right thing.[20]

6.3.1.3 Respect for the essential infrastructure

Where the essential conditions obtain, they constitute a deep and fundamental critical infrastructure, a commons, for any community of agents. Any human agent, reflecting on the antecedent and essential nature of the commons, must

---

Century' (2019) 2 *Frontiers in Artificial Intelligence* article 19 at 11 (on modern technologies and 'manipulation').

[18] An understanding of agency implicates both awareness and recognition of, as well as respect for, self-interest and the interest of other agents: so, an understanding of what it is to have the capacity for agency presupposes respect for the conditions for both self-interested agency and other-regarding agency. To cash out this argument, see Alan Gewirth, *Reason and Morality* (Chicago: University of Chicago Press, 1978); Deryck Beyleveld, *The Dialectical Necessity of Morality* (Chicago: University of Chicago Press, 1991) and, 'What Is Gewirth and What Is Beyleveld? A Retrospect with Comments on the Contributions' in Patrick Capps and Shaun D. Pattinson (eds), *Ethical Rationalism and the Law* (Oxford: Hart, 2017) 233.

[19] Shannon Vallor, *Technology and the Virtues* (New York: Oxford University Press, 2016) 203 (emphasis in original).

[20] See, too, for compelling commentary on the socio-technological threat to the commons for agency, Brett Frischmann and Evan Selinger, *Re-engineering Humanity* (Cambridge: Cambridge University Press, 2018). Similarly, see Sylvie Delacroix, 'Automated Systems and the Need for Change' in Simon Deakin and Christopher Markou (eds), *Is Law Computable?* (Oxford: Hart, 2020) 161.

Rethinking legitimacy 99

regard these infrastructural conditions as special. Indeed, from any practical viewpoint, prudential or moral, that of regulator or regulatee, the protection of the commons must be the highest priority.

Reasoning impartially, each human agent will see itself as a stakeholder in the commons; and, it will be understood that, for the benefit of all human agents, these essential conditions must be maintained and respected; precaution, prevention, and preservation is the name of this particular game. While respect for the commons' conditions is binding on all human agents, this does not rule out the possibility of prudential or moral pluralism. Rather, the commons represent the preconditions for both individual self-development and community debate, giving each agent the opportunity to develop his or her own view of what is prudent as well as what should be morally prohibited, permitted, or required. However, the practice of articulating and contesting both individual and collective perspectives (like all other human social acts, activities, and practices) is predicated on the existence of the commons.

6.3.2 The Second-Tier Regulatory Responsibility to Respect the Community's Fundamental Values

Beyond the fundamental stewardship responsibilities, regulators are also responsible for ensuring that the constitutive values of their particular community are respected. Just as each individual human agent has the capacity to develop their own distinctive identity, the same is true if we scale this up to communities of human agents. There are common needs and interests but also distinctive identities.

From the middle of the twentieth century, many nation-states have expressed their fundamental (constitutional) values in terms of respect for human rights and human dignity.[21] These values clearly intersect with the commons' conditions and there is much to debate about the nature of this relationship and the extent of any overlap—for example, if we understand the root idea of human dignity in terms of humans having the capacity freely to do the right thing for the right reason, then human dignity reaches directly to the commons' conditions for moral agency.[22] However, those nation-states that articulate their

---

[21] See Roger Brownsword, 'Human Dignity from a Legal Perspective' in M. Duwell, J. Braavig, R. Brownsword, and D. Mieth (eds), *Cambridge Handbook of Human Dignity* (Cambridge: Cambridge University Press, 2014) 1.

[22] See, e.g., Roger Brownsword, 'Human Dignity, Human Rights, and Simply Trying to Do the Right Thing' in Christopher McCrudden (ed), *Understanding Human Dignity* (Proceedings of the British Academy 192) (Oxford: The British Academy and Oxford University Press, 2013) 345; 'Developing a Modern Understanding of Human Dignity' in Dieter Grimm, Alexandra Kemmerer, and Christoph Möllers (eds),

particular identities by the way in which they interpret their commitment to respect for human dignity are far from homogeneous.

Put somewhat bluntly, whereas, in some communities, the emphasis of human dignity is on individuals having the right to make their own choices, in others it is on the constraints (in particular, relating to the sanctity, non-commercialisation, non-commodification, and non-instrumentalisation of human life) by which individual choice is limited.[23] These differences in emphasis mean that we frequently encounter protagonists on both sides of a debate invoking human dignity in support of their positions;[24] puzzlingly, according to some, there is dignity in dying (choosing to die) while, according to others, there is dignity in living (life being maintained). This also means that communities articulate in very different ways on a range of beginning-of-life and end-of-life questions as well as questions of human enhancement, the use of human embryos for research, property rights in detached human body parts, and so on.

It is, of course, essential that whatever the fundamental values to which a particular community commits itself, they should be consistent with (or cohere with) the commons' conditions. It is the commons that sets the stage for community life; and then, without compromising that stage, particular communities form and self-identify with their own distinctive values. Or, to make the same point in terms of the triple licence, the conditions set for the community licence must be compatible with the conditions that apply to the global licence.

6.3.3 The Third-Tier Regulatory Responsibility to Seek an Acceptable Accommodation of Interests

Within each community, there will be many debates about questions that do not implicate either the commons' conditions or the community's particular fundamental values. Judgements about benefits and risks, and about the dis-

---

Human Dignity in Context (Baden-Baden: Nomos; Oxford: Hart, 2018) 299; and, 'From Erewhon to Alpha Go: For the Sake of Human Dignity Should We Destroy the Machines?' (2017) 9 *Law, Innovation and Technology* 117.

[23] See Deryck Beyleveld and Roger Brownsword, *Human Dignity in Bioethics and Biolaw* (Oxford: Oxford University Press, 2001); Tim Caulfield and Roger Brownsword, 'Human Dignity: A Guide to Policy Making in the Biotechnology Era' (2006) 7 *Nature Reviews Genetics* 72; and Roger Brownsword, *Rights, Regulation and the Technological Revolution* (Oxford: Oxford University Press, 2008).

[24] For a particularly complex instance of this phenomenon, see C. Möllers, 'The Triple Dilemma of Human Dignity: A Case Study' in Christopher McCrudden (ed), *Understanding Human Dignity* (Oxford: The British Academy and Oxford University Press, 2013) 173 (case study of *KU v Finland*, Application no. 2872/02, 2008 at the European Court of Human Rights).

tribution of benefits and risks, might be varied and conflictual. Whether one favours seeking consensus or sharpening difference, dealing with a plurality of competing and conflicting views will be a challenge.

In many communities, these questions will be managed by a process of inclusive consultation and democratic deliberation structured by a concern that the governing regulatory framework should not 'over-regulate' and risk stifling potentially beneficial innovation, but nor should it 'under-regulate' and expose citizens to unacceptable risks.

At this level, the responsibility of regulators is to seek out an acceptable accommodation between the competing and conflicting interests of individuals and groups that are members of the community. Where the issues are both widely and deeply contested, the accommodation will be unlikely to satisfy everyone. There is no right answer as such; and, because the balancing exercise allows a broad margin for 'acceptable' accommodation, there are likely to be several regulatory positions that can claim to be reasonable while, conversely, we have no compelling reason to favour one such reasonable accommodation over another.[25] Inevitably, the process is somewhat 'messy'.[26]

These difficulties and contingencies notwithstanding, regulators will have a responsibility to act in good faith, both in reaching the accommodation and in keeping the position under review; and, correlatively, members of the community will have a responsibility to respond in ways that are compatible with both the fundamental values of their community and the maintenance of the commons' conditions.[27]

Accordingly, while, in some cases, a balancing approach is the appropriate regulatory response, in other cases, it is not. To put this more precisely: at the third-tier of regulatory responsibility (or, in relation to the social licence), a balancing of competing and conflicting preferences is appropriate; but, neither at the first tier (where the responsibility is to respect the commons' conditions) nor at the second tier (where the responsibility is to hold the

---

[25] See Roger Brownsword and Jeffrey Wale (n 8).

[26] Compare Richard E. Ashcroft, 'Could Human Rights Supersede Bioethics?' (2010) 10 *Human Rights Law Review* 639.

[27] As Mario Martini puts it in 'Regulating Algorithms' in Martin Ebers and Susana Navas (eds), *Algorithms and Law* (Cambridge: Cambridge University Press, 2020) 100, at 135:

What is needed…is a healthy balance between the risk of suffocating innovation and the foundations of a digital humanism. In the tradition of the Enlightenment era, the categorical imperative should point the way ahead for the digital world. Technology should always serve the people—not the other way around.

community true to its fundamental commitments and privilege its constitutive values) is such a balancing exercise appropriate.[28]

6.4 CONCLUDING REMARKS

There is much more to be said about this proposed rethinking of legitimacy. The idea of regulators having three tiers of responsibility goes beyond their responsibilities in relation to reliance on emerging technologies; and, importantly, it speaks to both the breadth and depth of regulatory responsibilities.[29] For our purposes, however, it supplies the key frame for our thinking about the substantive content of the rule of law and about the applications of technology that need to be monitored and controlled in all places as opposed to those which are subject only to community control and social licence.

To the extent that our point of departure is a Westphalian commitment to governance by rules, our thinking will be driven by a demand for 'legality' (meaning that the reasonable expectations that citizens have about the operationalisation of this form of governance should be met). This demand might or might not be embellished by a particular version of the rule of law. Either way, legality in conjunction with the rule of law pretty much takes care of regulatory legitimacy. However, once we move towards governance by machines and technological management, our thinking needs to be revised. The rule of law, duly rethought to connect with the new modalities of governance, and guided by the bigger picture of regulatory responsibilities, has to become the principal reference point for questions of legitimacy. Mireille Hildebrandt is right: if we do not undertake this rethinking, we have left the door open to a disempowering techno-managed future.[30]

---

[28] Noting the concession in n 14, where there are horizontal conflicts at either the first or second tiers, there might also need to be a 'balancing of values' at the relevant level. But, of course, there is no balancing between values at *different* levels; there, the lexical ordering resolves the conflict.

[29] See, e.g., Roger Brownsword, 'Migrants, State Responsibilities, and Human Dignity' (2021) 34 *Ratio Juris* 6.

[30] Nb, too, Leo Marx, 'Technology: The Emergence of a Hazardous Concept' (2010) 51 *Technology and Culture* 561 at 577:

The popular belief in technology as a—if not the—primary force shaping the future is matched by our increasing reliance on instrumental standards of judgment, and a corresponding neglect of moral and political standards, in making judgments about the direction of society.

PART III

Rethinking law and regulation in practice—
LawTech, RegTech, and technological
management

7. Rethinking legal and regulatory practice and the provision of legal services

7.1 INTRODUCTION

This third part of the book is about how we deal with what Karl Llewellyn called the 'law jobs', specifically how we deal with the 'trouble case' (disputes) and the preventive channelling of conduct (regulation).[1] Legal anthropologists have already provoked much rethinking in relation to these tasks; but, the context for their work has been simpler, very low-tech, societies.[2] By contrast, our focus is on LawTech and RegTech, on rethinking law and regulation in practice (with legal practice and regulatory functions now enabled by smart technologies). It is also about regulating conduct by 'technological management', where technologies (in a broad sense) are used to design places and spaces, products and processes, in ways that risks are managed by eliminating the practical options available to regulatees. While the purpose of LawTech, RegTech, and technological management is to provide legal services and perform regulatory functions, this does not, of course, exempt them from scrutiny for their legality, legitimacy, and compliance with the rule of law.

According to Richard Susskind, new technologies (particularly information technologies and AI) will be one of three key drivers of change in the practice of law (the other two being 'more-for-less' or value for money, and the liberalisation of traditionally restrictive legal practices).[3] These drivers suggest that there will be less demand for some traditional legal services because clients will become more adept at servicing their own needs and that the supply of some services will be more automated.[4]

---

[1] Karl N. Llewellyn, 'The Normative, the Legal, and the Law-Jobs: The Problem of Juristic Method' (1940) 49 *Yale Law Journal* 1355.

[2] See, e.g., Simon Roberts, *Order and Dispute* (London: Penguin, 1979).

[3] Richard Susskind, *Tomorrow's Lawyers* (2nd ed) (Oxford: Oxford University Press, 2017).

[4] On future trends for legal services, see, e.g., Deloitte, 'Future Trends for Legal Services' (June 2016), available at https://www2.deloitte.com/global/en/pages/legal/articles/deloitte-future-trends-for-legal-services.html (last accessed 21 February 2020).

Rethinking legal and regulatory practice and the provision of legal services   105

The turn to technology, however, will not stop at the delivery of traditional legal services. Regulators will employ smart tools that maximise the use of their resources in monitoring compliance and detecting non-compliance; dispute resolution both within and outwith the courts will be transformed;[5] and the control of crime will become increasingly high-tech. If a legal or regulatory process can be automated, the chances are that it will be;[6] and, if ex ante technological measures can be used to prevent wrongdoing, disputes, and conflicts, they will be so used—at any rate, unless a community has rejected the use of particular tools or reliance on a particular technological strategy. This reservation is not insignificant. In a report that assesses the early use of AI by the Federal Administrative Agencies, the authors point out that the stakes are high; there is much to be gained but also to be lost. Thus:

> Managed well, algorithmic governance tools can modernize public administration, promoting more efficient, accurate, and equitable forms of state action. Managed poorly, government deployment of AI tools can hollow out the human expertise inside agencies with few compensating gains, widen the public-private technology gap, increase undesirable opacity in public decision-making, and heighten concerns about arbitrary government action and power.[7]

Anticipating a future in which legal and regulatory functions are assisted or carried out by smart tools, the two outstanding features of the rethinking in this part of the book are automation (taking humans out of the loop) and prevention of wrongdoing, conflicts, and disputes (acting ex ante rather than responding in a remedial or corrective mode ex post). While the former is in line with governance by machines, the latter is in line with technological management.

---

[5]   See, further, https://remotecourts.org/ (last accessed 21 February 2021) where Richard Susskind writes:
> In the middle of March 2020, court buildings around the world began to close in response to the rapid spread of a newly identified coronavirus, SARS-CoV-2 (the 'virus'). Within days, alternative ways of delivering court service were put in place in many jurisdictions. The uptake of various technologies, especially video, was accelerated in the justice systems of numerous countries. There remain some skeptics and critics, but in light of the experience during the crisis, there is certainly greater acceptance now than in February 2020—amongst lawyers, judges, officials, and court users—that judicial and court work might be undertaken very differently in years to come. Minds have been opened and changed over the past few months. Many assumptions have been swept aside.

[6]   Generally, see Christopher Steiner, *Automate This* (London: Penguin, 2013).

[7]   David Freeman Engstrom, Daniel E. Ho, Catherine M. Sharkey, and Mariano-Florentino Cuéllar, *Government by Algorithm: Artificial Intelligence in Federal Administrative Agencies* (February, 2020) at 8; available at https://papers.ssrn .com/sol3/papers.cfm?abstract_id=3551505 (last accessed 10 April 2021).

In this chapter, we take a first look at the sweep of legal and regulatory, professional and lay, practices that are set to be rethought as a more technological approach is taken.

7.2 USING LAWTECH AND REGTECH: WHO, HOW, AND WHY?

In a well-known article, Ben Alarie envisages AI tools being employed, first by citizens and then by legal officials, to clarify how particular rules of law apply to specified facts.[8] The particular example on which Alarie focuses is that of the rules which determine whether a 'worker' is an employee or a self-employed contractor, this having many practical implications for the tax and benefit responsibilities and entitlements of the parties as well as for employers' liability. Over the years, the tests supported by the common law jurisprudence have changed somewhat but, even when the tests are relatively stable, they are not always easy to apply because each case has its own distinctive features. Moreover, where the question is posed in relation to legislative provisions the application of which hinges on the interpretation of the term 'worker'—for example, as in the Uber test-case in the UK, where the private car hire drivers argued (successfully) that they were 'workers' within the meaning of the relevant statutory employment law[9]—we not only hear echoes of the common law jurisprudence but also of the background employment purposes and policies.[10] So, if AI tools can enable parties to know where they stand in particular cases, this seems to be entirely beneficial, positively serving the rule of law ideal that there should be certainty as to the legal position and that there should be congruence between the rules as promulgated and the rules as administered by legal officials. Moreover, employing AI in this way does not disrupt the underlying assumption that agents will make their own autonomous decisions about compliance with the rules.

However, it is not difficult to imagine uses of AI that go well beyond this, putting a significant wedge under the idea of law as a mode of governance that is directed by humans who rely on rules. Beyond taking advice on the legal position, we can imagine disputes being resolved by machines (governance by machines) as well as conduct being channelled and confined not by prescriptive rules but by technological management. In this vision, the regulatory

---

[8] Benjamin Alarie, 'The Path of the Law: Toward Legal Singularity' (2016) 66 *University of Toronto Law Journal* 443, 445. Available at https://papers.ssrn.com/sol3/papers.cfm?abstract_id=2767835 (last accessed 24 January 2020).

[9] *Uber BV and others v Aslam and others* [2021] UKSC 5.

[10] For echoes of the common law test of 'degree of control', see ibid., para 95 et seq; and for the purposes and policies of the employment legislation, see para 70 et seq.

Rethinking legal and regulatory practice and the provision of legal services 107

enterprise is no longer rule-based and human-directed in the way that we traditionally conceive of law. Crucially, while regulatees might know precisely where they stand, this is no longer relative to a regime of rules but relative to an array of technologies that design out the practical option of 'non-compliance'. As we have said, once practice takes humans out of the legal and regulatory loop and once technological management replaces rules to channel conduct, we have a very different version of law. Here, the wedge under a human-centric enterprise and a rule-based practice is thick and significant.

In the following eight indicative cases, starting with the kind of unobjectionable case discussed by Alarie, we discuss a number of potential uses of technology in and around legal and regulatory practices. In these scenarios, it is as important to note who is using the technology (whether it is a legal subject or regulatee, or some legal officer or regulator, or a legal professional) as it is to note the purpose for which the technology is being used (and how this impacts on the autonomy of the legal subject or regulatee).

7.2.1 Using an AI Tool to Clarify the Legal Position I

Let us imagine that, long before the Uber test-case, Smith, one of Uber's drivers, uses an AI tool to clarify the legal position on a particular matter, to predict how the legal rules will be applied to a specified set of facts—for example, to clarify (as in Alarie's example) whether a particular working arrangement will be treated as an employment relationship or as a relationship between a client and an independent contractor (perhaps with a view to clarifying whether Uber would be vicariously liable for Smith's negligent driving); or, perhaps, some entirely unconnected matter such as whether the noise coming from building work on an adjoining property (and which is disturbing Smith's daytime sleeping) is so unreasonable as to constitute a common law nuisance. On the face of it, and assuming that the AI tool is reasonably reliable, such a consultative use is unproblematic. It is up to Smith to choose whether to use the tool and what to do with the advice given by it.

Let us suppose that Smith is advised by the tool that the claim (or defence) he has in mind is arguable but that the legal position is not entirely clear and predictable. On the basis of this feedback, Smith decides that he needs to take professional advice by consulting a lawyer. Possibly the lawyer to whom Smith turns for advice will also consult an AI tool; but, the lawyer's advice to Smith is more than a rehearsal of what the AI tool has advised. Again, provided that Smith knows exactly what he is getting for his money, this all seems to be unobjectionable.

We should also say that, in these hypotheticals, it makes no difference whether Smith is seeking to clarify his position relative to a legal rule that is mandatory (prohibiting or requiring certain action) or one that is optional (permissive or facilitative); and, it makes no difference whether Smith is using this tool as a prospective claimant or as a prospective defendant. Similarly, the nature of the rule is not material where it is a legal professional who uses an AI tool to assist in clarifying the legal position.[11]

7.2.2   Using an AI Tool to Clarify the Legal Position II

Let us imagine that Smith, now as a taxpayer, seeks guidance from the Revenue on whether a particular scheme will be treated as a lawful and permitted scheme of avoidance or as an unlawful evasion of liability. The status of 'guidance' given by the Revenue is somewhat problematic.[12] Nevertheless, in itself, the use of the tool seems unobjectionable.

That said, even as a matter of informal guidance, the view that we take of the use by a *regulator* of an AI tool is likely to be qualified. In particular, unless it is common knowledge that the Revenue uses tools in this way, there is likely to be a requirement that the Revenue should notify Smith that they have relied on a particular tool, or taken the tool's view into account in giving guidance back to Smith. If the guidance given by the Revenue becomes a formal decision, we would certainly expect the use of AI tools to be regulated and, of course, there would be procedures for appeal.

At first blush, we have not yet detected a serious issue about the use of LawTech or RegTech. These hypotheticals continue to treat the regulatory enterprise as rule-based and human-centric. The AI tool does not replace either the rules or their human interpreters. If the use of an AI tool enables regulatees to know precisely where they stand relative to the rules (and to plan with more confidence) and, at the same time, it enables regulators to apply and enforce the rules more accurately, this seems to be compatible with the ideals of the rule of law. And, so long as regulators and regulatees elect to use such tools and to act on their indications, human agency and autonomy is not compromised.

Nevertheless, the equivalence between AI tools being used to apply legal rules and principles and traditional 'coherentist' legal reasoning is only approximate. The AI tools might have been trained by reference to many examples of humans applying legal rules and principles but the tools lack the authenticity of a human who is trying to construct a compelling narrative that justifies reading the law in a particular way. In other words, the AI tools might simulate an exercise in coherentist legal reasoning but the logic that

---

[11]   Note, however, that there might be circumstances in which the use of AI tools is so widespread (and considered to be best practice) that legal professionals would be judged to be falling below the required standard of care if the tools were not used.

[12]   See Stephen Daly, *Tax Authority Advice and the Public* (Oxford: Hart, 2020).

drives the tools is not coherentist in the same way. Accordingly, while AI tools might outperform humans in a straightforward predictive context, and while applying the general principles of the cases to particular facts is functionally equivalent to coherentist reasoning, it does not follow that AI tools outperform humans in reasoning like a coherentist lawyer.[13] To this extent—and we might not be greatly concerned about this—the technological wedge is only a thin one.[14] However, if legal and regulatory decisions are to be outsourced to smart machines, this is a sea change in the mode of governance and we need to be alert to this wedge getting thicker.[15]

7.2.3 Using an AI Tool to Exercise One's Legal Powers (to Guarantee Compliance with Rules that Specify a Particular Optional Legal Facility)

Imagine that Smith wishes to make a will in a legal system where the rules do not require citizens to make a will (it is optional) but where the rules do prescribe a set of conditions to be observed (for example, conditions relating to a testator's signature and witnesses) before a will is to be treated as valid. Imagine, too, that Smith is aware that the courts are very strict in enforcing compliance with the conditions and that he is anxious not to slip up. Accordingly, in order to ensure that he makes a will that will be recognised as legally valid, Smith employs some will-drafting software. Such software, as the Legal Services Board points out in a recent report, may be either 'supportive' or 'substitutive'. Hence, 'if [the software] is used by a lay member of the public, [it] will almost certainly be wholly *substitutive* in nature. However, for an experienced lawyer, the software could be *supportive* in nature, as he or she could use their expertise to check that the document meets his or her client's requirements.'[16] For our purposes, let us assume that Smith is a lay person

---

[13]   See Rebecca Crootof, '"Cyborg Justice" and the Risk of Technological-Legal Lock-In' (2019) 119 *Columbia Law Review* 1.

[14]   But, nb, Frank Pasquale, 'A Rule of Persons, Not Machines: The Limits of Legal Automation' (2019) 87 *Geo. Wash. LR* 1.

[15]   See, further, the discussion in 7.2.6.

[16]   Legal Services Board, *Striking the Balance: How Legal Services Regulation Can Foster Responsible Technological Innovation* (London, April 2021) para 38. At para 35, the distinction between 'supportive' and 'substitutive' is drawn as follows:

> Up to now technologies have been mostly 'supportive' in that they have assisted persons in delivering legal services but not displaced their labour. However, some newer technologies are, or have the potential to be, 'substitutive' in that they can displace human labour.

At para 36, a distinction is also drawn between 'practical' and 'substantive' applications. Whereas the former are 'primarily intended to assist with the running of legal

whose use is substitutive in the sense that he is using an AI tool (or some other form of technological management) that guarantees that the will that is made will be recognised as valid and effective. Quite simply, if Smith tries to write his will in a way that is not compliant—for example, without adding his signature, or signing in the right place—the technology will prevent him from proceeding.

While we should be extremely cautious about the use of technological management by *regulators* (because it might compromise agency and autonomy), where it is a *regulatee* who freely elects to employ such technology, it is not so clear that there is a problem. That said, as Brett Frischmann and Evan Selinger caution, if we 'outsource' a task to a smart tool, there might be more at stake than the completion of a particular task:

> When deciding whether to outsource, we need to consider whether it's worth losing agency, responsibility, control, intimacy, and, possibly, knowledge and skill.[17]

Of course, if we could be confident that these risks would be confined to the one case in question—if we could be confident that we would only make one will and we would not make use of legal tools or other similar technologies on any other occasion—this might seem unduly alarmist. However, if the context is one in which our reliance on smart tools is 'creeping', then this is another matter. So, while the use of the particular technology in the particular case might be no more than a thinnish wedge under the law, we need to be careful. While Smith freely chooses a particular end (the making of a will) and the technology is a means to that end—features that seem both instrumentally rational and consistent with Smith's agency—we need to be careful that this does not evolve into habitual reliance that compromises Smith's agency.

7.2.4 Using Technologies to Enforce One's Legal Rights

Suppose that Smith uses blockchain to enforce his legal right to payment under certain contracts or obtains a web-blocking judicial order to prevent further infringement of his IP rights.[18] There are two questions that we might raise about this kind of use of technology.

---

practices', the latter 'are intended to assist with substantive legal work involved with the delivery of services to clients'.

[17] Brett Frischmann and Evan Selinger, *Re-Engineering Humanity* (Cambridge: Cambridge University Press, 2018), at 30.

[18] See, Mark Hyland, 'A critical evaluation of the effectiveness and legitimacy of webblocking injunctions' (2020) 12 *Law, Innovation and Technology* 30.

The first question is whether there is any element of over-enforcement. Are these tools being employed to achieve performance or compliance to which Smith is clearly entitled? If so, so far so good; but, if not, there is a cause for concern—especially so if Smith is involved in unlawful activities.[19] For example, if a payment is enforced but there are excusing conditions or exceptions that might be applicable, it is worrying that a contestable claim is enforced without contestation and without it being established that the technology is enforcing no more than Smith's legal entitlement. It is one thing for a payment to be ordered or a block to be put in place under a default judgment (where the defendant does not contest the claim or the order); but it is quite another thing for equivalent steps to be taken by default simply because the technology enables them to do so.

The second question is whether, even if there is no issue of over-enforcement, the means employed are legitimate. For example, there has been a question about whether web-blocking orders that may be legitimately employed against copyright infringers may also be employed lawfully against infringers of other kinds of IP (such as trade marks).[20] This is a traditional question about the scope of judicial authority. However, where tools such as blockchain are used outside the usual legal channels for enforcement and remedies, the co-existence of the technological option with the standard judicial option might present some interesting questions. This is a matter to which we will return in the next chapter.[21]

7.2.5   Using Tools to Assist with Official Decision-Making

We have already considered one example of officials (in the Revenue) using an AI tool to assist with their 'guidance'. However, there are many examples of legal officials making use of smart tools to guide their own decision-making, whether in relation to the best use of their resources, or to the treatment of a particular person.

How far, for example, might the courts rely on AI tools? Given the many potential applications of AI relating to different types of court and different

---

[19]   See, e.g., Thibault Schrepel, 'Collusion by Blockchain and Smart Contracts' (2019) 33 *Harvard Journal of Law and Technology* 117 (discussing unlawful collusive activities and the use of blockchain and smart contracts to 'punish' defectors).

[20]   For discussion, see Hyland (n 18).

[21]   See, 8.4.2. Also, see Karen Yeung, 'Regulation by Blockchain: The Emerging Battle for Supremacy Between the Code of Law and Code as Law' (2019) 82 *Modern Law Review* 207, and Roger Brownsword, 'Automated Transactions and the Law of Contract: When Codes are not Congruent' in Michael Furmston (ed), *The Future of the Law of Contract* (Abingdon: Routledge, 2020) 94.

types of judicial decision, this invites several questions, each of which asks whether a particular application would be unfair or violate due process.

For present purposes, we can restrict our remarks to the well-known case of *State of Wisconsin v Loomis*,[22] where the defendant denied involvement in a drive-by shooting but pleaded guilty to some less serious charges. The Circuit Court, having accepted the plea, ordered a Presentence Investigation Report (PSI) to which a COMPAS risk assessment was attached. This assessment, showing that the defendant presented a high risk of recidivism, was relied on by the Court, along with other sentencing considerations, to rule out probation. The defendant appealed on the ground that the Court's use of COMPAS violated due process.

Ruling against the defendant, the Wisconsin Supreme Court held (i) that 'if used properly' COMPAS would not violate due process and (ii) the Circuit Court had used the tool properly because 'its consideration of the COMPAS risk scores was supported by other independent factors'—in other words, 'its use was not determinative'.[23] The Court also identified a number of limitations and cautions that should be borne in mind when using such a risk-assessing AI tool, namely:

- The proprietary nature of COMPAS has been invoked to prevent disclosure of information relating to how factors are weighed or how risk scores are determined.
- Because COMPAS risk assessment scores are based on group data, they are able to identify groups of high-risk offenders — not a particular high-risk individual.
- Some studies of COMPAS risk assessment scores have raised questions about whether they disproportionately classify minority offenders as having a higher risk of recidivism.
- A COMPAS risk assessment compares defendants to a national sample, but no cross-validation study for a Wisconsin population has yet been completed. Risk assessment tools must be constantly monitored and re-normed for accuracy due to changing populations and subpopulations.
- COMPAS was not developed for use at sentencing, but was intended for use by the Department of Corrections in making determinations regarding treatment, supervision, and parole.[24]

If the *Loomis* principle is generalisable—and, we might want to pause before we do generalise it—it follows that judicial reference to AI assessments will be permissible but only as one relevant consideration; judges, on this view, may properly be assisted by AI tools but their reliance must not be complete; the indications given by an AI tool must not be determinative in the courtroom.

---

[22] 881 N.W.2d 749 (Wis. 2016).
[23] Ibid, paras 8 and 9; and, similarly, see paras 98–99.
[24] Ibid., at para 100.

Rethinking legal and regulatory practice and the provision of legal services   113

Or, in the language of the Legal Services Board, the proper use of AI tools by judges is 'supportive' rather than 'substitutive'.[25]

7.2.6   Using Tools to Make Official Decisions

Governance by machines implies that the decisions are actually made by the machines, rather like in high-frequency trading. For some communities, algorithms making trades in a millisecond and even the occasional flash-crash, might be no big deal. However, for other communities and in other domains, handing over decision-making to the machines is a serious wedge.

As we have just seen, in *Loomis*, the Wisconsin Supreme Court thought that the use of tools to *assist* judges (make sentencing decisions in criminal courts) was as far as we should go. What might we say in other domains, such as commerce, health, and employment?

In the Introduction to her book, *Weapons of Math Destruction*,[26] Cathy O'Neil recounts the troubling story of Sarah Wysocki, a fifth-grade school teacher in Washington, DC. Washington evaluated the performance of its school teachers by using a tool called IMPACT. The tool was designed to measure the added value given by a teacher year-on-year, with some complex algorithms attempting to make allowances for a range of variables that were independent of the teacher's input. At the end of the academic year 2010–11, Wysokci's IMPACT score was below the required threshold and she was duly dismissed.

Although Wysocki's dismissal was in line with Washington's policy, although it was indicated by the IMPACT score, and although there was no suggestion that there had been a technical malfunction, the case cried out for an explanation because the IMPACT score simply did not align with the high regard in which Wysocki was otherwise held as a teacher.

O'Neil suggests that the most likely explanation was that fourth-grade teachers had inflated their students' exam grades so that, when IMPACT was used to evaluate Wysocki's performance in relation to those (now fifth-grade) students, the baseline data on which the algorithms operated was inaccurate. However, where there is confidence (and, in some cases, over-confidence) in the technology, it is for those who contest the scores to come up with compelling counterevidence and, in this particular instance, this was something that Wysocki could not do.

What we should take from this is that, even if there is formally a right to challenge a decision made by a machine, and even a right to a hearing before

---

[25]   See 7.2.3.
[26]   (London: Penguin Random House, 2017).

114   *Rethinking law, regulation, and technology*

a human tribunal, this might not satisfy concerns that de facto the machine's decision is final. Moreover, if humans have greater confidence in machines than in their fellow humans, we might find that, over time, it becomes the right to a machine decision that is the fallback against human decisions—as, indeed, is already the case in some sports, such as tennis and cricket, where players are allowed a limited number of challenges against the on-court/pitch umpire, with the review being undertaken by what in effect is a technological court of appeal.[27]

That said, is it plausible to suppose that high-level judicial decision-making could be undertaken by a machine? Given the variety of disputes and adjudicative tasks, the socio-legal milieu within which judges act, and the dynamic context of courtroom hearings, John Morison and Adam Harkens conclude that 'while the technical capabilities of algorithmic tools can enable a closer working relationship between humans and machines within the justice system, it will remain a social process, although with potential new forms of interactions between individuals and technologies, producing new ways of resolving legal problems.'[28] It follows that fully automated justice is not on the near horizon. In short,

> [w]hile future technological developments may change this—or indeed policy wants and needs may give such [AI] tools overriding decision-making powers in preference to human actors—the present situation is at least one of transition, where justice provided through the use of these tools and platforms can be classified as *semi-automated*.[29]

Rather than putting humans out of the loop, this presages 'new institutional configurations of human-machine interaction, which are augmented in comparison with existing methods of decision-making'.[30]

---

[27]   Compare, too, Ryan Abbott, *The Reasonable Robot* (Cambridge: Cambridge University Press, 2020) at 9, imagining a future in which human drivers are held to the standard of self-driving cars, or the 'reasonable AI standard'.

[28]   John Morison and Adam Harkens, 'Re-engineering justice? Robot judges, computerised courts and (semi) automated legal decision-making' (2019) 39 *Legal Studies* 618, at 631.

[29]   Ibid., at 632 (emphasis in original).

[30]   Ibid., at 633. See, too, Dilan Thampapillai, 'The Law of Contested Concepts? Reflections on Copyright Law and the Legal and Technological Singularities', in Simon Deakin and Christopher Markou (eds), *Is Law Computable?* (Oxford: Hart, 2020) 223, 231 et seq; and, see, too, Simon Chesterman, *We the Robots? Regulating Artificial Intelligence and the Limits of the Law* (Cambridge: Cambridge University Press, 2021) Ch 9.

Much of this is echoed by Lyria Bennett Moses, who emphasises the link between human adjudication and rule of law values. Thus:

> A judge does not merely find legislation and cases, locate relevant provisions or ratio decidendi, and apply logic to deduce a result. Nor do judges reason statistically from historical data points. Instead, judges are a lynchpin for the rule of law, both in terms of their own decision-making processes and, through building trust and respect, encouraging a broader rule of law culture. Ultimately, judges decide what a decision should be, which is quite different to predicting what the decision will be. Even if machine learning could improve performance against rule of law values such as equal treatment, it could not be contestable on the same terms or take the internal point of view.[31]

So, even if the technologies overcome their 'clunkiness' and their 'bugginess', and even if their capabilities are hugely improved, they are not members of a community of humans who express their fundamental values in the rule of law and who agree the conditions on which they are prepared to accept governance by machines: adjudication by humans is not mechanical and especially so where the question is whether mechanical means of decision-making pass muster relative to whatever conditions have been set for the community licence and have been agreed as part of the social licence.

7.2.7 Using Tools to Improve Compliance with Mandatory Legal Rules

Let us suppose that regulators turn to AI tools as well as other kinds of technological instruments in order to improve compliance with mandatory legal rules. Here, the wedge gets thicker.

As is well known, there is a raft of technologies that might be deployed by regulators to improve compliance.[32] For example, there are technologies that record acts of non-compliance and that survey, locate, recognise, and identify regulatees; and there are AI tools that are designed to employ enforcement

---

[31] Lyria Bennett Moses, 'Not a Single Singularity' in Deakin and Markou (n 30) 205, 220.

[32] See Benjamin Bowling, Amber Marks, and Cian Murphy, 'Crime Control Technologies: Towards an Analytical Framework and Research Agenda' in Roger Brownsword and Karen Yeung (eds), *Regulating Technologies* (Oxford: Hart, 2008) 51; Amber Marks, Benjamin Bowling, and Colman Keenan, 'Automatic Justice? Technology, Crime, and Social Control' in Roger Brownsword, Eloise Scotford, and Karen Yeung (eds), *The Oxford Handbook of Law, Regulation and Technology* (Oxford: Oxford University Press, 2017) 705; and Roger Brownsword and Alon Harel, 'Law, Liberty and Technology—Criminal Justice in the Context of Smart Machines' (2019) 15 *International Journal of Law in Context* 107.

resources more effectively, as well as to risk-assess and risk-manage particular groups or individuals. In other words, technologies can improve regulatory performance by enhancing detection of non-compliance and correction of those who are not compliant.[33]

Where regulators rely on such technologies to support the legal rules, disincentivising and correcting non-compliance, we are still dealing with the enterprise of subjecting human conduct to the governance of rules. The greater the disincentivising effect, the thicker the technological wedge becomes. Long before we get to full-scale technological management of regulatee conduct, there is plenty of cause for concern (especially in relation to whether the use of the tools passes muster relative to the conditions for the particular community licence).

7.2.8 Using Technological Management to Guarantee Compliance with Mandatory Legal Rules

While legal rules might be mandatory on paper, in practice compliance by regulatees might be less than complete. The law, so to speak, is observed in the breach. In order to rectify this deficit, regulators might rely on various technical measures and tools that stop short of full-scale technological management; but, in the end, they might resort to restricting the practical options available to regulatees in particular places and spaces, or to limiting the affordances given by particular products or processes.

Taking the regulation of the speed of motor vehicles as his example, Pat O'Malley charts the hardening of technological control in the following terms:

> In the 'soft' versions of such technologies, a warning device advises drivers that they are exceeding the speed limit or are approaching changed traffic regulatory conditions, but there are progressively more aggressive versions. If the driver ignores warnings, data—which include calculations of the excess speed at any moment, and the distance over which such speeding occurred (which may be considered an additional risk factor and *thus* an aggravation of the offence)—can be transmitted directly to a central registry. Finally, in a move that makes the leap from perfect detection to perfect prevention, the vehicle can be disabled or speed limits can be imposed by remote modulation of the braking system or accelerator.[34]

When regulators make this final move, 'from perfect detection to perfect prevention', we have full-scale technological management. This is where the

---

[33] See, further, 9.2.3.
[34] Pat O'Malley, 'The Politics of Mass Preventive Justice', in Andrew Ashworth, Lucia Zedner, and Patrick Tomlin (eds), *Prevention and the Limits of the Criminal Law* (Oxford: Oxford University Press, 2013) 273 at 280.

technological wedge is both thick and problematic because (i) it displaces the idea of law as an enterprise of subjecting human conduct to the governance of rules and (ii) it compromises the exercise of human agency and autonomy. Unlike the earlier hypothetical in which Smith uses technological management to ensure that his will is validly made, motorists who are technologically managed as in O'Malley's example do not freely opt in to this form of control. Clearly, before any community authorises this kind of regulatory strategy, it needs to take a hard look at what it is endorsing: technological management might work, it might eliminate non-compliance, but at what price?

Taking stock, where smart tools are used by regulatees for the purposes of clarifying the legal position, the disruption is not too great; the technological wedge is relatively thin. The regulatory enterprise remains normative and rule-reliant; and regulatees continue to have the practical option of whether or not to comply with the rules. Similarly, if smart tools are employed to assist decision-makers, the wedge is relatively thin. However, once assistance gives way to reliance, and once occasional use becomes habitual, the wedge gets thicker. Further along the spectrum, where the use of smart tools is by regulators as part of a strategy of technological management that displaces normativity, rule-reliance, and the practical option of non-compliance, we have a very different scenario. This is where the wedge is altogether thicker. This is where the searching questions need to be asked.

7.3   CONCLUDING REMARKS

Driven by LawTech and RegTech, legal and regulatory practice is changing rapidly. Technological solutions drive out inefficiencies and promise a constructive competitiveness in what is traditionally a practice that is highly conservative. In the short run, the benefits are attractive; but care needs to be taken that, in the longer run, the technology does not come at too high a price for humanity.

As we have seen in our initial survey in this chapter, new tools are available to be used for legal purposes by both regulators and regulatees. With a range of different uses and different users, case-by-case analysis can obscure the bigger picture. In that bigger picture, we might see that, with the cumulative reliance on technologies, we are becoming habituated to the use of LawTech, RegTech, and technological management and making it easier for the wedge to become broader and thicker.

In the next two chapters, we can focus on the ways in which technological initiatives might, first, transform the practice of dispute settlement and resolution and then the control of crime.

8. Rethinking disputes and dispute resolution

8.1 INTRODUCTION

The Westphalian view, it will be recalled, is that the paradigms of law are national legal systems, conceived of as systems of primary rules directed at citizens supported by secondary rules that authorise certain bodies and persons to make and administer the primary rules. The logic of this view is that the reference point for legal disputes will be the rules of law, that processes will be orientated to the application of the rules to particular fact situations, and that the core of the dispute will concern the relevant rule, the application of the rule, or the facts. In all cases, the pathway for the dispute will lead to courts (or to court-like tribunals or arbitrators). According to this view of law, legal disputes take shape, are settled, or are resolved either in the courts or in the shadow of the courts. However, just as new technologies operate to de-centre the Westphalian view of law, rules as the primary instruments of law, and humans as the primary appliers of legal rules, so too they put pressure on the traditional court-centred view of disputes.

Once a Law 2.0 mentality takes hold, we will ask not only whether rules and regulations are fit for purpose, but also whether the courts (together with those professionals who provide advice and assistance to disputants) are fit for purpose. Notoriously, if we aspire to universal affordable justice, the civil justice system is not fit for purpose.[1] This was all too evident in Dickens' time; and it is still evident today that there is an iceberg of unmet legal need. For example, in the World Justice Project's report for 2019, the United Kingdom does relatively well, standing at 12 out of 126 globally, but the lowest mark

---

[1] Compare Jerold S. Auerbach, *Unequal Justice* (New York: Oxford University Press, 1976) at 12: 'In the United States justice has been distributed according to race, ethnicity, and wealth rather than need. This is not equal justice.' Similarly, see Benjamin H. Barton and Stephanos Bibas, *Justice Rebooted* (New York: Encounter Books, 2017) at p. 4: 'Mothers seeking child support, tenants fighting eviction, and laid-off workers claiming unemployment or disability benefits usually cannot afford lawyers. They routinely endure long delays and great difficulty navigating courts by themselves before they can receive justice.'

Rethinking disputes and dispute resolution 119

that it has for any one of the 44 indicators—and, what is more, the only mark below 0.60—is the mark of 0.53 for the 'accessibility and affordability' of civil justice.[2] By way of comparison, in the United States (which ranks 20 globally), the equivalent score is 0.46; but, in Denmark (ranked 1 globally) it is 0.76 and, in Norway (ranked 2 globally), it is 0.71. So, on these rankings, the position in the UK could be worse but it also could be very much better.

That said, there has been a good deal of rethinking about dispute settlement, with court-based adjudication being complemented by less formal arbitration, and by less adversarial conciliation and mediation. While these particular forms of alternative dispute resolution were not responses either to new technological challenges or to new technological opportunities, they have paved the way for more radical thinking. Thus, as a Law 3.0 mentality takes shape, online technologies supporting online activities invite a further rethink about how disputes might be resolved. As is well known, eBay's online Resolution Centre, operating in conjunction with PayPal, and handling more than 60 million disputes each year, has led by example.[3] Moreover, by giving buyers a money-back guarantee, it is a system that is designed to minimise conflicts. There are also, of course, many technologies that can be utilised to ensure that sellers are paid, whether these are smart shops[4] or blockchain-based transactions; and many ways of trying to resolve low-value high-volume cases by using a range of technologies (such as AI) to get cases settled and sorted.

Where disputes are higher value, or are more complex, old-style adjudication might still be appropriate. However, in many instances, the plan will be to

---

[2]   World Justice Project, *Rule of Law Index 2019*, at p 151; available at https://worldjusticeproject.org/sites/default/files/documents/ROLI-2019-Reduced.pdf   (last accessed 20 March 2021).

[3]   See Louis F. Del Duca, Colin Rule and Kathryn Rimpfel, 'eBay's De Facto Low Value High Volume Resolution Process: Lessons and Best Practices for ODR Systems Designers' (2014) 6 *Y.B. Arb. & Mediation* 204. For further particulars of the eBay system, see Barton and Bibas (n 1) 110–116. At 114–115, they say that 'The eBay system allowed for a massive, fully voluntary, and unprecedented experiment in human dispute resolution…By using the [dispute resolution] data to track customer satisfaction and future behavior,…[the] eBay team were able to tweak the system continuously to maximize settlements, minimize human involvement on the company side, *and* increase customer satisfaction and involvement.' But, nb, the Resolution Center is 'going away soon'; see https://resolutioncentre.ebay.co.uk/#:~:text=Resolution%20Centre%20will%20be%20going,eBay%20Sold%20and%20Purchase%20History (last accessed 27 June 2021).

[4]   Promoted by their sponsors as a frictionless shopping experience; resisted by their opponents as a 'dystopian, total-surveillance shopping experience': see Leo Kelion, 'Amazon Fresh till-less grocery store opens in London' BBC News, 4 March 2021, https://www.bbc.co.uk/news/technology-56266494 (last accessed 4 March 2021).

divert claims into regulated (no-fault) compensation schemes—for example, where there are personal injury claims arising from accidents involving automated vehicles or in hospitals. Where such schemes operate, claimants should no longer face an uphill, slow, and expensive adversarial struggle to establish complex questions of fault and causation. Where claims are not diverted in this way, technologies might be employed to clarify the parties' positions,[5] and to expedite settlement.

We can also anticipate LawTech (or LegalTech) being employed in non-contentious matters, such as giving advice to laypersons on financial planning or an amicable divorce, or ensuring that testators stay on the right track in drafting their wills.[6] Professional lawyers, too, will be using new technologies to assist them and, in many cases—disclosure and due diligence are stock examples—traditionally labour-intensive and time-consuming tasks will be automated.[7] Indeed, the development and application of LegalTech for a broad range of functions—from connecting lawyers to clients, to advice, assistance, and research—will be the order of the day.[8] A similar reliance on new tools can

---

[5]   Compare Benjamin Alarie, 'The Path of the Law: Toward Legal Singularity' (2016) 66 *University of Toronto Law Journal* 443.

[6]   For discussion, see Barton and Bibas (n 1) 124–130, especially concerning the services provided by LegalZoom [see, https://en.wikipedia.org/wiki/LegalZoom] and Rocket Lawyer [see, https://en.wikipedia.org/wiki/Rocket_Lawyer].

[7]   See, e.g., Richard Susskind and Daniel Susskind, *The Future of the Professions* (Oxford: Oxford University Press, 2015). See, too, *The Future of Legal Services* (London: the Law Society, 2016) 38, where technology is said to be impacting on legal services in the following ways: enabling suppliers to become more efficient at procedural and commodity work; reducing costs by replacing salaried humans with machine-read or AI systems; creating ideas for new models of firm and process innovation; generating work around cybersecurity, data protection and new technology laws; and, supporting changes to consumer decision-making and purchasing behaviours. For further prognosis, see, https://www2.deloitte.com/global/en/pages/legal/articles/deloitte-future-trends-for-legal-services.html.

[8]   Thus, according to Mark Fenwick, Wulf A. Kaal, and Erik P.M. Vermeulen, 'Legal Education in the Blockchain Revolution' (2017) 20 *Vanderbilt Journal of Entertainment and Technology Law* 351, 358–359 (footnotes omitted):

> Four categories of startups in Legal Tech can be distinguished. The first category includes startup companies that offer a range of online legal services, removing the in-person legal consultation process and guidance process for clients. The second…involves online 'matching' platforms that connect lawyers with clients. Such platform startups help consumers find a fitting lawyer without the costly involvement of a law firm. The third…use[s] AI tools to take over their lawyers' time-consuming and expensive legal research activities such as reviewing, understanding, evaluating, and reapplying contracts. Finally, startups with expertise in blockchain technology attempt to replace lawyers as intermediaries in certain types of transactions.

be expected, too, in relation to the work of the regulatory agencies (particularly concerning monitoring, reporting, and compliance) where an investment in RegTech, notably by the Financial Conduct Authority, is already a significant feature of the new legal landscape.[9]

Surveying this rapidly changing landscape and analysing the insinuation of technologies into dispute resolution, both in courts and out of courts, Ethan Katsh and Orna Rabinovich-Einy detect three key shifts as follows.[10] First, there is a shift from physical to virtual, or semi-virtual, settings: with this shift, individuals 'can access courts, evaluate their legal stance, communicate with the other party, and have a third party decide their dispute, all without having to physically attend the court or be restricted to court operating hours....' The second shift is 'from human intervention and decision making to automated processes'; and the third shift is 'from dispute resolution models that value confidentiality to models focused on collecting, using, and reusing data in order to prevent disputes....'[11] So, moving away from the processes that are characteristic of Law 1.0 court-centred dispute resolution, the shifts identified by Katsh and Rabinovich-Einy quickly take us to the Law 2.0 judgement that the physical courts alone are not fit for purpose, and then into a Law 3.0 conversation about automation and prevention.

That said, attachments to Law 1.0 processes persist and, as Katsh and Rabinovich-Einy ask, as we go through the shifts, we might wonder:

> Will parties who participate in these processes feel that they have received their 'day in court' and have been 'heard'? Will users perceive these processes as fair? Will judges sustain their neutrality and authority, and will courts, relying on algorithms, maintain their legitimacy?...
>
> Adopting technology in the courtroom opens up new opportunities not only for making our existing processes less expensive and cumbersome and more accessible at all hours. It could also change the very nature of court processes, with software playing an increasingly significant role in streamlining, resolving, and preventing claims. Indeed, there is promise for transforming our very understanding of the meaning of *justice*.[12]

While our ideas about what is convenient and what is efficient might remain fairly constant, there is no guarantee that citizens will judge that the gains in convenience and efficiency offset their questions about 'trust' in automated processes; and, the idea that our understanding of 'justice' might be trans-

---

[9] See https://www.fca.org.uk/firms/innovation/regtech.

[10] Ethan Katsh and Orna Rabinovich-Einy, *Digital Justice* (Oxford: Oxford University Press, 2017).

[11] See, Katsh and Rabinovich-Einy (n 10) 162–163.

[12] Ibid., at 164–165.

formed by these technology-driven forms of dispute-handling might seem less a promise than an unwelcome threat. If automated processes and technological dispute-handling are thought to be more about getting disputes *settled* rather than getting them settled *justly*, there might be resistance to rethinking the meaning of justice and, concomitantly, to the de-centring of courts, rules, and humans.[13]

This chapter starts by recalling two major ways in which our thinking about civil disputes has already been revised, namely: first, by rethinking traditional ideas of fault, liability, and compensatory responsibility; and, second, by developing alternative forms of dispute resolution (ADR) as well as mechanisms for online dispute resolution (ODR). We can then consider a couple of more radical revisions: while one revision focuses on the automation of civil justice (taking humans out of the decision loop), the other focuses on preventing disputes arising in the first place by making use of the ex ante technological management of risks and potential conflicts.

8.2   TWO LINES OF RETHINKING

There has already been much rethinking of civil justice. In this section, we highlight the rethinking of the connection between fault and compensatory

---

[13]   Famously, see Owen M. Fiss, 'Against Settlement' (1983–84) 93 *Yale Law Journal* 1073. Fiss argues that the case for settlement is dubious. Thus, at 1075, Fiss says:

> I do not believe that settlement as a generic practice is preferable to judgment or should be institutionalized on a wholesale and indiscriminate basis. It should be treated instead as a highly problematic technique for streamlining dockets. Settlement is for me the civil analogue of plea bargaining: Consent is often coerced; the bargain may be struck by someone without authority; the absence of a trial and judgment renders subsequent judicial involvement troublesome; and although dockets are trimmed, justice may not be done. Like plea bargaining, settlement is a capitulation to the conditions of mass society and should be neither encouraged nor praised.

When Fiss treats settlement as analogous to plea bargaining, he sees a system that defects from its public commitments. Adjudication is not about simply putting an end to the dispute or restoring the peace, there is more to it than that. According to Fiss (at p 1085), the role of adjudicators 'is not to maximize the ends of private parties, nor simply to secure the peace, but to explicate and give force to the values embodied in authoritative texts such as the Constitution and statutes: to interpret those values and to bring reality into accord with them. This duty is not discharged when the parties settle.' See, too, Riika Koulu, *Law, Technology and Dispute Resolution* (Abingdon: Routledge, 2019) (for concerns about the privatisation of dispute resolution and (coerced) enforcement).

Rethinking disputes and dispute resolution 123

responsibility; and the rethinking around ADR and, with developments in ICTs, the evolution of ODR.

8.2.1 Rethinking Traditional Ideas About the Connection Between Fault, Liability, and Compensatory Responsibility

Traditional thinking is that those who are at fault in relation to some harm or loss that is caused should bear the compensatory responsibility (the line of thinking is from blame to claim to compensation). Victims should look to wrongdoers (to the blameworthy) to correct the wrong. It follows that victims who seek compensation will need to identify the party who was at fault.

For example, in the case of *Carmarthenshire County Council v Lewis*[14] a nursery schoolteacher supervising a three-year-old child was distracted when a second child fell and was hurt. While the teacher was attending to the second child, the first child wandered off out of the school building and through an open gate onto an adjoining road. In order to avoid hitting the child, a lorry driver swerved, collided with a telegraph pole and was killed. The claimant was the lorry driver's widow. In these circumstances, the House of Lords (disagreeing with the lower courts) found that the teacher was not personally at fault—she had acted responsibly. However, it was held that the Council had failed to explain how the child had been able to get out of the school; and, without such an explanation, it was to be inferred that the County Council had failed to take reasonable precautions to prevent an unattended child leaving the school and causing an accident of this kind.

This was very much an exercise in Law 1.0 thinking. The principles of tort law were applied to determine whether, on the facts, the schoolteacher had failed to take reasonable care or whether the County Council was to blame in the steps that it had taken to keep the children safe when they were attending the school. If the defendants were not at fault, if they could not be blamed for the accident, they would not be required to pay compensation to the claimant; and, this would mean that, unless other eligible defendants could be identified, the claimant would not be compensated for her loss.

From a Law 2.0 perspective, this seems a somewhat unsatisfactory approach to the management of risks arising from the proximity of schoolchildren to roads carrying traffic. Instead of searching ex post for a party who might be characterised as being at fault in the particular circumstances, far better surely to establish ex ante who could best compensate for accidents of this kind and then place the liability on their shoulders. This would imply no blame but it would mean (i) that being at fault was not a condition for having the

---

[14]   [1955] AC 549.

responsibility to compensate and (ii) that not being at fault was not necessarily an exemption from the responsibility to pay compensation. Attribution of fault and allocation of compensatory responsibility become two independent matters.

Following this line of thinking, in many legal systems, we see attempts to take the complexity and unfairness out of accident claims by adopting 'no-fault compensation schemes' (such as that administered by the Accident Compensation Corporation in New Zealand)[15] or switching from fault-based liability to strict liability. For a long time, schemes of the former kind have been advocated as a rational response to the risk of road traffic accidents; and they are being touted again as the smart response to the risks presented by autonomous vehicles. Rather than tying compensatory liability to fault, the challenge is seen as being to articulate the most acceptable (and financially workable) compensatory arrangements that accommodate the interests in transport innovation and the safety of passengers and pedestrians. For example, one proposal (advanced by Tracy Pearl[16]) is that there should be an autonomous vehicle crash victim compensation fund to be financed by a sales tax on such vehicles. Of course, as with any such no-fault compensation scheme, much of the devil is in the detail—in particular, there are important questions to be settled about the level of compensation, whether the option of pursuing a tort claim remains open to victims, and what kind of injuries or losses are covered by the scheme.[17]

Similar thinking underlies product liability regimes. For instance, in the Recitals to Directive 85/374/EEC (on liability for defective products) we read:

> Whereas liability without fault on the part of the producer is the sole means of adequately solving the problem, peculiar to our age of increasing technicality, of a fair apportionment of the risks inherent in modern technological production.

Although the pathway to compensation is eased by removing the requirement that fault be proved, it is no part of this approach to the apportionment of risks to name, shame, and blame defendants where accidents happen or unintentional harm occurs. So, for example, in one of the leading US product liability

---

[15] See, https://en.wikipedia.org/wiki/Accident_Compensation_Corporation (last accessed 7 April 2021).

[16] See, Tracy Pearl, 'Compensation at the Crossroads: Autonomous Vehicles and Alternative Victim Compensation Schemes' (2018) 60 *William and Mary Law Review* 1827.

[17] Compare, Maurice Schellekens, 'No-Fault Compensation Schemes for Self-Driving Vehicles' (2018) 10 *Law, Innovation and Technology* 314.

cases, *Beshada v Johns-Manville Products Corp.*,[18] the defendant asbestos manufacturers argued that they could not reasonably know that their finished products supplied for use in the shipyards were still hazardous and could cause dust diseases. However, as the Supreme Court of New Jersey emphasised, in a product liability regime, arguments of this kind were not relevant. In his concluding remarks, Pashman J put the point thus:

> Defendants have argued that it is unreasonable to impose a duty on them to warn of the unknowable. Failure to warn of a risk which one could not have known existed is not unreasonable conduct. But this argument is based on negligence principles. We are not saying what defendants should have done. That is negligence. We are saying that defendants' products were not reasonably safe because they did not have a warning. Without a warning, users of the product were unaware of its hazards and could not protect themselves from injury. We impose strict liability because it is unfair for the distributors of a defective product not to compensate its victims. As between those innocent victims and the distributors, it is the distributors—and the public which consumes their products—which should bear the unforeseen costs of the product.[19]

In other words, product liability is not about individual fault or blame but about collective risk management; as the court expressed it, 'Strict liability focuses on the product, not the fault of the manufacturer.'[20] A finding that the defendants have been assigned the compensatory responsibility in the circumstances does not imply a negative judgment about the way in which they have conducted their business. Moreover, at least in theory, provided that the compensatory burden is spread across the community by insurance and pricing mechanisms, the risk is borne collectively.

Once we are thinking about disputes with a Law 2.0 mindset, we can just as easily rethink the principle of 'if blame then claim' as that of 'if no blame then no claim'. Strict liability disrupts the latter; legal immunities disrupt the former. So, for example, if we wish to minimise disputes about whether ISPs have taken reasonable care to avoid carrying objectionable or illegal content, we could either adopt a strict liability standard (which would be opposed by ISPs) or, equally well, confer an immunity on ISPs (which would be opposed by potential claimants). In the EU, and a number of other jurisdictions, the legal position initially adopted was that of a qualified immunity for ISPs (no liability provided that content was taken down reasonably promptly after

---

[18]   90 N.J. 191, 447 A.2d 539 (1982). For discussion (and defence of *Beshada*), see Christopher M. Placitella and Alan M. Darnell, '*Beshada v Johns-Manville Products Corp.*: Evolution or Revolution in Strict Products Liability?' (1983) 51 *Fordham Law Review* 801.

[19]   90 N.J. 191, at 209.

[20]   90 N.J. 191, at 204.

notice had been given). While this rethought the relationship between blame, claim, and compensation, and served to reduce disputes, it now strikes many commentators as over-protective of what were once small enterprises.[21]

8.2.2 ADR and ODR

In May 2013, the European Parliament and the Council of the EU adopted Directive 2013/11/EU on ADR for consumer disputes[22] and Regulation No 524/2013 on ODR for consumer disputes.[23] According to Article 1 of the former, the purpose of the Directive is 'to contribute to the proper functioning of the internal market by ensuring that consumers can, on a voluntary basis, submit complaints against traders to entities offering independent, impartial, transparent, effective, fast and fair alternative dispute resolution procedures'. Article 1 of the accompanying Regulation expresses its purpose in very similar terms, but emphasises 'the digital dimension' of the internal market. While the Directive and the Regulation signal an awareness of the problems that consumers might have, particularly in cross-border commerce, in accessing convenient, affordable, and fair dispute-resolution procedures, as well as an appreciation that these problems might impact on the confidence of consumers, these measures do not really represent a radical rethink. Courts, human decision-makers, and rules, but now aided incrementally by technologies that streamline and smooth the process, are still the gold standard for dispute resolution.[24]

---

[21] See, e.g., Marcelo Thompson, 'Beyond Gatekeeping: The Normative Responsibilities of Internet Intermediaries' (2016) 18 *Vanderbilt Journal of Entertainment and Technology Law* 783; and Lorna Woods and William Perrin, 'Internet Harm Reduction' (CarnegieUK Trust, 2019), available at https://d1ssu070pg2v9i .cloudfront.net/pex/carnegie_uk_trust/2019/01/27135118/Internet-Harm-Reduction -final.pdf (last accessed 30 June 2021). Moreover, reform is on the way: in the EU, see the Commission's proposal for a Digital Services Act, COM(2020) 825 final, Brussels 15.12.2020; and, in the UK, the draft Online Safety Bill was published in May 2021.

[22] Official Journal of the European Union L 165/63, 18.6.2013.

[23] Official Journal of the European Union L 165/1, 18.6.2013.

[24] Compare, Katsh and Rabinovich-Einy (n 10) at 155.
    The penetration of digital technology into courts is occurring in three phases. The first involves efficiencies and case management; the second connects with the growth of e-government, making more governmental information and new tools available to the public; and finally, change is occurring through an 'access to justice' prism under which some legal processes are conducted online and the traditional understanding of both 'access' and 'justice' is revisited. We are currently witnessing the early signs of the third phase in several jurisdictions, but for the most part, courts are still far from realizing the full potential of digital technology in enhancing access to justice by delivering digital justice.

First, both measures are less motivated by a fundamentally new approach to dispute resolution than by the long-standing logic of the Commission which targets obstacles to the development of a frictionless consumer marketplace. As Recitals 4 and 6 of the Directive candidly put it:

(4) Ensuring access to simple, efficient, fast and low-cost ways of resolving domestic and cross-border disputes which arise from sales or service contracts should benefit consumers and therefore boost their confidence in the market. That access should apply to online as well as to offline transactions, and is particularly important when consumers shop across borders.

(6) The disparities in ADR coverage, quality and awareness in Member States constitute a barrier to the internal market and are among the reasons why many consumers abstain from shopping across borders and why they lack confidence that potential disputes with traders can be resolved in an easy, fast and inexpensive way....

So, these are Law 2.0 measures that are in line with the Commission's regulatory policies for the growth of the consumer market.

Second, underlining the point just made, the thinking here is not Law 3.0. The ODR Regulation sets up a single point of entry gateway for consumer disputes, but it is a conduit to one of the ADR entities (see Article 9 of the Regulation setting out the process by which parties are to be invited to agree upon an ADR entity to which the dispute is to be referred). Moreover, these measures are not particularly concerned with automation; as if to reassure that humans will not be out of the loop, there are frequent references to the 'natural persons' in charge of the ADR.

Third, these instruments are very much about commerce and consumers (not, for example, about disputes relating to services provided by health professionals or concerning the provision of further or higher education, these being explicitly exempted by Articles 2(2)(h) and (i) of the Directive); and, even within this limited sphere, the availability of full-scale ODR on e-commerce platforms (such as eBay) might well mean that the practical significance of these EU initiatives is diminished.[25]

---

[25] For some insightful reflections on the development of ODR in both the EU and in the UK (further to the recommendations made by Lord Briggs in his *Civil Courts Structure Review: Final Report* (July 2016)), see Graham Ross, 'Developments in ODR and the online court' (May 2018), available at https://www.infolaw.co.uk/newsletter/2018/05/developments-odr-online-court/ (last accessed 10 March 2021). See, too, Department for Business, Energy and Industrial Strategy, *Resolving Consumer Disputes* (Final Report, London, 2018) assessing the effectiveness of ADR in the UK following the transposition of the EU Directive in 2015: available at https://assets.publishing.service.gov.uk/government/uploads/system/uploads/attachment_data/file/698442/Final_report_-_Resolving_consumer_disputes.pdf (last accessed 8 April 2021).

It should also be said that, so long as the proponents of ODR continue to regard the courts and judges as setting the gold standard for dispute resolution, they will invite the objection that ODR offers not only a second-class form of justice but also denies parties their 'day in court'.[26]

In this evolving landscape of ADR and ODR, where should we place the 'Online Court' (for England and Wales) as conceived by Lords Briggs' review of the structure of the civil courts, a concept about which there is a widely held view that its 'time has come'?[27] Responding to doubters, Lord Briggs concedes that there might well be 'setbacks, teething troubles, and unexpected difficulties';[28] nevertheless,

> the objective of making the civil courts more generally accessible to individuals and small businesses, for a just resolution of their simpler and small to modest value disputes at proportionate cost, fully justifies the risks in stepping a little into the unknown, and even the small risk that the time, money and effort about to be devoted to it may turn out to have been wasted.[29]

To fulfil this objective, a three-stage procedure is envisaged: first, there is an automated online triage stage designed to help litigants to articulate their claim, and to upload their key documents and evidence; second, there is a conciliation stage; and then, third, there is 'a determination stage, where those disputed cases which cannot be settled are determined by a judge, by whichever of a face to face trial, video or telephone hearing or determination on the documents is the most appropriate'.[30] For those who worry that humans might be removed from this procedure, we are reminded that 'the main form of conciliation at stage 2 is to be by human intervention, while all decisions about substantive rights are to be made by a judge'.[31] Indeed, we read that it would be a misconception to characterise the justice offered by the court as a form of ODR;[32] and that the name 'Online Court' is 'unsuitable' and apt to confuse.[33] In the light of these qualifications, while the project should be seen as a welcome attempt to improve access to justice, it is clearly not yet a radical embrace of technologies for dispute settlement and resolution.

---

[26]   Compare Julia Hörnle, *Cross-Border Internet Dispute Resolution* (Cambridge: Cambridge University Press, 2009) (for concerns about the fairness and integrity of ODR processes).

[27]   *Civil Courts Structure Review: Final Report* (July 2016), para 44.

[28]   Ibid.

[29]   Ibid.

[30]   *Final Report* (n 25) at para 6.4.

[31]   *Final Report* (n 25) at para 6.8.

[32]   Ibid.

[33]   *Final Report* (n 25) at para 6.120.

Rethinking disputes and dispute resolution

Picking up the story, the Briggs' proposal has been delayed and is now due for completion by December 2023; and, in the light of the reliance on various kinds of technologies as a response to the Covid-19 restrictions, there is now a view that, instead of thinking about an 'online court' as such, it would be helpful to recognise, alongside physical courts, various kinds of techniques for remote processing of disputes (audio, video, and online).[34] The pandemic has compelled us to get up to speed with platforms such as Zoom and Teams, in a way that makes remote working more familiar and routine. In this light, it might be that it is the pandemic in conjunction with the ODR advocates that has given the rethinking of dispute processing a decisive push.[35]

8.3   AUTOMATION

Incremental adoption of technologies that make dispute resolution smoother, more convenient, and more efficient is one thing; end-to-end automation of the process, however, is something else. Nevertheless, in our imaginary, the fully automated process of dispute resolution galvanises our rethinking. Thus, in many parts of the world, various forms of automated civil justice are being piloted. For example, according to a comment by Santosh Paul, China is leading the way in developing AI Internet Courts.[36] Thus:

> Hangzhou, a city in north China, powers the country's cutting edge technological revolution. It is here that the first justice delivery system run by AI was introduced in 2017. Beijing and Guangzhou quickly followed suit. The three AI Internet Courts in China are judging disputes relating to online transactions of sale of goods and services, copyright and trademark, ownership and infringement of domains, trade disputes, and e-commerce product liability claims.

Presumably these courts, operating 24/7, are seen as an efficient and effective way of processing civil disputes of the kind covered. On average, a trial lasts

---

[34]   See, Marialuisa Taddia, 'Shock to the System' *Law Society Gazette* (July 2020), available at https://www.lawgazette.co.uk/features/shock-to-the-system/5104867 .article (last accessed 10 March 2021).

[35]   See, e.g., https://remotecourts.org/. Compare, too, the drift of the discussion in Mark Findlay, *Globalisation, Populism, Pandemics and the Law* (Cheltenham: Edward Elgar, 2021) Ch 6. However, we should not ignore the many variables that can be in play and bear on whether a community 'buys into' ODR: see, e.g., John Clammer and Matthew Byrne, 'The Village Says "No": Why Online ADR is Not (Yet) Working in Rural India' (2021) 3 *Law, Technology and Humans* 133.

[36]   Published 28 May 2020: see https://www.barandbench.com/columns/is-artificial -intelligence-replacing-judging (last accessed 22 February 2021). See, too, Simon Chesterman, *We the Robots? Regulating Artificial Intelligence and the Limits of the Law* (Cambridge: Cambridge University Press, 2021) Ch 9.

28 minutes and the entire process, start to finish, takes 38 days. Technical support for the Hangzhou court is supplied by Alibaba and its subsidiaries; and it seems that blockchain technologies feature prominently in the technological array. While one of the attractions of reliance on such tools is that human bias and inconsistency is removed, in this instance, it is reported that there are actually serious concerns about both the independence and the impartiality of the courts. Just as there are humans and there are humans, there are technological designs and technological designs. Meanwhile, in Europe, it is Estonia that has the reputation of being in the vanguard of e-government; and, predictably, the development of robot judges (for small claims disputes) is one of the items on the Ministry of Justice's agenda.[37] What should we make of this? Are 'robot judges' next?[38]

In response, we can recall our discussion in the previous chapter. While machines might be able to outperform humans in predicting how an agreed rule might be applied to an agreed set of facts, judges not only have to decide cases, rather than predict outcomes, they also have to find the facts, draw inferences from the facts (about the intentions of the party), interpret and apply contested concepts in the agreed rules and principles, and determine which rule is the applicable rule. Accordingly, if smart machines are to outperform humans in all these respects, there is some way to go.[39] Smart tools will surely play a role in the judicial process, but reliance on 'robot judges' is another matter.

8.4 ACTING EX ANTE

According to Richard Susskind, one of the themes of his conversations with in-house lawyers is that dispute avoidance is to be preferred to even the neatest

---

[37] See, Eric Niiler, 'Can AI be a fair judge in court? Estonia thinks so' *Wired* (March 25, 2019) available at: https://www.wired.com/story/can-ai-be-fair-judge-court -estonia-thinks-so/ (last accessed 10 March 2021); and, Tara Vasdani, 'From Estonian AI Judges to robot mediators in Canada, UK', https://www.lexisnexis.ca/en-ca/ihc/ 2019-06/from-estonian-ai-judges-to-robot-mediators-in-canada-uk.page (last accessed 10 March 2021).

[38] See, e.g., Stephanie Condon, 'AI in the Court: Are robot judges next?' ZD Net, January 22, 2020 (focusing on the US): available at https://www.zdnet.com/article/ai-in -the-court-are-robot-judges-next/ (last accessed 12 March 2021). For deep reservations, see Lyria Bennett Moses, 'Not a Single Singularity' in Simon Deakin and Christopher Markou (eds), *Is Law Computable?* (Oxford: Hart, 2020) 205, 216–220.

[39] Compare Dilan Thampapillai, 'The Law of Contested Concepts? Reflections on Copyright Law and the Legal and Technological Singularities', in Deakin and Markou (n 38) 223. For in-depth analysis of the range of tools and techniques that might be applied to deductive and analogical legal reasoning, see Kevin D. Ashley, *Artificial Intelligence and Legal Analytics* (Cambridge: Cambridge University Press, 2017).

Rethinking disputes and dispute resolution 131

of resolutions;[40] that it is better, in Susskind's words, to put 'a fence at the top of a cliff rather than an ambulance at the bottom';[41] that there should be 'a shift from legal problem solving to legal risk management [this anticipating] a world in which legal problems are often dissolved before needing to be resolved'.[42] If we truly embrace Law 3.0 thinking, we should deploy the full range of our regulatory resources, including technical measures and technologies, to prevent disputes arising in the first place.

8.4.1 Prevention is Better than Dispute

The thought is simple and attractive: why not design our transactions and interactions in ways that reduce or eliminate the triggers for disputes? In our imaginary of automated futures, why not fully automated transactions, automated payment for automated provision of goods and services? If there are any technological glitches or errors, accounts will be automatically adjusted. Similarly, why not prevent accidents that cause injury to humans or damage to their property by taking humans out of the situation, whether as operators who cause the injury or damage or who are the parties injured? No doubt, implementing this simple thought is much less simple. Nevertheless, if we can automate the back end of disputes, why not also the front end?

8.4.1.1 If promises are made to be broken
If promises are made to be broken, then, to prevent disputes, we should focus on secured performance. In this spirit, imagine a world where commerce is, so to speak, a 'conversation conducted entirely among machines'.[43] Imagine, as Michal Gal and Niva Elkin-Koren foresee it, that

> [y]our automated car makes independent decisions on where to purchase fuel, when to drive itself to a service station, from which garage to order a spare part, or whether to rent itself out to other passengers, all without even once consulting with you.[44]

In that world, humans have been taken out of the transactional loop, leaving it to the technology to make decisions that humans would otherwise be responsible for making. The relevant humans include not only the primary contractors

---

[40] Richard Susskind, *Tomorrow's Lawyers* (Oxford: Oxford University Press, 2017).

[41] Ibid., at 95.

[42] Ibid., at 127.

[43] Per W. Brian Arthur, 'The Second Economy', *McKinsey Quarterly* (October 2011), quoted in Nicholas Carr, *The Glass Cage* (London: Vintage, 2015) at 197.

[44] Michal S. Gal and Niva Elkin-Koren, 'Algorithmic Contracts' (2017) 30 *Harvard Journal of Law and Technology* 309, at 309–310.

but also trusted third parties (such as banks that administer letters of credit or other documents in international trade).[45] For example, in the context of carriage of goods by sea, electronic bills of lading promise to be a smart response to the problem of ships reaching the port of discharge before paper bills; and, as Paul Todd has argued, the use of blockchain and smart contracts might be part of an even smarter response, overcoming a lack of trust in central registries.[46] Similarly, just like imperfect attempts to protect IPRs through contractual provisions, perhaps the required protections can be incorporated in relevant products and processes. In this world, transactional disputes between humans would be reduced or even eliminated, and if there are glitches to be resolved, this would be another conversation for the machines.

If this seems to project too far into the future, we can imagine instead a world in which performance of parts of the transaction at least can be entrusted to the technology. Most straightforwardly, as with smart contracts running on blockchain, the performance of those parts of the transaction that involve payments being made could be irreversibly entrusted to the technology. Let us suppose that a smart contract takes the form of a coded instruction for a 'payment' to be made by A to B conditional on the occurrence of some event (if x, then y). Where the 'event' is performance by B, then (provided that the technology is reliable) B will be paid and (provided that the 'performance' is as agreed) neither A nor B will have any grievance. There should be no dispute. Of course, there are provisos here; there is plenty to go wrong; and there are other ways for parties to ensure that they get paid. Nevertheless, this is a pointer to how technology might be used as a means of preventing disputes arising. There is more to smart shops than convenience; purchasers make their own selections and suppliers are assured of payment.

8.4.1.2 If humans are accidents waiting to happen

Humans, it might be said, are accidents waiting to happen. So, to prevent disputes arising, we should take humans out of accident scenarios. If we replace human operators with mechanical operators that are more reliable, this should reduce 'accidents'—this applies whether we are thinking about robots operat-

---

[45] For discussion of trust in banks as opposed to trust in other payment systems, see Iris H-Y Chiu, 'A New Era in Fintech Payment Innovations? A Perspective from the Institutions and Regulation of Payment Systems' (2017) 9 *Law, Innovation and Technology* 190.

[46] Paul Todd, 'Electronic Bills of Lading, Blockchains and Smart Contracts' (2019) 27 *International Journal of Law and Information Technology* 339. For reflections on the potential legal utility of blockchain registers, see John Quinn and Barry Connolly, 'Distributed Ledger Technology and Property Registers: Displacement or Status Quo' (2021) 13 *Law, Innovation and Technology* (forthcoming).

Rethinking disputes and dispute resolution 133

ing machines, or taking over the role of pharmacists in hospitals, or the automation of transport systems, and so on. Similarly, if we can take humans out of places where they are likely to be injured (in dangerous work environments, for example), we again should reduce accidents that cause harm to humans.

Imagine, then, that in the *Carmarthenshire* case, which we discussed earlier in the chapter, instead of a human schoolteacher supervising the children, we have a robot looking after the children. On these facts, what would we say about the liability of the robot or of the County Council who rely on the robot to look after the young children at the nursery school? This, of course, will depend on whether we are viewing the situation through the lens of Law 1.0, Law 2.0, or Law 3.0.

If we view the situation through the lens of Law 1.0, we will address it in a coherentist way. We will ask whether robot supervisors are analogous to human supervisors; can we treat robots as being 'personally' responsible or 'at fault'? If not, we have a problem. If robots are not to be treated as humans, how are we to treat them? As for the possible liability of the County Council, that is less problematic. Already, we take a somewhat pragmatic view (corporations can be treated as legal persons); and, guided by principles of corrective justice, we will ask whether it would be fair, just, and reasonable to hold the Council liable to compensate the injured parties.

If we view the situation through the lens of Law 2.0, our approach will be regulatory-instrumentalist. Here, the thinking would be that before schools are to be licensed to introduce robocarers, there needs to be a collectively agreed scheme of compensation should something 'go wrong'. On this view, the responsibilities and liabilities of the parties would be determined ex ante by the agreed terms of the risk management package. A regulatory-instrumentalist would want to assess the risks and benefits of relying on robot supervisors in publicly funded schools and then determine what would be an acceptable balance of interests (including what would be an acceptable compensatory scheme in the event of an accident).

However, if we view the situation through the lens of Law 3.0—which, of course, is the relevant lens for this part of the discussion—our approach will also be regulatory-instrumentalist but now with a technological dimension. In Law 3.0 we are thinking not only about the fitness of the rules but also about possible technical solutions. At the school, the technical solution might have been simply to keep the gate locked (in fact, there was considerable discussion about this in the case), or it might have involved a more complex technological fix—perhaps an invisible 'fence' at the edge of the schoolyard so that children simply could not stray beyond the limits. However, thinking about the puzzle in this way, the question would be entirely about designing the machines and the space in a way that collisions between schoolchildren and passing vehicles could not happen. That way, humans would not be harmed, there would not be grievances, and disputes would not arise.

Before we leave the scenario in *Carmarthenshire v Lewis*, imagine a further twist. Imagine that the lorry was not driven by a human but was fully autonomous and that it had been programmed to swerve if there was a risk of colliding with a human. If the vehicle were empty, the question would be about covering the costs of whatever damage was caused to the vehicle—a question that we can assume to be an everyday insurance matter. Let us suppose, though, the claim for compensation is by the widow of a passenger who was in, but not driving, the vehicle. What would we say about such a situation?

The first thing to say is that this reminds us that there are limits to preventing death and injury: try though we might, we cannot take all humans out of all potentially harmful situations. Fortunately, situations of this kind should arise only exceptionally and any questions about liability or compensation should have been settled way in advance of autonomous vehicles getting on the road. For many, the principal point of discussion would be whether the vehicle should have been programmed to save the life of the child at the possible expense of any passengers in the vehicle. In fact, one of the main questions generated by the development of autonomous vehicles has been the ethics of dilemmas of just this kind.[47] Let us suppose, though, that the community has debated the ethics, agreed on a standard design, and that the vehicle in question has the standard coding for situations of this kind. What can we now say about the question of legal liability?

According to Jonathan Morgan:

> From the industry perspective, liability is arguably the innovative manufacturer's greatest concern. The clashing interests raise in acute form the classic dilemma for tort and technology: how to reconcile reduction in the number of accidents (deterrence) and compensation of the injured with the encouragement of socially beneficial innovation? Not surprisingly there have been calls for stricter liability (to serve the former goals), and for immunities (to foster innovation). But in the absence

---

[47] For a small sample, see, Patrick Lin, 'The Ethics of Saving Lives with Autonomous Cars are Far Murkier than You Think' *WIRED*, 30 July 2013: available at https://www.wired.com/2013/07/the-surprising-ethics-of-robot-cars/ (last accessed 15 November 2016); and, 'The Robot Car of Tomorrow May be Just Programmed to Hit You' *WIRED*, 6 May 2014: available at https://www.wired.com/2014/05/the-robot -car-of-tomorrow-might-just-be-programmed-to-hit-you/ (last accessed 15 November 2016). Also, Jason Millar, 'You should have a say in your robot car's code of ethics' *Wired*, 9 February 2014 (available at: https://www.wired.com/2014/09/set-the-ethics -robot-car/) (last accessed 3 February 2017).

Rethinking disputes and dispute resolution

of any radical legislative reform, the existing principles of tort will apply—if only faute de mieux.[48]

This is surely right. If the regulation of an emerging technology is presented in a legislative setting, a risk-management approach is likely to prevail, with regulators trying to accommodate inter alia the interest in beneficial innovation together with the interest in risks being managed at an acceptable level. It will be a Law 2.0 conversation. On the other hand, if the question arises in a court setting, it is more likely that both litigants and judges will talk the coherentist talk of negligence and fault even though, as Morgan observes, the common law technique of reasoning by analogy via existing categories, far from being 'common sense', is 'obfuscatory'.[49] As Morgan says, the better way of determining the liability arrangements for autonomous vehicles is not by litigation but 'for regulators to make the relevant choices of public policy openly after suitable democratic discussion of which robotics applications to allow and which to stimulate, which applications to discourage and which to prohibit'.[50] That democratic discussion might well be conflictual but, having taken a position—that addresses both the ethical and the compensatory issues—regulators should at least be able to forestall disputes relating to particular incidents if not renewed discussion of the social licence for autonomous vehicles and, concomitantly, the fitness of the regulatory position.

8.4.2   Another Take on Congruence

In our earlier discussion of legality, we treated the Fullerian ideal of congruence as speaking to the accurate administration of the rules; or, where technologies are employed in the administration of the rules, the accurate translation and application of the rules. However, the tension between Law 1.0 thinking (in and around the courts) and Law 3.0 thinking (in and around new technologies of governance) prompts another thought about congruence.

The thought here is that the effects of employing technologies to prevent disputes arising should be congruent with orders or awards that courts would be prepared to make. So, for example, if a contract running on blockchain makes 'compensatory' payments to one of the parties that a court would not award—for instance, because a court would treat the amount of the payment as excessive (as a penalty) or because a court would calculate damages in a way

---

[48]   Jonathan Morgan, 'Torts and Technology', in Roger Brownsword, Eloise Scotford, and Karen Yeung (eds), *The Oxford Handbook of Law, Regulation and Technology* (Oxford: Oxford University Press, 2017) 522, 537.

[49]   Morgan (n 48) at 539.

[50]   Morgan (n 48) at 539.

that would come up with a different figure—then the technologies would not be operating in a way that was congruent with the operation of the courts applying the general legal principles of Law 1.0. Similarly, if the technology forced a performance by a seller that a court would not order (because courts are very sparing about making orders for specific performance), there would again be a question about congruence. This would all apply a fortiori if the parties were engaged in activities that were unlawful and if the technologically secured payments were due under illegal transactions or as a disincentive to defect from, say, anti-competitive agreements.[51]

As Karen Yeung has aptly observed, the co-existence of technologies of this kind with the background law and regulation might or might not be problematic.[52] If a lack of technological congruence with the background law (whether the general legal principles of Law 1.0 or, say, the consumer protection policies of Law 2.0) was found to be problematic, action would be required. It would be for regulators, acting in Law 2.0 mode, to intervene in order to clarify the law and to revise the social licence for the permitted use of the technologies at issue.[53]

8.5   CONCLUDING REMARKS

In the context of disputes, LawTech starts in a relatively modest and uncontroversial role. Criticisms of court-centred civil justice are legion: processes are slow and cumbersome; lawyers are expensive; and, as a result, access to justice is delayed or denied and unmet legal need continues to be unmet. To the extent that technologies can be deployed in ways that mitigate these complaints, that is all to the good. It is in this way that ADR and ODR respond to a situation that most commentators agree is unsatisfactory.

---

[51]   Compare, Thibault Schrepel, 'Collusion by Blockchain and Smart Contracts' (2019) 33 *Harvard Journal of Law and Technology* 117.

[52]   Karen Yeung, 'Regulation by Blockchain: The Emerging Battle for Supremacy between the Code *of* Law and Code as Law' (2019) 82 *Modern Law Review* 207.

[53]   For discussion, see Roger Brownsword, 'Smart Transactional Technologies, Legal Disruption, and the Case of Network Contracts' in Larry A. di Matteo, Michel Cannarsa, and Cristina Poncibò (eds), *The Cambridge Handbook of Smart Contracts, Blockchain Technology and Digital Platforms* (Cambridge: Cambridge University Press, 2019) 313; 'Automated Transactions and the Law of Contract: When Codes are not Congruent' in Michael Furmston (ed), *The Future of the Law of Contract* (Abingdon: Routledge, 2020) 94; and, 'Three approaches to the governance of decentralised business models: Contractual, regulatory and technological' in Roger M Barker and Iris H-Y Chiu (eds), *The Law and Governance of Decentralised Business Models* (Abingdon: Routledge, 2020) 51.

Rethinking disputes and dispute resolution

However, once we turn to technology to rethink disputes in a way that goes beyond this core project, we find a paradox. On the one hand, we look to technology to make it easier for disputants to seek resolution or settlement of their disputes; and we look to automation to expedite the process. Otherwise, disputants are being denied access to either a service or to justice. On the other hand, we also look to technology to make it more difficult for disputes to arise in the first place. On the one hand, we are trying to open up and facilitate the disputing process; on the other, we are trying to shut the door on disputes.

This paradox results from one prong of thinking that is attracted by the idea that we should try to reduce or even eliminate disputes by using technology to design out the causes of disputes. If grievances do not arise, disputes should be a thing of the past. At the same time, though, there is another prong of thinking that invites exploring the possibility of developing technologies that are able to resolve disputes in a way that outperforms any human. Our interest in AI-enabled judging machines is not so much efficiency or convenience but, if you believe it, expertise.

Finally, not only is there paradox, but there is also a degree of homology. For both prongs of our radical thinking (preventing disputes arising and automating dispute resolution), the lowest hanging fruit are similar, notably, dealing with debts. For one prong, through technological management, we can ensure that payments due are paid (paid on time and paid in full); and, for the other prong, it is simple enough for smart machines to order payment of debts that are clearly due (these are easy cases). For both prongs, the challenge is to take the technology to more difficult cases; and, for everyone, the underlying questions are: how far do we want our communities to be dispute-free zones; and, to what extent are we content for humans to be taken out of the loops of dispute resolution?

9. Rethinking crime, control, and channelling

9.1 INTRODUCTION

Of all areas of law, there is surely none that has been subjected to so much rethinking as that of criminal justice. Politicians constantly come up with new initiatives—to reduce crime, to divert youth offenders,[1] to pilot restorative justice,[2] to find new efficiencies in policing, to reduce recidivism, to relieve the pressure on overcrowded and outdated prisons, to criminalise this and that, to decriminalise the other (most controversially, the use of recreational drugs[3]), finally to find what works,[4] and so on. Slogans and sound bites abound— whether advocating short, sharp, shocks,[5] or a more reflective tackling of both

---

[1] For an overview, see Roger Smith, *Diversion in Youth Justice* (Abingdon: Routledge, 2018).

[2] From a huge literature, see, e.g. Howard Zehr, *The Little Book of Restorative Justice* (New York: Good Books, 2014), and James Dignan, *Understanding Victims and Restorative Justice* (Maidenhead: Open University Press, 2005).

[3] See, https://en.wikipedia.org/wiki/Drug_liberalization (last accessed 16 March 2021).

[4] Famously, see Robert Martinson, 'What works?—questions and answers about prison reform' (Spring 1974) *The Public Interest* 22, and the subsequent 'nothing works' thinking.

[5] As featuring in the Conservative General Election Manifesto in 1979, available at https://www.margaretthatcher.org/document/110858 (last accessed 14 March 2021). In the section addressing the deterrence of crime, we read:

> Surer detection means surer deterrence. We also need better crime prevention measures and more flexible, more effective sentencing. For violent criminals and thugs really tough sentences are essential. But in other cases long prison terms are not always the best deterrent. So we want to see a wider variety of sentences available to the courts....
>
> We need more compulsory attendance centres for hooligans at junior and senior levels. In certain detention centres we will experiment with a tougher regime as a short, sharp shock for young criminals. For certain types of offenders, we also support the greater use of community service orders, intermediate treatment and attendance centres. Unpaid fines and compensation orders are ineffective. Fines should be assessed to punish the offender within his means and then be backed by effective sanctions for non-payment....

crime and the causes of crime (similarly, being tough on crime and being tough on the causes of crime).[6] The noise is high-pitched and persistent, but the outcomes are unclear.

Finding a pattern in this rethinking is not easy. However, our interest is in picking out the voices that articulate the thinking of Law 2.0 and Law 3.0. While the former will advocate a more regulatory approach, the latter will advocate seeking out and employing technological solutions. From this perspective, we might surmise that the pattern of the rethinking of crime, control, and channelling is not dissimilar to that found in relation to the rethinking of disputes and civil justice. First, there is a certain amount of rethinking that is prompted not directly by technological innovation but by the realisation that the relevant legal and regulatory arrangements are not fit for purpose; second, new technologies coming on stream are adopted as tools that promise more effective performance; third, a vision of end-to-end automation, with humans out of the loop as responders to crime, drives the streamlining of processes and the use of smart decision-making tools; and, finally, the thought that the best of all worlds would be one in which criminal wrongdoing was prevented invites the use of technological management to reduce the practical opportunities for committing (or the need to commit) crimes.

While recognising some similarities in the general patterns of rethinking, we should not forget that the law and regulation of criminal justice is deeply contested, reflecting different valuations of 'crime control' and 'due process'.[7] Not everyone would agree that it is better that ten guilty persons go free than that one innocent person is acquitted; and, if anything, the tendency in the modern law has been to respond more urgently to concerns that the guilty might go free rather than to the concern that the innocent might be convicted. It also needs to be remembered that the criminal justice system speaks to more than private wrongs; crimes are wrongs against the community and the law has a public function to play. So, for example, while we might liken plea bargaining deals in the criminal justice system to settlement in civil disputes, we should be careful about drawing too easy comparisons.[8]

In this chapter, we start by noting some of the strands of a Law 2.0 approach, reflecting the rethinking of crime as a risk to be reduced and managed (including the use of technological instruments for this purpose); we then turn to the

---

[6]   From many examples, see Lambeth Labour, 'Tackling crime, tackling the causes of crime' (2 August, 2019) available at http://www.lambeth-labour.org.uk/2019/08/02/tackling-crime-tackling-the-causes-of-crime (last accessed 14 March 2021).

[7]   Seminally, see Herbert L. Packer, *The Limits of the Criminal Sanction* (Stanford: Stanford University Press, 1968).

[8]   Compare Peter Cane, *Responsibility in Law and Morality* (Oxford: Hart, 2002) Ch. 7.

more radical rethinking associated with Law 3.0, as we look to governance by machines (automation of processes in the criminal justice system) and technological management and the prevention of crime ab initio.

9.2 REGULATORY THEMES

In a much-cited essay, Malcolm Feeley and Jonathan Simon capture the regulatory character of the emergent criminal law and, concomitantly, the criminal justice system. According to Feeley and Simon, the aim of the system

> is not to intervene in individuals' lives for the purpose of ascertaining responsibility, making the guilty 'pay for their crime' or changing them. Rather it seeks to regulate groups as part of a strategy of managing danger.[9]

Putting this in other words, we can say that, characteristically, Law 2.0 thinking frames issues in terms of risk assessment, risk management, and risk communication. Here, we pick out three examples of this mode of rethinking criminal law and criminal justice: the recognition of (strict liability) 'regulatory' offences; the targeting of high-risk 'dangerous' persons; and the willingness to adopt technologies and tools that will serve criminal justice purposes.

9.2.1 Regulatory Offences

We have seen how, on the civil side, the law has rethought the link between personal fault, liability, and compensatory responsibility. In a similar way, we find that the traditional link between criminal intent (mens rea), guilt, and punishment has been rethought. In both cases, the emergence of new technologies is part of the story; however, the story is not so much about the development of technologies that can assist with regulatory purposes as about technologies that challenge traditional (Law 1.0) legal principles and the fitness of the regulatory environment.

Thus, in a seminal article, Francis Sayre remarks on the 'steadily growing stream of offenses punishable without any criminal intent whatsoever'.[10] In what was apparently a parallel, but independent, development in both England and the United States, from the middle of the nineteenth century, the courts accepted that, so far as 'public welfare' offences were concerned, it was acceptable to dispense with proof of intent or negligence. If the food sold

---

[9]   Malcolm Feeley and Jonathan Simon, 'Actuarial Justice: the Emerging New Criminal Law' in David Nelken (ed), *The Futures of Criminology* (London: Sage, 1994) 173, at 173.

[10]   F.B Sayre, 'Public Welfare Offences' (1933) 33 *Columbia Law Review* 55 at 55.

was adulterated, or if employees polluted waterways, and so on, sellers and employers were simply held to account. For the most part, this was no more than a tax on business; it relieved the prosecutors of having to invest time and resource in proving intent or negligence; and, as Sayre reads the development, it reflected 'the trend of the day away from nineteenth century individualism towards a new sense of the importance of collective interests'.[11]

In a modernising world, as Sayre recognises, the 'invention and extensive use of high-powered automobiles require new forms of traffic regulation;...the growth of modern factories requires new forms of labor regulation; the development of modern building construction and the growth of skyscrapers require new forms of building regulation',[12] and so on. However, Sayre emphatically rejects any suggestion that we should abandon 'the classic requirement of a *mens rea* as an essential of criminality',[13] saying:

> The group of offenses punishable without proof of any criminal intent must be sharply limited. The sense of justice of the community will not tolerate the infliction of punishment which is substantial upon those innocent of intentional or negligent wrongdoing; and law in the last analysis must reflect the general community sense of justice.[14]

In other words, so long as there is no stigmatisation or serious punishment of those (largely businesspeople) who act in ways that deviate from public welfare regulatory requirements, dispensing with mens rea is tolerable. However, what is not to be tolerated is any attempt to dispense with mens rea where the community sees the law as concerned with serious moral delinquency and where serious punishments follow on conviction. As Sayre puts it, 'For true crimes it is imperative that courts should not relax the classic requirement of *mens rea* or guilty intent.'[15] False analogies with public welfare offences, in order to ease the way for the prosecution to secure a conviction, should be resisted. He concludes with the warning that the courts should avoid extending the doctrines applicable to public welfare offences to 'true crimes', because this would be to 'sap the vitality of the criminal law'.[16] Still, this leaves vast swathes of regulatory crime to be created on a strict liability basis.

---

[11] Ibid., at 67.
[12] Ibid., at 68–69.
[13] Ibid., at 55.
[14] Ibid., at 70.
[15] Ibid., at 80.
[16] Sayre (n 10) at 84. Compare, R.A. Duff, 'Perversions and Subversions of Criminal Law' in R.A. Duff, Lindsay Farmer, S.E. Marshall, Massimo Renzo, and Victor Tadros (eds), *The Boundaries of the Criminal Law* (Oxford: Oxford University Press, 2010) 88 at 104: 'We must ask about the terms in which the state should address

142   *Rethinking law, regulation, and technology*

9.2.2   Dealing with the Dangerous

Some dangerous people (like suicide bombers) will not survive the commission of their crimes; and, others (like the 'Moors murderers', Ian Brady and Myra Hindley) will never be released back into the community. However, some dangerous people—people like the London taxi driver, John Worboys, who, in 2009, was convicted of 19 offences including one count of rape, five sexual assaults, one attempted assault, and 12 drugging charges[17]—might one day be released back into the community. Worboys was given an indeterminate custodial sentence (for the sake of public protection) with at least eight years to be served in prison. Following Worboys' conviction, the police received many other complaints from women who alleged that they had been drugged and assaulted by him. In January 2018, when the Parole Board decided that Worboys should be released, there was a wave of protest which led to a successful challenge in the High Court. In November 2018, the Parole Board duly changed its mind, concluding in effect that Worboys—now notorious as the 'black cab rapist'—was too dangerous to be released.

For those who take a risk perspective, there is a dilemma that might arise, and not infrequently does arise, where offenders who have served their specified tariff term in prison and who are due for release are still considered to be 'dangerous'—whether presenting a risk to a particular individual, or to a particular group or class of individuals, or to persons generally.[18] If the offender is released and quickly re-offends, victims will rightly argue that they have

---

its citizens when it seeks to regulate their conduct, and whether the tones of criminal law, speaking of wrongs that are to be condemned, are more appropriate than those of a regulatory regime that speaks only of rules and penalties for their breach.' According to Duff, where the conduct in question is a serious public wrong, it would be a 'subversion' of the criminal law if offenders were not to be held to account and condemned. For questions that might arise relative to the 'fair trial' provisions of the European Convention on Human Rights where a state decides to transfer less serious offences from the criminal courts to administrative procedures (as with minor road traffic infringements), see e.g., *Öztürk v Germany* (1984) 6 EHRR 409.

[17]   See BBC News, '"Black cab rapist" John Worboys to stay in prison', 19 November 2018: https://www.bbc.co.uk/news/uk-england-london-46265924 (last accessed 18 October 2020).

[18]   See, e.g., the protagonists in the dangerousness debate of the 1980s: Jean E. Floud and Warren A. Young, *Dangerousness and Criminal Justice* (London: Heinemann, 1981); Nigel Walker, *Punishment, Danger and Stigma* (Lanham, MD: Rowman and Littlefield, 1980); and Anthony E. Bottoms and Roger Brownsword, 'Dangerousness and Rights' in J. Hinton (ed), *Dangerousness: Problems of Assessment and Prediction* (London: George Allen and Unwin, 1983) 9, and 'The Dangerousness Debate after the Floud Report' (1982) 22 *British Journal of Criminology* 229. For more recent debates about protective sentencing, in particular, for analysis of the indeterminate sentence

been under-protected by the state. In cases such as that of Worboys—and, similarly, that of Usman Khan who, in November 2019, killed Jack Merritt and Saskia Jones at a prisoner rehabilitation conference at Fishmongers' Hall in London[19]—victims (actual and prospective) will complain that the system is letting them down. If, however, the offender is not released, and if in fact there would have been no further offending, no future victims, then an injustice is done to the offender. Those who campaign for the convicted and their rights will argue that the state should take the rights of those who are due for release from prison more seriously. However, in practice, because we will not know whether offenders who are not released would have re-offended (we will not know whether they are false positives), and because the popular media will ensure that we do know that an offender whose release is controversial has re-offended (we know whether they are false negatives), there is a strong pressure to keep supposedly dangerous offenders locked up.

So long as predictions of dangerousness are prone to error, there will be a difficult question of principle for criminal justice professionals: while utilitarians will tend to emphasise the importance of protecting the community, liberals will tend to emphasise the importance of respecting the rights of offenders. However, if the predictive tools employed by professionals were so accurate as to enable them to eliminate the false positives, but without also increasing the false negatives, this debate would be entirely academic. Accordingly, in the longer run, this might become purely a practical matter of designing tools that do the job. In fact, with huge leaps forward in AI, coupled with a willingness to employ AI predictive tools in the criminal justice system, it might be thought that we are already on the cusp of a breakthrough in predicting dangerousness. However, we should probably curb our enthusiasm: we should not underrate the challenge in bringing down the number of false positive predictions without also increasing the number of false negatives. Moreover, as Andrea Roth has acutely observed, while we might view AI tools as serving our 'desire for objectivity and accuracy, it is typically a desire for a particular type of accuracy: the reduction of false negatives'.[20]

---

of imprisonment for public protection, see Harry Annison, *Dangerous Politics: Risk, Political Vulnerability, and Penal Policy* (Oxford: Oxford University Press, 2015).

[19] Khan had been released from prison 11 months earlier. See David Brown and Duncan Gardham, 'Police and MI5 ignored lethal threat of charity's "poster boy"' *The Times*, 29 May 2021, p 6. Responding to critical remarks made by the inquest jury, the Home Secretary said that 'government and operational partners have taken important action to strengthen the supervision of terror offenders on licence and end the automatic early release of terrorist prisoners'.

[20] Andrea Roth, 'Trial by Machine' (2016) 104 *Georgetown Law Journal* 1245, 1252.

While the public might be reassured that, in any case where there is doubt about the matter, a supposedly dangerous offender will not be released back into the community, the reassurance would be all the greater if those who are judged to have dangerous behavioural characteristics were prevented from committing crimes in the first place. The thought that proactive prevention is better than reactive punishment foreshadows the most radical rethinking of criminal justice.

9.2.3 Using Technologies to Deter and Detect Crime and Determine Guilt

Potentially, technological tools can assist criminal justice professionals at all stages of the criminal justice system. For example, Ric Simmons reports that while the police in Los Angeles use prediction software to identify high-crime areas (to which areas, appropriate resources can then be deployed), the police in Fresno employ 'a software system called Beware to warn...officers of the threat level for the location of a 911 call' (the alert is 'green for safe, yellow for caution, and red for dangerous').[21] In Chicago, the police use predictive software to create a 'heat list' of the 400 people most likely to be involved in shootings or homicides;[22] again, this leads to appropriate resources being deployed to monitor the individuals in question. But, of course, there are many different technologies employed for a broad range of criminal justice purposes. Various kinds of sensing and surveillance technologies (including now drones), locating technologies, tagging and tracking devices, and recognition technologies might assist in deterring the commission of crime as well as in its investigation; as we have seen in an earlier chapter when we discussed the *Loomis* case, AI tools might guide decision-makers in relation to such matters as bail and punishment; and, there has been a lively debate about the potential of neurotechnologies to assist both the police and courts in assessing the credibility and truthfulness of persons who are witnesses or suspects and defendants.[23] From this growing repertoire of technological instruments, we can say a little more about the significance of big data, surveillance, and the 'new forensics'.

The new forensics, particularly the making, retention, and use of DNA profiles, has been with us for some time. In the United Kingdom, advocates of

---

[21] Ric Simmons, *Smart Surveillance* (Cambridge: Cambridge University Press, 2019) at 39.

[22] Ibid.

[23] See, e.g., Jeffrey Rosen, 'The Brain on the Stand', *New York Times* (11 March 2007), available at https://www.nytimes.com/2007/03/11/magazine/11Neurolaw.t.html (last accessed 14 March 2021).

crime control saw this biotechnological breakthrough as an important tool for the police and prosecutors; and the legislative framework was duly amended to authorise very extensive taking and retention of profiles. Even when legal proceedings were dropped or suspects were acquitted, the law authorised the retention of the profiles that had been taken. As a result, a DNA database with several million profiles soon was in place and, where DNA samples were retrieved from crime scenes, the database could be interrogated as an investigative tool (so that 'reasonable suspicion' could be cast on an individual, not by independent evidence, but by a 'match'). Precisely how much contribution to crime control was (or is) made by the profiles is hard to know. However, it was clear that the traditional rights of individuals were being subordinated to the promise of the new technology; and it was just a matter of time before the compatibility of the legislative provisions with human rights was raised in the courts. Famously, in the *Case of S. and Marper v The United Kingdom*,[24] the leading case in Europe on the taking (and retention) of DNA samples and the banking of DNA profiles for criminal justice purposes, the Grand Chamber in Strasbourg held that the legal provisions were far too wide and disproportionate in their impact on privacy. To this extent at least, individual human rights prevailed over the latest technology of crime control.[25] On the other hand, more recently, in a test case in the UK on the use of facial recognition technology by the police, the Court of Appeal ruled that, although the right to privacy was engaged, the restriction on that right was proportionate.[26]

Although DNA profiling and the 'new forensics' (including digital fingerprinting) offer important investigative resources, these technologies are still operating *after* the event, after a crime has been committed. However, as we move from Law 2.0 to Law 3.0, more radical thoughts occur. In big data, machine learning, and artificial intelligence, we see the opportunity for

---

[24]   (2009) 48 EHRR 50. For the domestic UK proceedings, see [2002] EWCA Civ 1275 (Court of Appeal), and [2004] UKHL 39 (House of Lords). See, further, Roger Brownsword and Morag Goodwin, *Law and the Technologies of the Twenty-First Century* (Cambridge: Cambridge University Press, 2012) Ch 4.

[25]   In the *Case of Gaughran v The United Kingdom* (Application n. 45245/15) (13 February 2020), with the Strasbourg jurisprudence having become more fine-grained, the UK was again held to have 'failed to strike a fair balance between the competing public and private interests' as a result of which its practice in retaining the DNA profiles, fingerprints, and photographs of persons *convicted of recordable offences* was held to have 'overstepped the acceptable margin of appreciation' such that the retention at issue constituted 'a disproportionate interference with the applicant's right to respect for private life and [could not] be regarded as necessary in a democratic society' (at paras 96–97).

[26]   *Bridges, R (On the Application Of) v South Wales Police* [2020] EWCA Civ 1058.

the automation of the criminal justice system and, more generally, we see the opportunity to act *before* the event by relying on technological management in order to prevent the commission of crime. This is a matter to which we will return after we have discussed the automation of criminal justice.

9.3   AUTOMATION

In a recent review of the take-up of technologies in the criminal justice system, Amber Marks, Ben Bowling, and Colman Keenan suggest that the direction of travel is

> [t]owards an increasingly automated justice system that undercuts the safeguards of the traditional criminal justice model. This system favours efficiency and effectiveness over traditional due process safeguards and is taking on a life of its own as it becomes increasingly mediated by certain types of technology that minimize human agency.[27]

In principle, in the case of some criminal offences and offenders, it should be possible fully to automate the process end-to-end. For example, in the case of road traffic offences, the process starts with the detection of a crime and the identification of the offender (employing, say, automatic number plate recognition), and it is followed by the automated issuing of the penalty notice and then enforcement of the payment.

Taking up the observation that the adoption of technologies for the sake of efficiency and effectiveness might come at the cost of due process, we start with some reflections on the tensions involved in the design of a criminal justice system; and then we reflect on the implications of taking humans out the loop.

9.3.1   Expectations, Criminal Justice, and Automation

We have many expectations with regard to the practice and performance of the criminal justice system, but the core expectation that the system will be just leaves unresolved the tension between procedural justice and substantive justice. It might well be that automated decisions enabled by AI would be more consistent than human decisions, but what price consistency if this simply perpetuates substantive injustice? It might also be true that we could reduce

---

[27]   Amber Marks, Benjamin Bowling, and Colman Keenan, 'Automatic Justice? Technology, Crime, and Social Control' in Roger Brownsword, Eloise Scotford, and Karen Yeung (eds), *The Oxford Handbook of Law, Regulation and Technology* (Oxford: Oxford University Press, 2017) 705, 705.

Rethinking crime, control, and channelling   147

the abuse of discretion by criminal justice professionals, but what price this improvement if there is an offset in the system's flexibility to dispense justice in the individual case? Moreover, what if, instead of decisions being made by occasionally biased humans, we hand over decision-making to machines that are systematically biased in ways that are both unacceptable and difficult to detect?

In a perceptive discussion, Vincent Chiao reflects on the expectations that we reasonably have of the criminal justice system and the need sometimes to accept trade-offs between competing expectations.[28] We expect, for example, that the decisions made by criminal justice professionals will be accurate and impartial (not biased), that they will also be 'intelligible' and transparent, that like cases will be treated alike but, at the same time, that justice will be individualised, and that decision-makers will be accountable. If the use of AI is to be acceptable, it has to (at least) match the performance of humans relative to these expectations. This might not be asking so much because, as Chiao sees it, the bar set by humans is pretty low—indeed, so low that it would be disappointing if risk assessment algorithms could not do better. The question, however, is whether AI can outperform humans (and, for that matter, random decision-making) across the board. Even if, as Chiao speculates, AI might prove to be more accurate than human decision-makers and no more compromised by upstream and systemic bias than humans in the criminal justice system, we should not be altogether sanguine about the development and application of AI. There are, as Chiao notes, reasons to worry about the *unregulated* private development of the technologies; and we might also pause over the possibility that the increased use of predictive algorithms not only turns criminal law and criminal justice over to technocrats and experts, but also detaches it from the public re-enactment of a society's moral code.

There is also a persistent concern (highlighted by the court in *Loomis*) that proprietary interests in the technology might inhibit disclosing how it works coupled with the concern that, where an 'explanation' is actually given, it might prove to be largely meaningless to suspects and defendants. Yet, humans are not always able to explain their own behaviour or the behaviour of those with whom they interact. Moreover, as Chiao points out, there are many tools and processes (from air travel to pharmaceuticals) which humans happily use without being able to explain how they work. If AI has to explain itself, once again, the bar is not high.

---

[28] Vincent Chiao, 'Fairness, accountability and transparency: notes on algorithmic decision-making in criminal justice' (2019) 15 *International Journal of Law in Context* 126.

Perhaps, then, in our quest for intelligibility, the critical question is not whether we can understand how the algorithms work, but whether we can be given reasons for the decision that we accept as a reasonable justification. In other words, it is not causal explanation that matters so much as normative justification. If the operations of AI are not easily explained, that might not be too important; but, if AI simply 'does not do' justifications, if it cannot give reasons for its decisions, then we have a fundamental problem. This would be like being ruled by super-intelligent beings from another planet who are far smarter than we are but who cannot communicate with us.

If one of the potential benefits of AI is that it might discipline human discretion in the criminal justice system, then might it discipline the discretion that the police notoriously have in their operational practices (that is, discretion as to *who* to police, *where* to police, *what* to police, *how* to police, and so on) as well as in their interpretation of so many legal rules that hinge on 'reasonableness' (such as the reasonable suspicion standard for a stop and search or for an arrest)? One step in this direction is the introduction of body worn cameras/videos (BWVs).[29] On the face of it, BWVs promise to make policing more transparent which, in turn, should have a positive impact on the fairness and accuracy of policing. However, so long as there is a residual discretion about when to switch on BWVs, we might wonder whether the promise of the technology will be realised in practice. Moreover, because of the data-capture involved in the use of BWVs, there are concerns about the fair collection and processing of personal data as well as deeper anxieties about privacy.

Taking stock, we can see that, even where AI is used only to assist criminal justice professionals, there are questions about whether our expectations about the performance of the system are better realised with or without these technologies. Moreover, one wonders whether these thin wedges will become thicker as techno-enthusiasm takes over. Given that BWVs (like roadside traffic cameras) can be made much smarter and connected to other smart machines, there is the prospect of the technologies actually taking over the policing and the enforcement rather than advising and assisting humans who do such work.

9.3.2   From Humans Being 'in the Loop' to Being 'out of the Loop'

In an earlier chapter, we discussed the way in which Article 22 of the General Data Protection Regulation raises a cautionary flag in relation to certain classes of decision where such decisions are based solely on automated processing.[30]

---

[29]   For discussion, see Ben Bowling and Shruti Iyer, 'Automated policing: the case of body-worn video' (2019) 15 *International Journal of Law in Context* 140.

[30]   See section 5.3.3.

Rethinking crime, control, and channelling 149

This general caution is mirrored in the Law Enforcement Directive[31] (lest automated processing in the criminal justice system should put humans out of the loop); and, in the United Kingdom, section 50 of the Data Protection Act 2018 further elaborates these safeguards by treating the right to human intervention as essentially a right to request that the data controller should reconsider the decision or take a new decision that is not based solely on automated processing.[32] As we noted earlier, there are a number of nice points of interpretation arising from these provisions. However, even if the interpretive issues can be satisfactorily resolved, it remains to be determined just how effective the possibility of recourse to human intervention will prove to be.

In an age when AI and automated decisions outperform humans, how realistic, reasonable, or rational is it for humans, having reconsidered the matter, to override the automated decision? As Hin-Yan Liu has argued in an insightful commentary, humans become vulnerable because of their now perceived inferiority to smart machines.[33] Thus:

> A general vulnerability that erodes our means of resisting AI power involves a narrative about perceived or actual human inferiority. This has the effect of eroding human confidence and ability in challenging and countering AI, stoking the automation bias whereby proximate human beings acquiesce to AI 'recommendations', and effectively relegate human overseers to mere button-pushers. As this is a form of categorical superiority, because AI can be pitted against the human being, that has not emerged before it threatens to blindside us entirely. As well as being unprecedented and therefore difficult to identify, however, it will be hard to recognise this form of erosion in available responses because it is nebulous by affecting the very orientation of human beings in relation to AI. As such, the subtle yet pervasive narrative of human inferiority suggests a great weakness in our collective ability to respond to and regulate AI.[34]

If smart machines, rather than humans, begin to set the standards for road safety, and if in the criminal justice system, as Chiao moots, AI might prove more accurate than human decision-makers, then (as Liu implies) the possibility of bringing humans back into the loop might be little more than an empty gesture. On the one hand, as with many ostensibly remedial pathways, the gradient is simply too steep; even for those prospective complainants who know about the availability of a remedy, the cost and complexity of pursuing a complaint is just too great. On the other hand, the humans who are brought

---

[31] Directive 2016/6801.

[32] See, too, ss 96 and 97 of the Act concerning automated processing by the intelligence services.

[33] Hin-Yan Liu, 'The power structure of artificial intelligence' (2018) 10 *Law, Innovation and Technology* 197.

[34] Ibid., at 222.

back into the loop might be reluctant to gainsay the automated decision—in which case, this will further disincentivise individual complainants. Not only do we know that 'repeat players' tend to do better in disputes than 'one-shot' players,[35] we can anticipate that automated decision-makers will prove to be repeat players with a vengeance. If humans are to be brought back into the loop, and if smart machines are to be effectively monitored, it is probably not at the behest of individual complainants. Rather, it will be left to regulatory bodies to undertake ex ante licensing of AI and ex post audit of its performance.[36]

9.4   ACTING EX ANTE

The popular film, *Minority Report*, is one version of the imaginary of preventive justice. On the face of it, it is better to prevent criminal wrongdoing rather than to react after the crime has been committed; it is better to act ex ante rather than ex post; and, if new technologies help us to make effective ex ante interventions, so much the better. More power, as it were, to the technologies.

However, even in our imaginaries, things do not always go as planned; and, even where interventions are effective, they might not be acceptable. For example, in Nick Harkaway's dystopian novel, *Gnomon*, we are invited to imagine a United Kingdom where, on the one hand, governance takes place through 'the System' (an ongoing plebiscite) and, on the other, order is maintained by 'the Witness' (a super-surveillance state, 'taking information from everywhere' which is reviewed by 'self-teaching algorithms' all designed to ensure public safety).[37] When citizens are asked to cast their votes on a draft Monitoring Bill, in which it is proposed that permanent remote access should be installed in the skulls of recidivists or compulsive criminals, some object that this crosses a red line. Indeed, for those citizens who are guided by liberal values and respect for human rights, this (fictitious) bill probably crosses more than one red line.

Even without such dramatic forms of anticipation and intervention, there are many reasons to be concerned about the drift towards ex ante prevention that is facilitated by new technologies. For example, there is a concern that, as technological prevention moves into the foreground, the state is no longer quite so central to the orchestration of public debate about what is right and what is wrong (in other words, there is a privatisation of morality); and, at the same time, there is a fear that there might be some loss of a productive

---

[35]   Famously, see Marc Galanter, 'Why the "Haves" Come Out Ahead: Speculations on the Limits of Legal Change' (1974) 9 *Law and Society Review* 95.

[36]   Compare our discussion in section 4.3.4.

[37]   Nick Harkaway, *Gnomon* (London: William Heinemann, 2017) at 11.

interaction between legal and social norms. There is also a concern that what is 'technologically viable' will come to dominate debates about the nature and scope of the ex ante measures that are employed, resulting in a lack of sensitivity in relation to false positives as well as the breadth and depth of the practical restrictions that are imposed. In short, there is a cluster of concerns about the potential de-centring of public deliberation and debate and about the prospects for democracy, due process, and liberal values.

Where the technologies that enable and shape a predictive and preventive approach to criminal justice are themselves underwritten by utilitarian thinking—as often will be the case—then it will be those who do *not* subscribe to a Benthamite theory of punitive justice who will be troubled. Hence, for Andrew Ashworth and Lucia Zedner, the concern is precisely that 'the preventive endeavour' is becoming detached from the constraining principles of due process and respect for human rights.[38] According to Ashworth and Zedner, while it is widely accepted that the state has a core duty to protect and secure its citizens,

> [t]he key question is how this duty…can be squared with the state's duty of justice (that is to treat persons as responsible moral agents, to respect their human rights), and the state's duty to provide a system of criminal justice…to deal with those who transgress the criminal law. Of course, the norms guiding the fulfilment of these duties are contested, but core among them are the liberal values of respect for the autonomy of the individual, fairness, equality, tolerance of difference, and resort to coercion only where justified and as a last resort. More amorphous values such as trust also play an important role in liberal society and find their legal articulation in requirements of reasonable suspicion, proof beyond all reasonable doubt, and the presumption of innocence. Yet, the duty to prevent wrongful harms conflicts with these requirements since it may require intervention before reasonable suspicion can be established, on the basis of less conclusive evidence, or even in respect of innocent persons. The imperative to prevent, or at least to diminish the prospect of, wrongful harms thus stands in acute tension with any idealized account of a principled and parsimonious liberal criminal law.[39]

When, as Ashworth and Zedner observe, the practice is to resolve the tension in favour of prevention, and when the latest technologies (including AI and machine learning) offer instruments that promise to enhance predictive accuracy and preventive effectiveness, liberal concerns are inevitably heightened.

In particular, there might be questions about the accuracy of the particular technology (about the way that it maps onto offences, or in its predictive and pre-emptive identification of 'true positive' prospective offenders, and so

---

[38]   Andrew Ashworth and Lucia Zedner, *Preventive Justice* (Oxford: Oxford University Press, 2014).

[39]   Ibid., at 251–252.

152   *Rethinking law, regulation, and technology*

on).[40] Moreover, if technological management is characterised as an exercise in risk management, a certain number of false positives might be deemed to be 'acceptable'. However, liberals should resist any such characterisation that purports to diminish the injustice to those individual agents who are wrongly subjected to restrictive measures;[41] the values of liberty and due process are not to be bypassed in this way.[42]

In what follows we can consider whether concerns about false positives in the context of preventive measures are comparable to core due process concerns about the punishment of the innocent; and then we can consider whether smart prevention (employing technological management) should be categorically rejected by members of any community with moral aspirations

---

[40] See, further, Christina M. Mulligan, 'Perfect Enforcement of Law: When to Limit and When to Use Technology' (2008) 14 *Richmond Journal of Law and Technology* 1 http://law.richmond.edu/jolt/v14i4/article13.pdf (last accessed 11 August 2018); and Ian Kerr, 'Prediction, Pre-emption, Presumption' in Mireille Hildebrandt and Katja de Vries (eds), *Privacy, Due Process and the Computational Turn* (Abingdon: Routledge, 2013) 91.

[41] Compare *United States v Salerno and Cafaro* (1987) 481 US 739, where one of the questions was whether detention under the Bail Reform Act 1984 was to be treated as punishment or as a 'regulatory' measure. The majority concluded that 'the detention imposed by the Act falls on the regulatory side of the dichotomy. The legislative history of the Bail Reform Act clearly indicates that Congress did not formulate the pretrial detention provisions as punishment for dangerous individuals…. Congress instead perceived pretrial detention as a potential solution to a pressing societal problem…. There is no doubt that preventing danger to the community is a legitimate regulatory goal' (at 747).

[42] Compare the minority opinion of Marshall J (joined by Brennan J) in *US v Salerno and Cafaro* (n 41 at 760:

> Let us apply the majority's reasoning to a similar, hypothetical case. After investigation, Congress determines (not unrealistically) that a large proportion of violent crime is perpetrated by persons who are unemployed. It also determines, equally reasonably, that much violent crime is committed at night. From amongst the panoply of 'potential solutions,' Congress chooses a statute which permits, after judicial proceedings, the imposition of a dusk-to-dawn curfew on anyone who is unemployed. Since this is not a measure enacted for the purpose of punishing the unemployed, and since the majority finds that preventing danger to the community is a legitimate regulatory goal, the curfew statute would, according to the majority's analysis, be a mere 'regulatory' detention statute, entirely compatible with the substantive components of the Due Process Clause.
>
> The absurdity of this conclusion arises, of course, from the majority's cramped concept of substantive due process. The majority proceeds as though the only substantive right protected by the Due Process Clause is a right to be free from punishment before conviction. The majority's technique for infringing this right is simple: merely redefine any measure which is claimed to be punishment as 'regulation,' and, magically, the Constitution no longer prohibits its imposition.

Rethinking crime, control, and channelling 153

(particularly liberal communities). Not all rethinking should be welcomed and, where a community is committed to liberal values and human rights, measures of prevention and risk management, just as much as punishment for wrongs actually done, have to match up to these commitments. If a community is to pursue a strategy of preventive technological management, it needs to be supported not only by a social licence (that reflects the general acceptability of the approach) but also by the particular community licence—and, above all, of course, by the global commons licence.

9.4.1 True and False Positives: Belief and Actuality

When we say, in the context of an agent having been convicted of a crime, that we believe that the agent is a true positive, we mean that we believe (typically, on the basis of the evidence and the relevant standard of proof) that the agent did commit the offence. If, in this context, we say that we believe that the agent is a false positive, we mean that we have grounds for believing that the agent did not commit the offence. In both cases, though, there is an 'actuality' (the commission of the crime and who committed it) against which, in principle, our classification of the agent can be cross-checked. If that actuality is at odds with our classification, our classification is incorrect. Even if we have grounds for believing that an agent committed the crime, and even if by the standards of the criminal justice system we have grounds for characterising the agent as a true positive, that is an incorrect classification if the agent did not actually commit the crime. If an agent did not actually commit the crime, that agent is innocent no matter that all the evidence points to the guilt of the agent. In the final analysis, when there is a tension between the judgment of the criminal justice system and the actuality, it is the latter that is the arbiter of our innocence and our guilt.

Now, it might be objected that this paradigm cannot be translated to the case of an agent who, rather than being convicted of an offence is restricted by preventive measures. Quite simply, this is because, in the context of smart prevention, there is no analogue for the actual commission of the offence. In that context, if we say that an agent is a true positive, we mean that we believe that the agent is correctly classified as one who would have gone on to commit an offence; and, if we say that an agent is a false positive, we mean that we believe that the agent is incorrectly classified as one who would have gone on to commit an offence. However, so the objection runs, because the matter was not actually put to the test, we cannot meaningfully discuss the truth or falsity of the proposition that, but for the preventive intervention, the agent would have committed the offence. The most that we can do is form a belief about whether the agent would or would not have done so. There is no 'actuality' against which our classification of the agent can be cross-checked, no actuality to act as the arbiter of innocence or guilt.

That said, insofar as we are classifying agents on the basis of our reasonable beliefs, there is some comparability between the classification of agents as true or false positives in both the context of conviction and punishment and prevention. To be sure, the evidence that is treated as relevant to the belief differs from one context to another. In the context of conviction and punishment, the focus is on the conduct of the agent; but, in the context of smart prevention, where the profile provides the evidence, the assessment is less about conduct and more about character and circumstances.[43] In both cases, moreover, our beliefs can be reviewed and revised depending on the evidence. If we could always access the actuality in the context of an offence having been committed, this comparability would not be significant—because we would do just that and eliminate false positives. In other words, although *in principle* there is an actuality against which to cross-check the correctness of our characterisation of agents as innocent or guilty, in practice, we simply do not have access to it. The reality is that, in practice, criminal justice practitioners operate in a world of procedural propriety and reasonable grounds for belief. Whether we are characterising an agent who is punished or an agent who is prevented as a true or a false positive, our description is based on our beliefs. In practice, what will prompt a reclassification (from true positive to false positive) is not some kind of revelation of whether the agent 'actually did it' or 'would have done it' but new evidence and a fresh appraisal of one's beliefs and the grounds for one's beliefs. The media might talk the talk of whether some agent was 'actually innocent' of the crime but, for practitioners, it is a question of following the right process and forming beliefs that are based on reasonable grounds.[44]

Given that, in practice, the characterisation of agents who are convicted of crimes as true or false positives operates in a realm of justified belief without recourse to an independent actuality, there is no problem in treating the characterisation of agents who are subjected to preventive measures as true or false positives. In both cases, punished agents and prevented agents, the labelling of an agent as a true or false positive reflects a belief largely based on evidential grounds.

---

[43] Compare, Nicola Lacey, *In Search of Criminal Responsibility* (Oxford: Oxford University Press, 2016) esp at 170–171.

[44] Compare Richard Nobles and David Schiff, *Understanding Miscarriages of Justice* (Oxford: Oxford University Press, 2000).

9.4.2 Smart Prevention, Community Values, and the Commons

In the chorus of condemnation and criticism that typically follows a terrorist outrage—such as the London bombings in July 2005 or the bombing at Manchester Arena in May 2017—we find too many questions and too few answers. While many of the questions will be about the adequacy of the response to the incident, there will also be questions about whether it could or should have been prevented. However, if rules and their sanctions do not deter suicide bombers, how are we to prevent similar outrages? If rules will not do the preventive job, we might wonder whether the smarter approach is to look for technological solutions.

Already, the emphasis of the global response to terrorism is to 'prevent and combat' it.[45] The intelligence services are expected to monitor 'high risk' persons and intervene before they are able to translate their preparatory acts (which themselves might be treated as serious criminal offences) into the death of innocent persons. However, while smart prevention, where predictive technologies are brought together with preventive technologies to manage the relevant risks (and even to target and 'take out' particular individuals), might share precisely the same regulatory purposes as counterpart rules of the criminal law, it differs from the traditional criminal justice response in three important respects.[46]

First, whereas punishment operates after the offence has been committed, smart prevention operates before offences are committed; smart prevention is an ex ante, not an ex post, strategy. Second, whereas traditional criminal justice might invest in more effective deterrence of crime, smart prevention invests in more effective anticipation, interception, and deflection of crime. Third, and crucially, smart prevention does not give agents either moral or prudential reasons for compliance; rather, it focuses on reducing the practical options that are available to agents. The question is whether, even if smart prevention is more effective than the traditional rules of the criminal law, it is compatible with a community's commitment to liberal values, with its understanding of just punishment, and above all with respect for the commons' conditions. Just like any other smart intervention, smart prevention needs to meet the terms of the triple licence.

---

[45] See the UN Global Counter-Terrorism Strategy, https://www.un.org/counterterrorism/un-global-counter-terrorism-strategy (last accessed 16 May 2021).

[46] Moreover, while a community might think that it is acceptable for the state to take lethal preventive precision measures against targeted terrorists in distant lands, it might regard the use of drones (for surveillance and preventive strike purposes) as a totally unacceptable response to domestic crime.

However, before we respond to these questions, an important caveat is in order. As Bernard Harcourt cautions, one of the objections to predictive criminal justice is that it tends to amplify historic discrimination against minority and ethnic groups.[47] Indeed, questions have already been raised in the US about the hidden racial bias of apparently colour-blind algorithms used for bail and sentencing decisions.[48] If smart prevention exacerbates the unfairness that is otherwise present in criminal justice practice, it cannot be the strategy of choice. Accordingly, when comparing and contrasting smart prevention with traditional ex post criminal justice strategies, we will do so on a *ceteris paribus* basis.

In order to focus our response to the questions raised about smart prevention, we should ask whether the proposed measures are compatible with the community's moral aspiration as well as how such a preventive strategy compares with more traditional strategies for controlling crime.

9.4.2.1 Smart prevention and moral aspiration

Where a community has moral aspirations, it might be thought to be important that members should not only comply with legal rules but also comply freely and with an understanding of the moral thinking that guides governance. Ideal-typically, citizens will be disposed to comply and to comply for the right reason. In such a community, three deviations from the ideal-type will be a cause for concern: those who are disposed to comply but not for the right reason; those who are generally disposed to comply but who, in a particular case, have more compelling moral reasons against compliance (the case of conscientious objection); and, those who are not disposed to comply.[49] Where those who are not disposed to comply become a serious concern, a strategy of smart prevention might appeal. However, before a community with moral aspirations (especially a liberal community) embraces this 'solution', there are several considerations that will give it pause.

First, the community might judge that, for reasons of both moral development and moral opportunity, it should maintain rule-guided zones of conduct. The thinking is that it is in such zones that there is an accounting for conduct,

---

[47] Bernard E. Harcourt, *Against Prediction: Profiling, Policing, and Punishing in an Actuarial Age* (Chicago: The University of Chicago Press, 2007).

[48] Sam Corbett-Davies, Emma Pierson, Avi Feller, and Sharad Goel, 'A computer program used for bail and sentencing decisions was labelled biased against blacks. It's actually not that clear' *The Washington Post* (17 October 2016). Compare, too, Cathy O'Neil, *Weapons of Math Destruction* (London: Allen Lane, 2016).

[49] See, Deryck Beyleveld and Roger Brownsword, 'Punitive and Preventive Justice in an Era of Profiling, Smart Prediction and Practical Preclusion: Three Key Questions' (2019) 15 *International Journal of Law in Context* 198.

that such accounting is one of the ways in which moral agents come to appreciate the nature of their most important rights and responsibilities, and that this is how in interpersonal dealings agents develop their sense of what it is to do the right thing.[50] While the significance of the complexion of the regulatory environment is a somewhat under-researched topic,[51] the community is surely right to pause: smart prevention should not be allowed to crowd out moral reason.

Second, smart prevention is designed to reduce, indeed eliminate, non-compliance. However, the community might hesitate to treat this as an unqualified good. Smart prevention works by taking the option of compliance (as previously understood) off the table. While the resulting pattern of behaviour might be 'compliant', it is hardly the case that members are 'complying'. They simply have no practical choice in the matter. Moreover, as we have already indicated, smart prevention also treats the reasons for compliance (including the right reasons) as irrelevant. The ideal-typical case is no longer the benchmark.

Third, a compelled pattern of compliance removes the most conspicuous opportunities for conscientious objection. Given the salience of direct acts of conscientious objection, smart prevention takes out a significant prompt for a moral examination of the legal measures. If the community is to live up to its aspirations, it will pause before it removes such a prompt for members to engage in collective and critical moral reflection.

For each particular community, there will need to be deliberation about the pros and cons of smart prevention. To keep faith with its aspirations, the community will need to maintain a clear moral narrative that backs its preventive strategy, and it will probably do well to confine the strategy as well as ensure that the voices of conscientious objectors can still be heard. However, we should not forget that, beyond the aspirations and concerns of each particular community, there is the universal concern that the commons' conditions should not be compromised. Even if the members of a particular liberal community are satisfied that their reliance on smart prevention strikes a reasonable balance between reducing non-compliance and respecting the community's moral aspirations, we need to be satisfied that patterns of compliance do not

---

[50] Compare, too, Anthony Duff's caution against changing the (rule-based) regulatory signals so that they speak less of crime and punishment and more of rules and penalties: R.A. Duff, 'Perversions and Subversions of Criminal Law' in Duff, Farmer, Marshall, Renzo, and Tadros (n 16) 88, esp at 104. According to Duff, where the conduct in question is a serious public wrong, it would be a 'subversion' of the criminal law if offenders were not to be held to account and condemned. See, too, the argument in Alon Harel, 'The Duty to Criminalize' (2015) 34 *Law and Philosophy* 1.

[51] See, Roger Brownsword, 'Lost in Translation: Legality, Regulatory Margins, and Technological Management' (2011) 26 *Berkeley Technology Law Journal* 1321.

come at the cost of the essential context for agency. It bears repetition that smart prevention, like all other technological applications, must meet the terms of the triple licence.

9.4.2.2 Comparing smart prevention with other strategies

Assuming a background of moral education and awareness, how does smart prevention compare with moral and prudential strategies for discouraging and dealing with serious crime? And, how do those latter strategies compare with one another?

First, how does smart prevention compare with ex post moral reason applied in a penal setting? According to Anthony Duff, the state should respect citizens as autonomous agents and should treat offending agents as ends in themselves.[52] Whether, like Duff, we take a Kantian perspective or a liberal rights-based approach, we see that, even within traditional institutions of criminal justice, there is a further opportunity for moral education, both at the trial and, post-conviction, in rehabilitative penal institutions. In both phases, trial and post-trial punishment, the state should engage in a moral conversation;[53] criminal law and punishment should be seen as 'a unitary enterprise of dialogue and judgment in which law-abiding citizens, defendants and convicted offenders are all called to participate'.[54] However, even when practised in an exemplary fashion, this ongoing dialogue with the criminal does not guarantee the safety of innocent agents; and, where the decisive educational intervention comes only after innocent agents have already been harmed, this might seem to be too little too late. The thought persists that smart prevention might be a better option—and, at any rate, it might be a better option if its preventive measures could be suitably integrated into the community's moral narrative.

Second, a strategy that relies on adjusting the prudential disincentives against offending—for example, by intensifying surveillance or by making the penal sanctions themselves even more costly for offenders—invites a two-way comparison: first, with a strategy that relies on moral reason; and, second, with smart prevention. How might a prudential strategy fare if compared in this way? Although the criminal justice system that relies on prudential reasons remains a communicative enterprise, the register is no longer moral. Such

---

[52] R.A. Duff, *Trials and Punishments* (Cambridge: Cambridge University Press, 1986).

[53] As Duff (n 52) puts it at 238:
Punishment, like moral blame, respects and addresses the criminal as a rational moral agent: it seeks his understanding and his assent; it aims to bring him to repent his crime, and to reform himself, by communicating to him the reasons which justify our condemnation of his conduct.

[54] Ibid.

a deviation from the ideal-type of a communicative process that focuses on *moral* reasons might be judged to be a cost in and of itself; and, if the practical effect of prudentialism, for both compliers and offenders, is to crowd out moral considerations,[55] the consequences involve a cost. Nevertheless, the selling point for such a prudential strategy is that agents who are capable of making reasonable judgements about what is in their own interest will respond in the desired (compliant) way and that this will protect innocent agents against avoidable harm. Of course, this sales pitch might be overstated. There is no guarantee that regulatees will respond in the desired way to a switch from moral exhortation to prudential sanctions;[56] and, neither is there a guarantee that they will make the overall prudential calculation that regulators expect. The problem is that agents might continue to opt for non-compliance, and prudentialism is powerless to stop them from so doing. At this point, smart prevention becomes the relevant comparator. If we want to reduce the pos-sibilities for regulatees to respond in their own way to the state's prudential signals, smart prevention looks like a serious option. To be sure, smart pre-vention gives up on any idea of a communicative process, moral or prudential. Practical options are simply eliminated; agents are disabled or incapacitated, or they are presented with places, products, and processes that limit their possi-bilities for non-compliance. If smart prevention can outperform prudentialism, and if its restrictions can be integrated into the community's moral narrative, this looks like a serious candidate.

Third, as we have just said, smart prevention might offer more effective protection than any other strategy. However, if it cannot be integrated into the community's moral narrative, this is a major cost; and if it means that we lose what is otherwise an opportunity to reinforce the moral message or to re-educate those who have not internalised the moral principles, this is again a cost.[57] Stated shortly, this is the dilemma: if we act ex post, for some inno-cent agents, the state's moral reinforcement might be too late; but, if the state employs smart prevention ex ante, we might weaken the community's moral narrative and we might not realise that, for some agents, there is a need for moral reinforcement.

---

[55] For relevant insights about the use of CCTV, see, Beatrice von Silva-Tarouca Larsen, *Setting the Watch: Privacy and the Ethics of CCTV Surveillance* (Oxford: Hart, 2011).

[56] Being exhorted to do the right thing is one thing; being fined for doing something might be viewed, not as a response to moral wrong, but simply as a tax on conduct: see U. Gneezy and A. Rustichini, 'A Fine is a Price' (2009) 29 *Journal of Legal Studies* 1.

[57] Compare Michael L. Rich, 'Should We Make Crime Impossible?' (2013) 36 *Harvard Journal of Law and Public Policy* 795.

By way of a provisional conclusion, it is suggested that it is not obvious which strategy should be prioritised or which combination of strategies will work best in protecting relevant goods while also assisting the community to realise its moral aspirations. Whatever strategy is adopted, its impact will need to be monitored; and, so far as smart prevention is concerned, a key challenge is to find ways of it being fully integrated into the community's moral narrative.

9.5   CONCLUDING REMARKS

The range and utility of the tools that are available to the officers and agencies of law enforcement has never been greater. The criminal justice system, in all respects, is increasingly technological. However, while the rethinking of criminal law and criminal justice might not yet extend to full-scale automation (taking humans out of the loop) and prevention by technological management, this looks like the direction of travel. It seems to be a matter of when, not if.

If the momentum of technological development and application is not to be decisive, each community will need to reconsider (and even reverse) its rethinking of criminal justice. For those communities that value governance by humans and by rules, there are red lines to be drawn. For communities that do not have such commitments, it might be acceptable to allow criminal justice to travel in this direction—indeed, in some such communities, the burden of justification might be on those who argue that the transition should be more gradual.

That said, even if a particular community is entirely comfortable with the direction of travel relative to its own fundamental values, that speaks only to the community licence. No community, no matter how comfortable with automated and preventive criminal justice, should employ technologies in the criminal justice system where this would compromise the commons' conditions; such is the non-negotiable constraint imposed by the commons licence.

PART IV

Rethinking legal and regulatory institutions

10. Rethinking national legal and regulatory institutions

10.1 INTRODUCTION

As will be clear from the discussion in Part III, the rethinking of law, regulation, and technology has considerable practical implications for many legal and regulatory institutions, particularly the courts. However, there are also questions to be raised about the institutional framework for our engagement with new technologies—questions about how to engage with new technologies, about the span of engagement and review, and about how to develop a deeper understanding of what makes for a successful engagement.[1]

While there might be more than one institutional design that is fit for purpose, it is suggested that there are two essential conditions for any adequate design. One condition, the 'governance' condition, is that there is a clear understanding in the community about who (or which body) has the relevant responsibility in relation to the regulation of emerging technologies and about the operating procedure. If this condition were to be met, everyone would be clear about questions of competence; and, the bodies charged with the responsibilities would be properly resourced. The other condition, the 'intelligence' condition, is that the community has arrangements in place to gather up, synthesise, and disseminate whatever lessons can be taken from experience of engaging with new technologies. Intelligent engagement with emerging technologies presupposes systematic and reflexive learning.

Relative to these two essential conditions, institutional design and practice in the United Kingdom falls short. Crucially, in the UK, there is no institutional hub with the responsibility to gather together our intelligence about regulating emerging technologies; we might have some intelligence or 'know-how', but we have no repository for it. Taking Rumsfeldian ignorance to another level, not only do we not know what we do not know, we do not know what we do know. While the former might be excusable, the latter surely is not. Moreover, there is no clear understanding about who is responsible for making the initial

---

[1] See Roger Brownsword, 'Law Disrupted, Law Re-imagined, Law Re-invented' (2019) 1 *Technology and Regulation* 10.

engagement with an emerging technology; there is no clear allocation of responsibility for review; there is no body to audit our performance; there is no sense of whether we are getting better at regulating emerging technologies; and, unless things have gone very well or very badly, there is no sense of how they have gone and whether there is anything to be learned from our regulatory experience. Indeed, it seems to be largely a matter of happenstance as to who addresses which technology and what regulatory issue; and there is absolutely no pattern or consistency in how such matters are addressed.

This notwithstanding, some would hold up the UK as an example of how to regulate emerging technologies. Often, it is the way in which the UK engaged with emerging techniques for assisted conception that is claimed to be exemplary. As is well known, in the late 1970s, when techniques for assisted conception were being developed and applied, but also being seriously questioned, the response of the UK government was to set up a Committee of Inquiry chaired by Mary Warnock. In 1984, the Committee's report (the Warnock Report) was published.[2] However, it was not until 1990, and after much debate in Parliament, that the framework legislation, the Human Fertilisation and Embryology Act 1990, was enacted. We could spend some time debating whether this process itself was exemplary (on the face of it, it was unwise to bring together relatively uncontroversial techniques for assisted conception with highly controversial questions about the use of human embryos for research purposes), or whether it was the regulatory product that was the model to follow (a legislative framework, setting up a regulatory agency to license relevant activities), or whether it was neither, or both; but that would be a diversion. The point is that, whatever we make of this particular example, it has not been adopted here in the UK as the standard operating procedure for engaging with new technologies—indeed, as we have said, there is no such procedure.[3]

Looking at practice in the United Kingdom but also going beyond our shores, the fact of the matter is that legal and regulatory responses to emerging technologies seem to vary from one technology to another, from one legal

---

[2]   *Report of the Committee of Inquiry into Human Fertilisation and Embryology* (London: HMSO, Cm. 9314, 1984).

[3]   In 2001, the Human Fertilisation and Embryology (Research Purposes) Regulations 2001/188 were passed (in order to extend the purposes for which the HFEA could license research using human embryos). This was a controversial measure and there were protracted parliamentary debates in both Houses. However, in this instance, the select committee charged with exploring the issues raised by 'cloning' and the use of human embryos for stem cell research purposes did not sit until *after* the Regulations had been passed. For commentary, see Roger Brownsword, 'Stem Cells, Superman, and the Report of the Select Committee' (2002) 65 *Modern Law Review* 568.

system to another, and from one time to another. Sometimes, there is extensive public engagement, sometimes not. On occasion, special commissions (such as the now-defunct Human Genetics Commission in the UK) have been set up with a dedicated oversight remit; and there have been examples of standing technology foresight commissions (such as the US Office of Technology Assessment);[4] but, often, there is nothing of this kind. Most importantly, questions about new technologies sometimes surface, first, in litigation (leaving it to the courts to determine how to respond) and, at other times, they are presented to the legislature (as was the case with assisted conception).

If we are to do better than continue to 'muddle through', we need to rethink how we engage with emerging technologies. In this chapter our rethinking starts by sketching some options that might meet the essential design conditions, following on from which we develop just one particular approach; and then we elaborate on the idea of a rethought understanding of 'coherence' which should inform not just the work of the courts but all bodies charged with governance responsibilities. This discussion, which will be limited to national institutions, will be extended to regional and international institutions in the following chapter.

10.2 MEETING THE ESSENTIAL DESIGN CONDITIONS

What kind of arrangements might ensure that the essential design conditions are met? In principle, a number of governance patterns or procedures might work. For example, a community might adopt a Warnock-like process as its standard operating procedure for engaging with emerging technologies; or, it might take the Human Genetics Commission as its model, establishing a new commission or agency for each new technology; or it might allocate responsibility to specialised bodies that engage with all technologies but focus on just one aspect of the engagement; or, it might combine elements of these approaches in a quest for the optimal mix. Whichever design is adopted, the community must ensure that it also takes good care of the intelligence function. To earth this discussion, we can focus on just two options: a technology-specific agency model (option 1) and a differentiated functions model (option 2).

---

[4] On which, see Bruce Bimber, *The Politics of Expertise in Congress* (Albany: State University of New York Press, 1996) charting the rise and fall of the Office and drawing out some important tensions between 'neutrality' and 'politicisation' in the work of such agencies.

10.2.1 A Technology-Specific Model (Option 1)

In her discussion of the regulation of synthetic biology, Alison McLennan offers an example of the kind of agency that we might consider adopting as the basis for a design that allocates responsibility technology by technology.[5]

McLennan argues in favour of establishing 'a unique institution for the bespoke regulation of synthetic biology...a Synthetic Biology Agency'.[6] The mission of the agency would be to permit 'synthetic biology to proceed in a way that is most able to create societal benefit...while implement[ing] a regime of risk assessment for environmental harm which is underpinned by the precautionary principle, in recognition of the high degree of uncertainty surrounding synthetic biology's potential impacts'.[7] Given this mission, McLennan envisages the agency as having extensive and enduring responsibilities in relation to the ongoing governance of synthetic biology. For example, she envisages the agency engaging with the DIY community and exercising oversight over it; taking responsibility for regulatory policy in support of innovation, including encouraging the sharing of essential synbio tools; undertaking public engagement and adaptive governance activities; reviewing the stage of technological development, commissioning studies, identifying gaps in risk research, and reviewing the impact and effectiveness of regulatory mechanisms; and so on.[8] In short, so far as synthetic biology is concerned, this would be an all-purpose agency, serving as the regulatory hub for this particular technology and its applications.

This invites two questions. First, would it be sensible to set up an agency with this particular technology-specific remit; and, second, building on McLennan's approach, would it be smart to develop a network of such agencies to engage with new technologies?

Responding to the first question, McLennan offers four reasons in support of such a strategy: these are reasons concerning better coordination of governance, a concentration of expertise, cross-fertilisation across policy and regulation, and collaboration.

First, the model 'would help to address the current "patchwork" array of regulatory measures in place for synthetic biology and the problem of coordination between agencies'.[9] Second, this would serve to concentrate and generate relevant institutional expertise. Third, 'cross-fertilisation in policy making

---

[5]   Alison McLennan, *Regulation of Synthetic Biology* (Cheltenham: Edward Elgar, 2018).

[6]   Ibid., at 353.

[7]   Ibid., at 354.

[8]   Ibid., at 354–356.

[9]   Ibid., at 356.

can be achieved' where the full range of regulatory challenges (concerning, in particular, connection, prudence, effectiveness, and legitimacy) 'interact with each other'.[10] Fourth, such an agency model would 'foster the continuation of work that has already begun in bringing together professionals within the different scientific fields...and professionals in social sciences such as law, sociology, ethics, policy and public awareness of science'.[11]

This leads to the second question. If a community were to adopt McLennan's approach to engagement with synthetic biology as its standard template, it would set up similar agencies for additive manufacturing, for blockchain, for AI and machine learning, and so on. However, a number of challenges would need to be addressed.

One of the challenges with such an approach would be to know when the time is right to invest in a new agency (presumably, if the right time is not self-evident, it would be when the government or other funders judge that a particular emerging technology is sufficiently significant). For example, would there be an agency for augmented reality or for deepfake technology?[12] Or, would these technologies be treated as less than significant, or the establishment of an agency premature?

Another challenge might be to deal, not so much with new kinds of technology but with 'older' and with convergent technologies. Would there be new agencies for older technologies? Would there be a bespoke agency for convergent technologies, or would the lead responsibility be taken by an existing agency? No one would want to encourage 'turf wars' between agencies.[13]

Most importantly, perhaps, it would be imperative that the intelligence gathered by these agencies did not remain buried in an array of regulatory silos. For example, the Synthetic Biology Agency might have important intelligence about the DIY synbio community that it could share with the 3D Printing Agency and, possibly, with other agencies dealing with distributed technologies.[14] Whatever intelligence there is in each agency would need to be collected, synthesised, and disseminated. So, in addition to the technology-specific agencies, there would need to be a body that is responsible for such collection, synthesis, and dissemination.

---

[10] Ibid.

[11] Ibid.

[12] Compare Roger Brownsword, *Law 3.0: Rules, Regulation and Technology* (Abingdon: Routledge, 2020) Ch 6.

[13] Compare Albert C. Lin, 'Size Matters: Regulating Nanotechnology' (2007) 31 *Harvard Environmental Law Review* 349.

[14] Compare Albert C. Lin, 'Herding Cats: Governing Distributed Innovation' (2018) 96 *North Carolina Law Review* 945.

10.2.2 A Differentiated Functions Model (Option 2)

A second option would be to identify the principal governance functions (or legal and regulatory tasks) and then allocate responsibilities function by function rather than technology by technology.

For example, let us suppose that the community identifies the following as the principal responsibilities to be allocated: (i) an anticipatory responsibility (of foresight and horizon-scanning); (ii) a responsibility for making the first response to an emerging technology; (iii) a responsibility for making the initial 'intervention' (whether a measure of hard or soft law, regulation or governance); (iv) a responsibility for monitoring how the response operates in practice; and (v) an auditing responsibility. There will also need to be clarity about such matters as to whom these bodies are accountable, and how those who are responsible should proceed. Most importantly, let us suppose, too, that the community envisages that a central hub will have responsibility for gathering together, synthesising, and disseminating all that we learn from our experience of engaging with new technologies; and, that the hub will liaise with and coordinate the activities of a set of nodes charged with the lead responsibilities.

One of the challenges faced by this model would be integrating with existing institutions. In a community that already has a constitutionally authorised scheme of governance as well as civil society bodies that engage with governance, there will need to be a clear understanding about how the hub and nodes are to interface with existing institutions. In principle, it is envisaged that the nodes will play a coordinating role by working with whatever other bodies (in both the public sector and civil society) are addressing the relevant matters. In practice, of course, this might not be entirely straightforward; and even if it is relatively straightforward initially, the relationships between the hub, the nodes and the networks of governance will inevitably evolve.

Elaborating on this option, in the next section we sketch the nature and scope of the particular responsibilities assigned to the nodes and then the role of the hub, receiving regulatory intelligence from the nodes and cascading intelligence back through the nodes.

10.3 A DESIGN ELABORATED

The design to be elaborated is option 2, this comprising four nodes, each with its own particular responsibility, a body with the auditing responsibility and, at the heart of the design, an intelligent hub.

10.3.1 Node 1: Anticipatory Responsibility

The first node would have a foresight and horizon-scanning responsibility.[15] Governments, of course, dedicate some resource to anticipating future trends, challenges, and opportunities; but, not necessarily with a focus on emerging technologies, and not necessarily with the legal and regulatory framework in mind.[16] To state the obvious, this node would need to be working closely with the innovation and technology communities; it would need to be thinking not only about the governance challenges that technologies on the horizon might present but also about how those technologies might present opportunities, both as regulatory tools and as responses to policy problems;[17] like other nodes, it would feed into the hub; and, distinctively, it would have a close working relationship with the node that is responsible for making the first response.

There are precedents for bodies that play a role that is of a similar or related kind. For example, the Nuffield Council on Bioethics quite recently set up a Horizon Scanning Advisory Group (comprising a sub-set of members of the Council) which carries out its 'horizon scanning programme by holding workshops, engaging with a wide range of organisations and individuals, and by monitoring literature and news, across a wide geographical area and different fields of interest and expertise'.[18] The role of the group is to feed into the Council's forward thinking by identifying developments in biological and medical research that will inform the Council's planning and work priorities. In particular, the developments flagged up by the group might be candidates

---

[15] See Kerstin E. Cuhls, 'Horizon Scanning in Foresight—Why Horizon Scanning is Only Part of the Game' (2020) *Futures and Foresight Science* https://doi.org/10.1002/ffo2.23. Cuhls defines 'foresight' as 'the systematic debate of complex futures'; note that the debate is structured, that it is complex (taking a holistic view), and that it is about possible, probable, and preferable futures (in the plural). By contrast, 'horizon scanning' plays an exploratory role in forward-looking activities, serving 'to explore futures, "emerging issues", and signals of all kinds, and to evaluate the importance of "things to come"'.

[16] There is a UK Government Horizon-Scanning Programme Team which has published, inter alia, reports on AI and on big data; however, it seems to be relatively inactive. For such information as there is about this team, see https://www.gov.uk/government/groups/horizon-scanning-programme-team (last accessed 11 February 2021).

[17] See, e.g., Government Office for Science (Foresight), *The Future of Food and Farming: Challenges and Choices for Global Sustainability* (London, 2011) (re potential use of GM crops): available at https://assets.publishing.service.gov.uk/government/uploads/system/uploads/attachment_data/file/288329/11-546-future-of-food-and-farming-report.pdf (last accessed 11 February 2021).

[18] See https://www.nuffieldbioethics.org/what-we-do/horizon-scanning (last accessed 11 February 2021).

for an 'in-depth' review. If a topic is to be selected, it should 'come within the broad sphere of research in the medical or biological sciences, align with the Council's strategic plan, and fit within a balanced portfolio of work'. The group would also want to be persuaded that the topic was new, timely, raising significant ethical issues, and policy relevant, and that the Council would be able to make a distinctive contribution.[19] If a topic is selected, the Council will forward it to the funders' governing board for approval.

While the group is clearly engaging with horizon-scanning for new developments in technology, its focus (in line with the traditional mission of the Council itself) is on biotechnologies and largely health care, its brief is to consider the ethics (which can mean all sorts of things), and it will not proceed if it feels unable to make a distinctive contribution. As such, this is not quite in line with the script for what would be the lead node for anticipating technologies that invite legal and regulatory attention, but it is a move in the right direction.

10.3.2   Node 2: The Responsibility as First Responder

The node that is charged with acting as first responder has a key responsibility. First responders often lay out the basics (concerning the technology and its potential benefits and risks, as well as the governance questions) in a way that will enable both the public and policy makers to begin thinking about the issues. Although a number of bodies in the UK make a valuable contribution when they perform this role, it is unclear whose responsibility it is to lead as first responder. We might wonder why, for example, it was the Royal Society that acted as the first responder to machine learning[20] rather than one of the other academies (the British Academy was, at the time, working on data governance) or the Nuffield Council on Bioethics.

If we are looking for a model as a first responder, particularly a first responder node that liaises closely with the body that has the responsibility for making the initial legal and regulatory response, we might consider the body that originally was the Group of Advisers on Ethical Implications of Biotechnology (which operated from 1991 to 1997) and its successor, the European Group on Ethics in Science and New Technologies (EGE). The mandate of the EGE was renewed by Commission Decision (EU) 2016/835, Article 2 of which provides that the 'task of the EGE shall be to advise the Commission on ethical questions relating to sciences and new technologies and the wider societal implications of advances in these fields'.

---

[19]   Ibid.
[20]   See, The Royal Society, 'Machine learning: the power and promise of computers that learn by example' (London, April 2017).

To this end, the EGE is charged with identifying, defining, and examining ethical questions raised by such advances, and with providing 'guidance in the form of analyses and recommendations that shall be oriented towards the promotion of ethical EU policymaking, with due regard to the Charter of Fundamental Rights of the European Union'. There are many questions to ask about the EGE—including, for example, how it fits into the governance landscape, what precisely its role is, and whether its business is ethics in general or human rights in particular.[21] However, for our purposes, it is the still limited range of its inquiries that is striking. While the original group, rather like the Nuffield Council on Bioethics, was focused on biotechnologies, the successor group (again, not unlike the Nuffield Council on Bioethics) has occasionally extended its range. For instance, the EGE has published Opinions on ICTs (in 2012), energy (in 2013), and security and surveillance technologies (in 2014). Nevertheless, its work is dominated by biotechnologies and by ethics; and, we might think it telling that when AI loomed large as a potentially major development for Europe, the Commission appointed an ad hoc independent expert group (with a much larger and quite different membership from the EGE) to advise on the ethical framework.[22]

10.3.3 Node 3: The Responsibility for the Initial Intervention

Given the review undertaken by the first responders, the initial 'intervention' might take a number of forms, from hard law to soft law, and with public regulators or private bodies taking the lead. We should also include at this stage those co-regulatory interventions such as the use of regulatory sandboxes and the articulation of policy prototypes.[23]

---

[21] See, e.g., Alison Mohr, Helen Busby, Tamara Hervey, and Robert Dingwall, 'Mapping the Role of Official Bioethics Advice in the Governance of Biotechnologies in the EU: The European Group on Ethics' Opinion on Commercial Cord Blood Banking' (2012) 39 *Science and Public Policy* 105; and Aurora Plomer, 'The European Group on Ethics: Law, Politics and the Limits of Moral Integration in Europe' (2008) 14 *European Law Journal* 839.

[22] For the report of this high-level expert group (*Ethics Guidelines for Trustworthy AI*, 2019), see https://www.ccdcoe.org/uploads/2019/06/EC-190408-AI-HLEG -Guidelines.pdf (last accessed 8 April 2021); for more on the group, its work, and its place within the EU digital strategy, see https://digital-strategy.ec.europa.eu/en/ policies/expert-group-ai (last accessed 8 April 2021). Compare, though, the European Group on Ethics in Science and New Technologies, *Statement on Artificial Intelligence, Robotics, and 'Autonomous' Systems* (Brussels, 2018).

[23] See, e.g., https://www.bbva.com/en/what-is-regulatory-sandbox/ (on regulatory sandboxes) and https://openloop.org/lets-experiment/ (on policy prototypes) (both last accessed 13 May 2021).

In democratic polities, there will be institutions that are competent to respond to questions that might be raised about the legality of emerging technologies; and there will be institutions that are competent to (indeed, expected to) respond should it be felt that new laws or regulatory interventions are required. We are assuming, however, that, along with the other nodes, each of which is to be treated as independent from the established legal and political institutions, there will be a node that is responsible for the initial formal response. This immediately raises the question of how such a node, sitting alongside the established institutions, should relate to the latter. In particular, what would be the relationship between this node and the executive and legislative branches of government?

One possibility is that the node would operate rather like the Law Commissions in the United Kingdom, engaging with legal questions, issuing consultation papers, and publishing reports which typically make recommendations along with draft bills. There was a time when the Commission's bills were processed along a fast track in Parliament; and this might be the model for the node's recommendations and draft bills: or, it might be that, as with the Law Commission nowadays, the node's bills would simply join the queue for legislative processing.

Another possibility, right at the other end of the spectrum, is that the node would do little more than nudge the legislature into action, largely leaving it to the existing parliamentary resources (the specialist committees and research units, such as the Parliamentary Office of Science and Technology (POST)[24]) to take the matter forward. However, the more that the node left it to the established institutions to make the formal response, the more important it would be to ensure that the insights from the first responder node were taken forward; and, if there had been no prior consultation exercise, it would be essential to ensure that any formal response was properly informed (including properly informed by public engagement).

That said, the conventional wisdom (insofar as we can so describe it) is that, in the earlier stages of a technology's development, hard law interventions

---

[24] According to its website, 'POST produces impartial, non-partisan, and peer-reviewed briefings, designed to make scientific research accessible to the UK Parliament. The briefings come in the form of POSTnotes and POSTbriefs. Timely and forward thinking, they cover the areas of biology and health, energy and environment, physical sciences and computing, and social sciences', see https://post.parliament.uk/about-us/ (last accessed 14 February 2021). In the last couple of years, topics covered by POSTnotes (which are four-page briefing documents) include: drones; human germ-line gene-editing; brain–computer interfaces; 3D bioprinting in medicine; online extremism; edge computing and cloud computing; interpretable machine learning, and remote sensing and machine learning; and AI and health care.

are more problematic than soft law codes and guidance. So, for example, with a focus on the regulation of nanotechnology, Bärbel Dorbeck-Jung and Marloes van Amerom[25] identify soft law as having the following strengths: the flexibility, agility, and scope for experimentation in governance to cope with uncertainty and the need for change and adaptation;[26] allowing for 'a range of possibilities for interpretation and trial and error processes without the constraints of uniform rules and threat of sanction'; allowing for diversity, simplicity, and speed; reducing negotiation costs (because the norms are not binding and the stakes, therefore, are lower); and, supporting the internalisation of the norms (the 'social basis of legitimacy').[27]

It is apparent from these points in favour of soft law that it is not only the challenge of regulatory connection that might be eased; in particular, the final point in the list underlines the better prospects for regulatory effectiveness where regulatees have some ownership of the code. However, the flexibility and informality of self-regulation can give rise to concerns about the basis for reliance and compliance; soft law might tend towards 'races to the bottom', with compromises leading to 'lower quality, efficacy and safety standards'; and, while negotiation costs might be reduced, transaction costs might be increased if the norms and codes of guidance need constant adaptation and change.[28] There is also the important concern that soft law as the product of self-governance might invite the prioritisation of self-interest over the public interest.

This prompts the thought that the smart regulatory approach should be to strive for the optimal mix of soft law with hard law – and, possibly, the thought that the mix should change (becoming harder) as the technology develops, as more is known about it, and as its risk profile becomes clearer. Relative to such an approach, Dorbeck-Jung and van Amerom see the UK as relying on a predominantly soft law strategy for dealing with nanotechnologies, this being well suited to an initial phase of 'evidence gathering, standardization, public

---

[25] Bärbel Dorbeck-Jung and Marloes van Amerom, 'The Hardness of Soft Law in the United Kingdom: State and Non-State Regulatory Activities Related to Nanotechnological Development' in Hanneke van Schooten and Jonathan Verschuuren (eds), *International Governance and Law* (Cheltenham: Edward Elgar, 2008) 129.

[26] There is, of course, a huge literature addressing the 'soft law' governance of emerging technologies, where the context is one of both uncertainty and moving targets: see, e.g., Stefan Kuhlmann, Peter Stegmaier, and Kornelia Konrad, 'The tentative governance of emerging science and technology—a conceptual introduction' (2019) 48 *Research Policy* 1091 (relating tentative governance to 'reflexive', 'anticipatory', 'adaptive', 'experimentalist', 'explorative', 'distributive', and 'mixed' governance).

[27] Dorbeck-Jung and van Amerom (n 25), at 133–134.

[28] Ibid., at 134.

dialogue, funding of research and development, and international and national collaboration'.[29] The subsequent challenge is to achieve a smart 'hybridization of soft and hard law'.[30]

10.3.4 Node 4: The Monitoring Responsibility

The node having the responsibility to monitor the impact of the initial formal response might find itself, like the previous node, having to align its activities with established institutions for monitoring. To the extent that the initial formal response puts in place a regulatory agency to monitor compliance (as was the case, for example, with the Human Fertilisation and Embryology Act, 1990), the node would be monitoring the performance of the agency; but, where there are no other arrangements for monitoring the impact of the formal response, it would be for the node to ensure that the impacts were assessed. As with all the other nodes, the lessons learned would be fed back to the hub.

10.3.5 The Auditing Responsibility

The body responsible for auditing the performance of the nodes in engaging with emerging technologies would need to stand outside the set of nodes, checking their individual performance but also their interactions and performance as a set.

The audit would check more than whether a particular node adequately did what it was supposed to do. The auditing body, with the benefit of hindsight, would be in a position to assess whether precautionary measures were well founded and, conversely, whether proactive support for a technology was well founded. Were the feared risks actually reasonable ones, and were they reasonably managed? Were the promised benefits of a technology actually realised? If soft law measures or industry self-governance were relied on, was the public interest properly protected? To what extent were intellectual property rights a problem for the effective operation of the nodes?

---

[29] Ibid., at 143. Compare, too, Gregory N. Mandel, 'Regulating Emerging Technologies' (2009) 1 *Law, Innovation and Technology* 75, highlighting the opportunities for win–win cooperation and information-sharing in the pre-competitive stages of a technology's development.

[30] Dorbeck-Jung and van Amerom (n 25), at 146. Even if this has yet to be accomplished in relation to nanotechnologies, there are many examples of soft law codes of practice that are nested within hard law statutory frameworks – as is the case, for example, with the regulation of human fertilisation and embryology.

174 *Rethinking law, regulation, and technology*

Following up questions of this kind, the auditing body would need to liaise closely with the hub so that it could make an effective input into our accumulating intelligence about the regulation of new technologies.

10.3.6   The Intelligent Hub

The intelligent hub is critical to this—and, indeed, to any other—design. If we already knew what we know and what we did not know, we might feel the need for a hub was overstated; but, equally, we might see a role for such a hub in enhancing our intelligence and understanding of how to engage with emerging technologies. However, the bar here is remarkably low. There is so much that we do not know about how, when, or why to regulate, about what works and does not work, and about the assumptions that we make. For example, is it right that we tend to overestimate the short-term benefits of new technologies but underrate their longer-term impact? Is it right that our enthusiasm for technologies whose promoters promise immediate benefits for human health and well-being does us no favours?

To give one example, Collingridge's dilemma—concerning the optimal timing of a regulatory intervention—is hardly new;[31] and, yet, it persists. We know that there is a dilemma, but we do not know how to deal with it. Governments like to claim that they have taken the right (regulatory) measures at the right time. Characteristically, in 'Law 2.0' (regulatory) conversations, the right measures are treated as those that 'neither over-regulate nor under-regulate'; and the right time is 'neither too early nor too late'. But, what does this tell us about whether our default should be a proactive or a reactive approach? While the risk with the former is that we are 'too early' as a result of which we risk over-regulating (impacting negatively on innovation) or missing the target, the risk with the latter approach is that we are 'too late' as a result of which we are now unable to correct for under-regulation against relevant risks. But, which approach should be our default and why do we not have more 'know-how'? Similarly, as we have mentioned already, should it be soft law or hard law that is our regulatory default?

At the intelligent hub, the team might appreciate that the timing question looks rather different depending upon which of the levels of regulatory responsibility is at issue. Typically, the puzzle is set in the context of regulators setting the terms of the 'social licence' for the technology and its applications; here, it is true, that the default is not obvious. However, where the question concerns the compatibility of an emerging technology and its applications

---

[31]   As formulated in David Collingridge, *The Social Control of Technology* (New York: Frances Pinter, 1980).

Rethinking national legal and regulatory institutions 175

with the particular 'community licence', and, a fortiori, where the question is whether the technology and its applications pass muster relative to the 'global commons licence', then a proactive and precautionary approach has to be the default. If the commons' conditions are compromised (whether by climate change, pandemics, or super-surveillance), if the critical infrastructure is weakened, this is a script for catastrophe or dystopia. Here, the rule must be 'better too early than too late', or 'it is never too early'. Similarly, where there are concerns about the red lines of a particular community being crossed, early action by regulators is surely in order.

That said, none of this will happen unless there is an intelligent hub. So, whatever clarification might be brought to bear on our regulatory thinking, the opportunity will be missed unless it is being developed by a team who focus on just the questions that would be the responsibility of the hub. No doubt, governance of emerging technologies is complex; but the design point is simple. If we want to have an intelligent approach to the governance of new technologies, we need a hub to gather, develop, and disseminate that intelligence.[32]

10.4 A NEW COHERENTISM

An essential element in living with Law 3.0 is the articulation of a 'new coherentism', reminding regulators of two things: first, that their most urgent regulatory focus should be on the maintenance of the commons' conditions; and, second, that whatever their interventions, and particularly where they take a technocratic approach, their acts must always be compatible with the preservation of the commons.

In future, the courts—albeit the locus for traditional coherentist thinking—will have a continuing role to play in bringing new coherentism to bear on the use of technological measures (with a central question being whether a particular use meets the terms of the triple licence). In other words, it will be for the courts to review the legality of any measure that is challenged relative to the authorising and constitutive rules; and, above all, to check that particular instances of technological management are consistent with the commons-protecting ideals that are inscribed in the rule of law.[33]

With a new coherentist mindset, it is not a matter of checking for internal doctrinal consistency, nor checking that a measure is fit for its particular regu-

---

[32] Appropriately, Title VI of the European Commission's proposal for a Regulation on AI, COM(2021) 206 final (Brussels, 21.4.2021) establishes a new European Artificial Intelligence Board, one of the functions of which is to collect and share best governance practices amongst the Member States.

[33] Compare Ken Coghill, 'Existential Public Value' (2021) *International Journal of Public Administration*, doi: 10.1080/01900692.2021.1875234.

176 *Rethinking law, regulation, and technology*

latory purpose. Rather, a renewed ideal of coherence should start with the paramount responsibility of regulators, namely, the protection and preservation of the commons. All regulatory interventions should cohere with that responsibility. This means that the conditions for both human existence and the context for flourishing agency should be respected. In line with such thinking, in 2017, when researchers met at Asilomar in California to develop a set of precautionary guidelines for the use of AI, it was agreed (in Principle 21) that 'risks posed by AI systems, especially catastrophic or existential risks, must be subject to planning and mitigation efforts commensurate with their expected impact'.[34] Quite rightly, the researchers took their responsibilities seriously; governance in all respects needs to be informed by the spirit of new coherentism.

In some respects, the courts' role in undertaking new coherentist review would not be dissimilar to their role in undertaking judicial review. Suppose, for example, a government responds to a pandemic, such as Covid-19, by introducing a legislative package of infection-controlling measures. There are provisions about surveillance, about the use of new test-and-trace technologies, about curfews, about the collection of patient data (with no requirement for consent), about the use of an AI tool to decide which patients should be given priority for beds in hospital ICUs, and, in due course, about who should be given priority for a vaccine and about vaccine passports. While some will push back against these measures, arguing especially that they infringe privacy, the government insists that it is dealing with an 'emergency', that the circumstances are 'unprecedented', and that citizens have 'a civic duty' to accept and cooperate with these measures.

Now, if a court were asked to review these measures in the spirit of new coherentism, its first task would be to determine at which level (the commons, the community, or the social) the arguments have purchase.

On the one side, what is to be made of the appeal to privacy? As is well known, a popular view is that this right should be applied in a 'contextual' way.[35] However, the court might point out that there is Context and there are contexts. There is Context (in the sense of the commons) and then there are many contexts that rely on the integrity of the commons. So, if it is judged that privacy reaches through to the interests that agents necessarily have in the commons' conditions, particularly in the conditions for self-development and agency, it is neither rational nor reasonable for agents, individually or collectively, to authorise acts that compromise these conditions (unless they do so

---

[34] Available at https://futureoflife.org/ai-principles/?cn-reloaded=1 (last accessed 26 April 2021).
[35] Seminally, see Daniel J. Solove, *Understanding Privacy* (Cambridge, Mass.: Harvard University Press, 2008), and Helen Nissenbaum, *Privacy in Context* (Stanford: Stanford University Press, 2010).

in order to protect some more important condition of the commons).[36] That is, as Bert-Jaap Koops has so clearly expressed it, privacy has an 'infrastructural character', 'having privacy spaces is an important presupposition for autonomy [and] self-development'; without such spaces, there is no opportunity to be oneself.[37] On this reading, privacy is not so much a matter of protecting goods (informational or spatial) in which one has a personal interest but protecting infrastructural goods in which there is either a common interest (engaging first-tier responsibilities) or a distinctive community interest (engaging second-tier responsibilities).[38]

On the other side, while a bald appeal to 'civic duty' cuts no ice, the appeal to unprecedented circumstances and to an emergency might engage exceptions that are either explicit or implicit in the community's constitutive values—or, they might go even deeper to the commons itself. After all, a pandemic is more than an epidemic, and a potentially lethal virus for which we have no vaccine is more dangerous than a virus that is not lethal or for which we do have a vaccine. Given these considerations, a court might judge that there is a plausible argument that the existence conditions of the commons are under threat, that plausibility is sufficient for precautionary steps, and that at least some of the measures are prima facie legitimate. In undertaking this review and assessment, the courts would seem to be asking familiar questions about, inter alia, the 'proportionality' of a particular measure. However, 'proportionality', like precaution, has to be read within the three-tiered structure of responsibilities and regulatory considerations that I am proposing. What we judge to be a proportionate restriction on freedom of movement and association relative to an uncertain threat to the global commons is one thing; what we judge to be a proportionate impingement on these freedoms where there is no such threat but there is a desire to reduce illness or crime is something else; and what we judge to be a reasonable or proportionate balance of interests at the level of a social licence is something else again.

Having completed this first task, a court might find that while the measures are designed to minimise damage to the existence conditions of the commons, they do impinge upon the privacy interest as it relates to the agency context of

---

[36] Compare Maria Brincker, 'Privacy in Public and Contextual Conditions of Agency', in Tjerk Timan, Bryce Clayton Newell, and Bert-Jaap Koops (eds), *Privacy in Public Space* (Cheltenham: Edward Elgar, 2017) 64.

[37] Bert-Jaap Koops, 'Privacy Spaces' (2018) 121 *West Virginia Law Review* 611, 621.

[38] Compare the list of prohibited practices in Title II of the European Commission's proposal for a Regulation on AI, COM(2021) 206 final (Brussels, 21.4.2021). The practices listed are considered unacceptable relative to Union values and include 'AI-based social scoring for general purposes done by public authorities'.

the commons. It might be possible to relieve some parts of this tension, but let us suppose that there comes a point where the court has to decide which takes priority: is it the existence conditions or the agency context?

That is a very good question. It is not a question that can be answered by appealing to how we define ourselves as the particular community that we are, nor by relying on our community's reading of the priority. It cannot be so answered because this is a question for all humans; it is a question about the commons in which we all have an interest and upon which our particular communities rely. This points to the need for international coordination, for global institutions that are committed to new coherentist thinking. For example, national courts might be required to refer questions to an international panel for guidance; or there might already be global agreement on the priorities within the commons' conditions. To be sure, the thought might occur that, given the state of international relations, this is simply wishful thinking. This, it must be conceded, is a fair point; and, it is a thought that we must confront in the next chapter.

10.5   CONCLUDING REMARKS

The way in which a community engages with rapidly emerging technologies will be shaped by whatever background understanding there is about the questions that need to be asked, about who is responsible for asking them, and about the appropriate actions to be taken. Where there is such an understanding, this might well be articulated in a particular institutional design. Of course, simply because there is a certain understanding and, concomitantly, that understanding is reflected in the institutional design, it does not guarantee that the arrangements will be fit for purpose. Nevertheless, a community that approaches matters in this way is on the right track.

In this chapter, we have been considering the rather different case of a community that has no clear understanding about how to engage with new technologies, no allocation of institutional responsibility, and a practice that is happenstance. In such a community, there might be occasions when it gets things right, but the general approach is wrong and the particular arrangements are clearly not fit for purpose.

The proposal in this chapter is that we need to rethink how to engage with emerging technologies. In particular, we need to think about the kinds of institutional design that would structure and support intelligent and informed conversations about engagement with new technologies. Most importantly, we have proposed that each community needs to have an institutional hub that gathers intelligence about the regulation and governance of (as well as governance by) new technologies. The intelligence so gathered can then be cascaded through the regulatory community and to the general public.

Of course, there are many challenges facing a proposal that seeks to infuse a culture of new coherentist thinking while interfacing with historic legal institutions and regulatory arrangements. Nevertheless, if we have a sense of what the ideal design might be and if we understand what the right questions are, our rethink should improve our chances of successful engagement.

11. Rethinking international legal and regulatory institutions

11.1 INTRODUCTION

Recalling the ambition of new coherentist thinking, no technological instruments should be applied for regulatory purposes unless they meet the terms of the triple (global, community, and social) licence. But, of course, the commons is not confined to particular nation-states. The conditions for human existence on planet Earth are relevant to all nation-states and can be impacted by each nation-state's activities. The same applies where nation-states interfere with the conditions for flourishing agency beyond their own national borders. Whether in relation to the conditions for human existence[1] or for the enjoyment of human agency,[2] there can be cross-border spill-over effects. Accordingly, if the essential infrastructure for human social existence is to be secured, this implies that there needs to be a considerable degree of international coordination and shared responsibility.[3]

In this chapter, it will be argued that this is the time to work towards establishing a new international agency both to coordinate our thinking about the governance of emerging technologies and to assume the responsibilities of regulatory stewardship for the global commons.

No doubt, such a proposal will be resisted by states who judge that such an agency would impact negatively on their national interests. Moreover, even from a less partial perspective, many might judge that this is simply not a good idea. For example, some might judge that the positives associated with centralisation are outweighed by its negatives;[4] and, while some might

---

[1] See Roger Brownsword, 'Migrants, State Responsibilities, and Human Dignity' (2021) 34 *Ratio Juris* 6.

[2] See, e.g., the critique of our 'information societies' in Shoshana Zuboff, *The Age of Surveillance Capitalism* (London: Profile Books, 2019).

[3] See David A. Wirth, 'Engineering the Climate: Geoengineering as a Challenge to International Governance' (2013) 40 *Boston College Environmental Affairs Law Review* 413, esp. at 430–436.

[4] For a very helpful identification and assessment of the relevant considerations, see Peter Cihon, Matthijs M. Maas, and Luke Kemp, 'Fragmentation and the Future:

support the idea of a G20-based coordinating committee for the governance of technologies such as AI, and what is more see it as taking responsibility for 'global stewardship', they will resist a centralised international cyber regime complex as 'neither feasible nor desirable'.[5] Similarly, the World Economic Forum reports that 'from a pool of approximately 200 experts, not one proposed a new, supranational, treaty-based organization to take on the challenge of global technology governance'.[6] Evidently, this reflects concerns about the funding of supranational bodies as well as their 'falling global legitimacy'.[7] Concerns about legitimacy and (lack of) trust are also prominent in the UN Secretary-General's *Strategy on New Technologies*,[8] which contemplates new technologies being deployed in the service of existing mandates (thus, '[e]ngagement with new technologies should be seen as a necessary component of successful mandate implementation—not a new mandate');[9] and, which plans to respond to technology-related threats to international peace and security where they 'are not covered by existing instruments or processes'.[10] Although much of the thinking in this *Strategy* is in line with stewardship of the global commons—and, indeed, with the idea that, subject to respect for the global commons, it is for each community 'to determine how they wish to maximize the benefits and minimize the risks of the technologies shaping their future'[11]—my argument is that we do need a new mandate guided by a distinctive and dedicated approach and that we might need bespoke international laws and new international agencies to take this project forward.[12]

Investigating Architectures for International AI Governance' (2020) 11 *Global Policy* 545.

[5]   Thorsten Jelinek, Danil Kerimi, and Wendell Wallach, *Coordinating Committee for the Governance of Artificial Intelligence* (Task Force 5, Saudi Arabia 2020) at 5 and 6.

[6]   World Economic Forum, *Global Technology Governance: A Multistakeholder Approach* (Geneva, October 2019) at p 13. But, we should note the interesting proposal for an international AI agency in Simon Chesterman, *We the Robots? Regulating Artificial Intelligence and the Limits of the Law* (Cambridge: Cambridge University Press, 2021) Ch 8.

[7]   Ibid.

[8]   UN, September 2018, available at https://www.un.org/en/newtechnologies/images/pdf/SGs-Strategy-on-New-Technologies.pdf (last accessed 26 April 2021).

[9]   Ibid., at p 11.

[10]   Ibid., at p 17.

[11]   Ibid., at p 9.

[12]   Compare, e.g., Seth D. Baum and Grant S. Wilson, 'The Ethics of Global Catastrophic Risk from Dual Use Bioengineering' (2013) 4 *Ethics in Biology, Engineering and Medicine* 59; Grant Wilson, 'Minimizing global catastrophic and existential risks from emerging technologies through international law' (2013) 31 *Virginia Environmental Law Journal* 307; and Dennis Pamlin and Stuart Armstrong, 'Twelve

Essentially, there are two principal challenges to the fitness of international regulatory agencies: one is that the self-serving national tendencies that are characteristic of international relations coupled with the disproportionate power and influence of some nation-states militates against the effective operation of global agencies; and, the other is that agencies need to be careful to avoid over-reaching (by impinging improperly on national sovereignty) lest this compromises their legitimacy.

In this chapter, we start with a short reality check, a check on both international relations and international agencies which explains why international governance tends to be underpowered and less effective than it should be. Against this background, and mindful of the challenges of both effectiveness and legitimacy, we then make some proposals for the development of an intelligent global hub, charged with the responsibilities of regulatory stewardship. Given this reality check we proceed on the assumption that a proposal, coming out-of-the-blue, for a new international regulatory agency would be unlikely to command sufficient support (or, even if sufficiently supported to be established, would not function properly). Accordingly, in rethinking the design of our international institutions, we focus on incremental steps towards establishing such a hub. Starting with regional hubs that collate national intelligence, the thinking is that this could evolve into a global body that coordinates intelligence from the regional hubs; and, then, that this body might take on regulatory stewardship and have oversight where new technologies are being deployed for the purpose of mitigating risks to the global commons (as with geo-engineering initiatives) or strengthening the commons' conditions.

11.2 INTERNATIONAL RELATIONS AND AGENCIES: A REALITY CHECK

Whatever the ideal institutional design, we have to take into account the realities of both international relations and the operation of international agencies, such as the many bodies that operate under the aegis of the United Nations, the IMF, the World Bank, and the World Trade Organization. While, given the extensive literature on the nature of international law and the dynamics of international relations,[13] it might seem a contradiction in terms to suggest that we can speak *briefly* to the state of international relations and then to agencies, in the present context, this is as much as we can do.

---

risks that threaten human civilisation: The case for a new risk category' (Oxford: Global Challenges Foundation, 2015) 182 (mooting the possibility of establishing a global risk organisation, initially only with monitoring powers).

[13] A good starting point is Harold Hongju Koh's review essay, 'Why Do Nations Obey International Law?' (1997) 106 *Yale Law Journal* 2599.

11.2.1 International Relations

The context for international relations is that of sovereign nation-states interacting and transacting against an historic backcloth of conflict; and, although global institutions may be designed for cooperation, the background of national sovereignty, national interest, and historic conflict is always present.

Formally, the relations between nation-states are regulated by international law. However, even in the Westphalian view, international law is less than complete. To the extent that law is supposed to ensure that might is not right, international law underachieves. Rather than limiting the exercise of sovereign national power, too often, international law is viewed by those with the might as a resource to be worked in the service of showing relevant power plays to be 'right'—as a tool to 'legitimate' action.[14] Moreover, when the jurisdiction of the principal court depends on voluntary acceptance by the parties, we might say that the effectiveness of the international legal rules is largely dependent upon the willingness of the nation-states to respect the rules and institutions of the international legal order.

In this context, as Gerry Simpson highlights, the makers and subjects of international law have different amounts of power and influence, different intentions (some are more well intentioned than others), different levels of commitment to collective responsibilities, and different degrees of civilisation.[15] To start with, there are both functioning states and failed states. Amongst the former, while many states are good citizens of the international order (respecting the rules of international law), there are also superpowers (who play by their own rules) and rogue states (who play by no rules). If the regulatory stewards were drawn from the good citizens, that might be fine insofar as an agency so populated would be focused on the right question and motivated by concerns for the common interest of humans. However, we have to doubt that they would be in any position to ensure compliance with whatever precautionary standards they might propose let alone be mandated to introduce measures of technological management.

Once upon a time, nation-states pursued their interests in openly militaristic ways. Without giving up their arsenals, nation-states now have other

---

[14] See, Martti Koskenniemi, 'The Fate of Public International Law: Between Technique and Politics' (2007) 70 *Modern Law Review* 1; and Ian Hurd, *After Anarchy: Legitimacy and Power in the UN Security Council* (Princeton: Princeton University Press, 2007).

[15] Gerry Simpson, *Great Powers and Outlaw States* (Cambridge: Cambridge University Press, 2009).

options. The distributed denial-of-service (DDoS) attack on Estonia in 2007 is a well-known case in point.[16] The impact of the attack was considerable:

> Members of the Estonian Parliament went for four days without email. Government communications networks were reduced to radio for a limited period. Financial operations were severely compromised, ATMs were crippled, and Hansabank, the largest bank, was forced to close its Internet operations. Most people found themselves effectively barred from financial transactions while the attacks were at their height. Estonia responded by closing large parts of its network to people from outside the country, and a consequence was that Estonians abroad were unable to access their bank accounts.[17]

More than a decade on from the Estonian outage, the lines—between war, crime, and politics, and between militia and civilians—can seem even more blurred. Wars are now fought in more than one dimension—physical, narrative, and discursive;[18] the instruments of war are both kinetic and non-kinetic; and the targets include national critical cyber-infrastructures.

In a world of 'hybrid warfare'—a term that nowadays connotes an approach that draws on a range of instruments, including 'terrorism, insurgency, criminality, and conventional operations, along with the extensive use of information operations'[19]—an attack might take more than one form including cyberattacks on 'military command and control, air traffic control systems, hospital power supplies, the electricity grid, water supplies, nuclear power, satellite communications, Internet attacks on the banking system, and cyberattacks on dams/water supply and other eco threats'.[20] When cyber chiefs warn

---

[16] Compare, too, Richard Norton-Taylor, 'Titan Rain – How Chinese Hackers Targeted Whitehall', *The Guardian*, 5 September 2007, p 1. One notch down from such incidents are the denial-of-service attacks launched by pro-Wikileaks 'hactivitists' in December 2010: see, e.g., Cahal Milmo and Nigel Morris, 'Prepare for all-out cyber war' *The Independent*, 14 December 2010, p 1.

[17] House of Lords European Union Committee, *Protecting Europe Against Large-Scale Cyber-Attacks* (Fifth Report, Session 2009–2010) para 11, Box 1.

[18] See David Patrikarakos, *War in 140 Characters* (New York: Basic Books, 2017).

[19] Lawrence Freedman, *The Future of War: A History* (London: Allen Lane, 2017) at 223. See, too, Sascha-Dominik Dov Bachmann and Anthony Paphiti, 'Russia's Hybrid War and its Implications for Defence and Security in the United Kingdom' (2016) 44 *Scientia Militaria, South African Journal of Military Studies* 28; and Sascha-Dominik Dov Bachmann and Håkan Gunneriusson, 'Russia's Hybrid Warfare in the East: The Integral Nature of the Information Sphere' (2015) 16 *Georgetown Journal of International Affairs* 198.

[20] Bachmann and Paphiti (n 19) at 31.

that the only question about an attack that disrupts critical infrastructure is not if but when, there is real cause for concern.[21]

One of the most alarming implications of such attacks are drawn out in a recent report from Chatham House.[22] This is that cyberattacks might disable nuclear command, control, and communication systems but also that inadvertent nuclear launches might stem from reliance on false information and data.[23] As Lawrence Freedman rightly says, the term 'information war' invites confusion: it might refer to 'measures designed to disable systems dependent upon flows of information'; or it might refer to 'attempts to influence perceptions by affecting the content of information'.[24] In the former sense, we are talking about 'engineering', in the latter 'about cognition'.[25] Either way, though, there is plenty to worry about. Threats to the global commons abound.[26]

But, surely, the United Nations could and should act against such attacks, threats, and plain wrongdoing? Evidently, matters are not so simple. The application of historic legal instruments to modern technologies (such as cybertechnologies and drones) is far from clear;[27] and, even if there were a way, we cannot assume that there would be a will. While all Member States of the United Nations are formally equal, the reality is that some are more equal than others, this being exemplified by the constitution of the Security Council. Not only are the five permanent members of the Security Council amongst 'the most important actors on the world stage, given their size, their economic and financial weight, their cultural influence, and, above all, their military might',[28] they have the power to veto (and, in practice, they do veto) decisions that the Council would otherwise make. Not surprisingly, this has led to widespread criticism of the undemocratic and unrepresentative nature of the Council; to questions about its legitimacy;[29] and, crucially, to criticism of the veto which

---

[21]   Ewan MacAskill, 'Destructive attack on UK a matter of "when, not if" warns cyber chief' *The Guardian*, 23 January 2018, p 1.

[22]   Beyza Unal and Patricia Lewis, *Cybersecurity of Nuclear Weapons Systems: Threats, Vulnerabilities and Consequences* (London: The Royal Institute of International Affairs, Chatham House, 2018).

[23]   See, too, Freedman (n 19) Ch 21.

[24]   Freedman (n 19) at 227.

[25]   Ibid.

[26]   See, too, Jelinek et al (n 5).

[27]   For discussion, see, e.g., Marco Roscini, *Cyber Operations and the Use of Force in International Law* (Oxford: Oxford University Press, 2016).

[28]   Gert Rosenthal, *Inside the United Nations* (Abingdon: Routledge, 2017) 95.

[29]   See, David D. Caron, 'The Legitimacy of the Collective Authority of the Security Council' (1993) 87 *American Journal of International Law* 552 (advocating, independence, accountability, oversight, and participation as promoters, albeit not guarantors, of legitimacy).

enables the permanent members to subordinate their collective responsibilities (for the commons' conditions) to their own national priorities.[30]

Taking stock: while international relations should be characterised by zero tolerance for reckless endangerment of the global commons, the reality is that practice ranges from mere insouciance to outright disregard and reckless endangerment. The accumulation of weapons of mass destruction (WMD) should not be tolerated; nor should lower-level non-kinetic or cyber threats which might provoke dangerous responses. If an agency of global regulatory stewards were to be put in place, it would not be coming to a practice of respect that is in good order. The commons is already under severe stress.

11.2.2   International Agencies

To state the obvious, there are a great many international agencies and transnational bodies, some of which are specifically concerned with emerging technologies, particularly with setting technical standards.[31] However, when it comes to international agencies whose remit is the governance of emerging technologies, arguably, as the World Economic Forum has put it in a white paper, the governance landscape is 'relatively sparse'.[32] While 'global governance is obliquely dominated by provisions around trade, financial and intellectual property regimes...very few of these would be specifically focused on the latest emerging technologies, and all would seem a bit out of date.'[33]

Even if the landscape were less sparse, there might be work to be done. Simply because an agency operates at international level it does not mean that it will have the right focus; and, it certainly should not be assumed that its global position will insulate it against the politics and pathologies of national regulatory agencies or governance bodies. International agencies are similarly susceptible—indeed, possibly, even more susceptible[34]—to the risks of regu-

---

[30]   Generally, see Rasna Warah, *Unsilenced: Unmasking the United Nations' Culture of Cover-ups, Corruption, and Impunity* (Bloomington: AuthorHouse, 2016); John Pilger, 'John Pilger reveals how the Bushes bribe the World' *New Statesman*, 23 September 2002, available at https://www.newstatesman.com/node/192550 (last accessed 11 April 2021).

[31]   Notably, the International Organization for Standardization (ISO), the International Electrotechnical Commission (IEC), and the Institute of Electrical and Electronics Engineers (IEEE).

[32]   World Economic Forum (n 6) at p 12.

[33]   Ibid.

[34]   Compare Roland Vaubel, 'Principal-agent problems in international organizations' (2006) 1 *Review of International Organizations* 125, at 136, pointing out that where organisations are not controlled by voters or by national governments, and where they interact with powerful interest groups, then 'corruption is likely to be widespread'.

latory capture and corruption;[35] to 'horse trading';[36] to a shortage of resources and expertise; to conflicts created by their funding sources; and to inter-agency turf wars.[37] These are all risks that could inhibit the work of regulatory stewards whose mandate is to protect the global commons.

Where an agency's mission is expressed in new coherentist language, that is a good start. However, experience shows that, where the missions of international agencies include a number of objectives (such as trade, human rights, and environmental concerns), or where there is a dominant objective (such as the control of narcotics), value commitments (to human rights) will tend to be overridden ('collateralised')[38] or even treated as irrelevant ('nullified').[39] Now, while it is one thing for the international community to unite around what it takes to be its shared prudential interests and, in so doing, to give less weight to its interest in certain aspirational values, respect for the commons' conditions should never be collateralised or nullified in this way. Accordingly, to keep this imperative in focus, if the regulatory stewards are located within an international agency, their mission must be limited to the protection of the commons; and acceptable collateralisation or nullification must be limited to non-commons matters.

---

[35] See, e.g., Abigail C. Deshman, 'Horizontal Review between International Organizations: Why, How, and Who Cares about Corporate Regulatory Capture' (2011) 22 *European Journal of International Law* 1089.

[36] See Axel Dreher, Jan-Egbert Sturm, and James Raymond Vreeland, 'Global horse trading: IMF loans for votes in the United Nations Security Council' (2009) 53 *European Economic Review* 742.

[37] See, e.g., Roberto Andorno, 'Global bioethics at UNESCO: in defence of the Universal Declaration on Bioethics and Human Rights' (2007) 33 *Journal of Medical Ethics* 150 (on the competence of UNESCO relative to the WHO).

[38] See, e.g., Sheldon Leader, 'Collateralism' in Roger Brownsword (ed) *Global Governance and the Quest for Justice Vol IV: Human Rights* (Oxford: Hart, 2004) 53; and, on trade and public health, see Deshman (n 35). For the particular case of the WTO, see Daniel Wüger and Thomas Cottier (eds), *Genetic Engineering and the World Trade System* (Cambridge: Cambridge University Press, 2008); Robert Howse, 'Adjudicative Legitimacy and Treaty Interpretation in International Trade Law: The Early Years of WTO Jurisprudence', in J.H.H. Weiler (ed), *The EU, the WTO, and the NAFTA* (Oxford: Oxford University Press, 2001) 35, and Joanne Scott, 'On Kith and Kine (Crustaceans): Trade and Environment in the EU and WTO' ibid at 125.

[39] On the nullification of human rights in the context of narcotics control, see Richard Lines, *Drug Control and Human Rights in International Law* (Cambridge: Cambridge University Press, 2017).

11.2.3   Is This Unduly Pessimistic?

Responding to this sketch, it might be objected that much of the evidence is 'merely anecdotal' and that, anyway, it does not amount to a systemic problem. No doubt, a good deal of the evidence is 'anecdotal' and some of the story-tellers might have axes to grind. Nevertheless, when the breadth and depth of anecdotes reaches a certain level, they need to be taken seriously; moreover, in some studies, the shape of a particular story has been confirmed in quantitative studies that reveal a more general pattern.[40]

A priori, we can assume that where nation-states conduct themselves in self-interested (nationalistic) ways, they will not be keen to cooperate with one another unless it is clearly to their advantage. Moreover, where the particular nation-states do not trust one another, proposals for cooperation will raise concerns (on both sides) that, if they do cooperate and the other side defects, this will leave them in a worse position than if they had declined to cooperate. On this analysis, there might be occasions when the circumstances do favour self-interested cooperation, but they will be relatively rare. When there is such an opportunity for cooperation, it needs to be seized.

This prompts the thought that such circumstances might obtain just now.[41] Climate change coupled with the pandemic hurts all nation-states. True, some are hurt more than others, but maybe we should be thinking that this is just the right time to be proposing an agency that would have responsibility for stewardship of the global commons. Whether international relations are largely dictated by prudential (rational self-interested) reasoning, or by considerations of fairness, or by interactive processes and concerns about reputation, maybe we now have a rare window of opportunity.[42] If that is right, we should certainly press for it, and press hard for it; but we will continue our discussion on a less sanguine reading of our current circumstances.

11.3   INTERNATIONAL DESIGN RETHOUGHT

Rethinking the design of our international institutions might proceed in two stages.[43] As a first step, an international agency, serving as a hub for our reg-

---

[40]   See, e.g., the study by Dreher et al (n 36).
[41]   As suggested by Mark Coeckelbergh giving a paper at a conference on 'Regulating UncertAInty' (Sant'Anna, Pisa, 9 April 2021).
[42]   For the root reasons for cooperation and compliance, see Koh (n 13).
[43]   Compare the two-stage proposal in Jelinek et al (n 5) at p 8. A coordinating forum is proposed as an 'intermediate step' on the way to a coordinating committee: 'Such a light version of [the committee] would not require any reform, but would invite major stakeholders to discuss the goals, principles, and institutions of a future coordi-

ulatory intelligence, would be put in place as a natural evolution from the networks of national and regional hubs; in a sense, this would be no more than the completion of an institutional design that is already implicit in the networks of national and regional hubs. The second step would be to shape the mission of the international hub so that it clearly engaged new coherentist thinking, specifically in relation to the preservation and maintenance of the global commons and particularly in relation to proposals to employ technological measures for the protection of the commons. Although this second step would be building on an existing agency, it would be more challenging than the first step.

11.3.1 First Step: Building on the National and Regional Hubs

If we imagine that each state puts in place an intelligent hub with nodes (along the lines proposed in the previous chapter), the national hubs will be gathering intelligence about how to engage with and regulate emerging technologies (including intelligence about governance by machines and technological management). If we imagine, too, that region by region these national hubs are in a dialogue with regional hubs, there will already be an intelligent governance network operating with a two-way cascade of intelligence (this being fed up from the national hubs and then fed back down by the regional hubs). To propose a global hub would now seem like a natural extension of the network, enabling the intelligence garnered and synthesised by the regional hubs to be further processed and disseminated by the global hub.

One of the attractions of this design would be that the network would have information about a broad range of governance approaches that would enable the regional and global hubs to compare and contrast different regulatory approaches. There would be no need to characterise this as a regulatory competition; there would be no prizes for those nations that seemed to have the best regulatory approaches. However, this would be a coordinated way of assessing the positive and negative features of different regulatory approaches always being sensitive to context.[44]

---

nating committee as well as the risk…. Participation would be on a voluntary, but recurring basis to ensure a continuation of the debate and follow up with joint declarations and tasks.'

[44] Compare Natalie A. Smuha, 'From a "race to AI" to a "race to AI regulation": regulatory competition for artificial intelligence' (2021) 13 *Law, Innovation and Technology* 57.

11.3.2 Second Step: a Stewardship Remit for the Agency

Building on the global intelligent hub, the proposal would be that the remit of the agency should be sharpened and extended. The sharpening would be to make the agency a global resource and repository of governance intelligence in relation to emerging technologies; and the extension would be to bring stewardship of the global commons into the mission.

Primarily, the stewardship mission would be to ensure that regulators worldwide take their global responsibilities seriously. The days of insouciance, wanton neglect, and reckless disregard for the global commons have to be consigned to history. Given the scale of the challenge, we should not get too far ahead of ourselves. Nevertheless, if, in a new era, regulators at any level were proactively to propose measures to protect the global commons, this would need to be cleared by stewards at the agency—who would need to be satisfied that the measures would be effective and that they would not have unintended negative effects. The stewards would also need to consider the transnational implications of the strategy being employed. In practice, the most controversial aspect of this remit would be its application to proposals to employ technological measures (such as geo-engineering[45] or gene drives[46]) for the purpose of protecting or enhancing the commons.

The stewards would need to be independent. This is not to say that they would have no interest—all humans have an interest in the protection of the commons—but this would not be a conflicting interest. However, self-serving national interests would be conflicting and the regulatory stewards would need to be insulated lest such conflicts and influence adversely affected their focus or otherwise impeded international cooperation in protecting the commons.

It is suggested, too, that the stewards would be headed by lawyers who would lead a team of all the relevant talents. Moreover, the role of the lawyers would not be confined to clearing up what are in effect Law 1.0 questions coming from non-lawyer members of a cross-disciplinary panel. The agency would be infused with Law 3.0 thinking.

For sure, nation-states who do not want to yield any of their sovereign power to an agency of this kind will find objections. However, some who are more detached in their assessment of the proposal might also object on the ground that the agency would be over-precautionary, over-bureaucratic, and unwilling

---

[45] Jesse L. Reynolds, 'Solar Climate Engineering, Law, and Regulation' in Roger Brownsword, Eloise Scotford, and Karen Yeung, *The Oxford Handbook of Law, Regulation and Technology* (Oxford: Oxford University Press, 2017) 799.
[46] Benjamin Capps, 'Gene drive gone wild: exploring deliberative possibilities by developing One Health ethics' (2019) 11 *Law, Innovation and Technology* 231.

to sanction experimental techniques. Clearly, the proposed design would need to be sensitive to a raft of objections, some more appropriate than others.

As with any international agency, one of the key questions about the hub would be its legitimacy.[47] In particular, it would be important to emphasise that the agency would take a restricted view of its cosmopolitan responsibilities. Its focus would be strictly on the global commons; it would have no competence to rewrite the constitutive values of particular communities (competence in relation to such matters would be strictly for the community and its own institutions); and, in sharing its governance intelligence, it would be acting purely in an advisory role. In short, the agency would fully respect the principle of regulatory cosmopolitanism.[48]

To whom would the agency be responsible and for what? In principle, the agency would be accountable to all humans. Quite simply, each and every human is a stakeholder in the commons. Moreover, some might argue that the responsibility should extend to future generations of humans. How, in practice, appropriate mechanisms of reporting and accounting could be put in place to reflect this view would be a matter for discussion. It might be tempting to say that we should simply place our trust in the integrity and expertise of the regulatory stewards, but we know that if the stewards get things wrong, the consequences could be catastrophic.

11.4   CONCLUDING REMARKS

The current practice of international relations reflects far from ideal conditions for any sustained protection of the global commons. The short-sighted pursuit of national interest has to be overcome. The key to this, as Neil Walker has rightly remarked in relation to global law, is 'our ability to persuade ourselves and each other of what we hold in common and of the value of holding that in common'.[49] In other words, all parties need to understand that our future prospects depend on the preservation of the global commons. If there is one thing that we humans do have in common, it surely is our dependence on the global commons. Accordingly, to propose that there should be an international

---

[47]   Nb our earlier remarks in 11.1.

[48]   See, Roger Brownsword, *Rights, Regulation and the Technological Revolution* (Oxford: Oxford University Press, 2008) Ch 7; and, Kwame Anthony Appiah, *Cosmopolitanism* (London: Penguin, Allen Lane, 2006). While the global agency might respect local competence, we should not discount the possibility of nation-states abusing this jurisdiction (e.g., by arguing that their regulatory measures concern only community issues and, thus, are not subject to agency approval).

[49]   Neil Walker, *Intimations of Global Law* (Cambridge: Cambridge University Press, 2015) at 199.

agency with a mission to preserve the commons should be well received by many, but to have any chance of success, all nation-states need to be on board.

In this chapter, it has been suggested that an organic approach to the development of such an agency might have better prospects than simply proposing it cold. The idea is that this agency would evolve from the network of intelligent hubs to become not only a global hub but also to assume the responsibilities of stewardship. Even if there is general acceptance and little resistance to such an agency, there are still some very difficult questions to answer, particularly concerning the accountability of the stewards. Moreover, the burden of responsibility on the agency would be enormous; if mistakes were made, they could prove to be catastrophic.

We started with a reality check and we can end with what David Kaye rightly characterises as 'an undeniable truth about world politics', namely that:

> we are diverse, we have interests that may be difficult to reconcile, but we must find processes that build confidence in decisions about their reconciliation and solution, and ultimately about the exercise of power.[50]

It is against this backcloth that the many challenges of building institutions that serve our shared interest in the stewardship of the global commons must be confronted.

---

[50] David Kaye, 'Legitimacy, Collective Authority and Internet Governance: A Reflection on David Caron's Study of the UN Security Council (2019) 37 *Berkeley Journal of International Law* 289, 301.

PART V

Rethinking the institution of law, authority, and respect

12. Rethinking the authority of law

12.1 INTRODUCTION

In this fifth part of the book, we begin to rethink fundamental questions about the authority of law and about why we should respect the law (just because it is 'the law'). In both cases, when we bring technology into our thinking about law and regulation, we find that this has a disruptive effect on the traditional debate about such questions. It is not so much that technology encourages us to switch sides in the traditional debate but that it introduces a radically different dimension to the debate. However, before we get to the questions that now come on to our agenda, there are three preliminary remarks to be made.

First, it is far from clear what precisely is being claimed or questioned when the 'authority' of, or 'respect' for, the law are at issue. For the purposes of our discussion, we will treat the authority of law as relating to the title of those who claim to be properly authorised to undertake legal functions and respect for the law as a demand that citizens should defer to the law and comply with legal decrees and decisions simply because they represent the law.[1] In both cases, whether we are focusing on authority or respect, the question is: why is the fact that this is the law determinative? What is so special about the law?

Second, what we make of the case for authority or respect seems to be very closely related to matters of legitimacy. If a claim to authority is a claim to legitimate title and the demand for respect claims that the relevant decrees or determinations are legitimate, one way or another, whatever tests of legitimacy are in play will need to be satisfied. If those tests are undemanding in relation to recognising authority, they are likely to be more demanding in relation to claims for respect; and, conversely, where a demanding standard for authority is set and met, this will be likely to lead quite quickly to acknowledging that respect is appropriate.

---

[1] A standard reference point is Joseph Raz, *The Authority of Law* (Oxford: Oxford University Press, 1979), in which the discussion is dominated by the concept of authority (rather than respect) and by the idea of deferring to authoritative sources (even, given such a source, refraining from making one's own practical case-by-case judgements).

Third, following on from the previous point, in this chapter, we will assume a relatively undemanding standard for authority (which basically remits the question to the formal constitutional allocation of functions and authority). However, although this serves as the baseline view in this chapter, in the next chapter, when we address the question of respect for the law, we will introduce a second baseline view which is more demanding.

Bearing in mind these preliminary points, we can turn to the baseline view of authority and then how it might be rethought in a context where we have a choice as to the mode of governance—a choice between, on the one hand, a human enterprise of governance by rules assisted by technical measures and technology or, on the other, governance by machines and technological management.

12.2   THE BASELINE VIEW OF LEGAL AUTHORITY

We can take the baseline position in relation to the authority of law as being rooted in the Westphalian idea of law. In Hart's articulation of this concept of law, any question about the authority (title) of a body or person undertaking a legal function (or claiming to act in a legal capacity) hinges on there being an appropriate mandate in an authorising rule.[2] In the case of legislative and judicial bodies, this authorisation might be explicitly declared in the founding constitutional rules; in other cases, the authorisation will be found in rules that have themselves been made by authorised rule-makers.

The traditional jurisprudential puzzle with this account is that the chain of title takes us back to the constitution, or the rule of recognition, or the last norm of positive law, or some such apex rule within the particular legal system. This means that, in the final analysis, the system purports to be self-validating. It means that the plausibility of all claims to authority within the system are contingent on acceptance of the apex rule as the ultimate test of authority. However, this contingency is the Achilles' heel of the baseline view of authority.

There are a number of responses to this problem, to the apparently unauthorised nature of the apex authorising rules themselves. One response, famously advanced by Hans Kelsen, treats this as a logical problem: because there seems to be no end to the chain, we need a logical full stop. Kelsen's proposal is that we should presuppose a hypothetical rule (the 'Basic Norm' in Kelsen's terminology) that stands just outside the legal system and which authorises the apex

---

[2]   HLA Hart, *The Concept of Law* (Oxford: Clarendon Press, 1961).

rule.[3] However, this does not actually preclude someone asking on what basis the Basic Norm is itself authorised but, more importantly, it is pure fiction and it does nothing to answer the practical and normative questions raised by citizens. Another response is to present the apex rule as the agreed reference point for testing authority, supported by stable official practice. However, since it is precisely the authority of these officials that is at issue, this is no support whatsoever. Giving this a different spin, it might be said that the reference point is agreed in accordance with a social contract which means that the members of the community are precluded by their consent from disputing the apex rule as the test. Again, though, while this might be sound in principle, in practice it is also pure fiction.[4] A further response is to trace the authorisation to an accepted moral or religious source. This form of justification connects to the second baseline view that we will bring into the discussion in the next chapter. Here, suffice it to say that, while this might be plausible in some contexts, it lacks plausibility where communities have stopped believing in the divine right of kings, or similar justificatory narratives. Finally, taking a more pragmatic view, it might be said that we simply have to accept the social facts of official practice: relative to the (officially recognised) apex authorising rules, but only relative to those rules, we can have a reasoned discussion about whether a particular person or body has authority and is acting within the terms of their authority; beyond that, however, there is nothing worth discussing. Yet, if this is the best that we can do when citizens question the strong demands that are made for recognising and respecting law, this simply is not good enough.

What this means is that the baseline view of legal authority is already in trouble once we take a hard look at it. However, for present purposes, let us suppose that we are prepared to accept the apex rule as the test. The question then is how our baseline thinking about the authority of law might be impacted by a switch from governance by rules (together with technical measures and some technological support) to governance by machines and technological management. What should we make of 'the emergence of "algorithmic authority" as the legitimate power of "code" to direct human action and also to impact which information is considered true'?[5]

---

[3] Hans Kelsen, *The Pure Theory of Law* (2nd ed) (Berkeley: University of California Press, 1967).

[4] Compare Deryck Beyleveld and Roger Brownsword, *Consent in the Law* (Oxford: Hart, 2007).

[5] Emre Bayamlıoğlu and Ronald Leenes, 'The "Rule of Law" Implications of Data-Driven Decision-Making: A Techno-Regulatory Perspective' (2018) 10 *Law, Innovation and Technology* 295, at 295.

12.3 RETHINKING AUTHORITY

In an extended discussion, Chris Reed and Andrew Murray have already undertaken a major exercise in rethinking the authority of law.[6] Their central point is that, whatever the plausibility of claims to authority in offline analogue legal systems, these do not translate across to the online environments of cyberspace. In the latter, where individuals are presented with a plurality of authority and legitimacy claims, the self-validating claims of national legal systems will not suffice. Summing up their analysis in four key points, Reed and Murray say:

> The first [point] is that law has two main sources of authority: that deriving from the lawmaker's constitution, which in the case of state law is clear authority only for persons physically present in the state's territory; and the authority which comes from acceptance of a rule by a community. The second is that jurisprudence in cyberspace is exclusively concerned with the second source of authority, and needs to identify it at the level of individual rules rather than considering the authority of the entire body of the lawmaker's output. Third, laws compete for authority in cyberspace, and they compete with social and other norms as well as other laws, so that the authority of a law and also the demands it is able to make depend on how well it does in that competition. Finally, although lawmakers may be able to do little to enhance their authority claims, they can certainly weaken them by failing to establish the legitimacy of those claims and by impairing the rule of law through making authority claims which go beyond the boundary of the lawmaker's community.[7]

Taking acceptance by the individual as focal, Reed and Murray's claim is that 'the legitimacy, efficacy and normative acceptance of law norms in the online environment are predicated upon their acceptance by the community and by the individual in that community.'[8] In other words, claims to authority are not vindicated by constitutional declaration or by the practice of officials who are authorised by such declaration, but depend on recognition and acceptance by the community and its individual members.

There are two particular points to emphasise here. First, the radical challenge to legal authority that is presented by actors in cyberspace is not that there is a persistent problem about working out which legal system is most closely connected with a particular online transaction or interaction. This certainly is a problem, but it is the familiar problem faced by private international lawyers

---

[6]   Chris Reed and Andrew Murray, *Rethinking the Jurisprudence of Cyberspace* (Cheltenham: Edward Elgar, 2018).

[7]   Ibid., at 234–235.

[8]   Ibid., at 228.

in figuring out the applicable law.[9] That said, we should not conclude that there is no real problem; that this is just an exercise in advanced conflicts of laws. The real problem and the radical challenge to legal authority comes when actors in cyberspace do not ask whether it is the rules of legal system A or legal system B or C that are applicable but, rather, why they should recognise the authority of any legal system (over their own modes of self-governance or codes of online conduct).

Second, although, in cyberspace, we will find technical measures that support rules as well as some technological management, Reed and Murray's rethinking is not driven by these new modes of governance. Their rethinking of authority still assumes that the legal enterprise is articulated through the governance of rules. This is in no sense a criticism of their analysis; it simply notes that, even without assuming new forms of governance, or without reimagining law, we can undertake a major rethink of legal authority where cybertechnologies are in the relevant regulatory space. However, our question does assume a different type of governance—whether the type that we assume is governance by rules in conjunction with technical measures or governance by machines with technological management. Given such modes of governance, our question is what we should make of claims to legal authority when applied not only to whatever rules remain, but in particular to the technical measures that support the rules or the technologies that supplant the rules and take over legal and regulatory functions.

The baseline claim to the authority of legal rules is, as we have said, unconvincing in traditional environments;[10] and, as Reed and Murray argue, it needs to be rethought in cyberspace. In the former case, the constitution cannot be the last word on authority; and, in the latter case, it is not clear which constitution, if any, should be taken as decisive. Nevertheless, if the authority of technical measures or of technologies were to be claimed, would a reference back to the constitution be any more decisive or appropriate?

The question of whether a reference back to the constitution would be decisive is pretty straightforward. Where the question is about the authority of a body or person to employ technical measures alongside rules, in principle, this is no different from the question of authority in relation to the use of the rules. Of course, the particular constitutional features of a legal system might

---

[9]   Compare Uta Kohl, *Jurisdiction and the Internet: Regulatory Competence over Online Activity* (Cambridge: Cambridge University Press, 2007).

[10]   We should note, too, that the traditional idea of legal authority has already been problematised in transnational legal scholarship—and, what is more, it has been problematised in ways that are analogous to those identified by Reed and Murray. See, e.g., Roger Cotterrell and Maksymilian Del Mar (eds), *Authority in Transnational Legal Theory* (Cheltenham: Edward Elgar, 2016).

Rethinking the authority of law   199

have different and distinct authorising arrangements for the use of rules and for the use of technical measures. So, it would not always follow that a body that is authorised to use rules in the performance of some legal or regulatory functions is also authorised to use technical measures; it might be that a separate body or person is authorised for the latter. At all events, to the extent that the particular constitutional arrangements do confirm the title of the body or person in question to use technical measures, it will be no more convincing than any other authority question that is remitted to the apex rules. So, for example, if we were to question whether a robot discharging legal functions has authority, we might be able to trace the authorisation back to a human or body of humans and then back to the constitution; but, unless the apex authorisation is conceded, we do not have a compelling answer to our question.

Where the question of authority is raised in relation to governance by robots or by machines (with humans out of the loop) or by technological management (where citizens have no choice other than to 'comply'), the question of whether a reference back to the constitutional authorisations is appropriate is a more difficult one. And, the reason why it is more difficult is because we need to ask whether we can meaningfully talk about the title of the robots or machines or the technological management. Is it still meaningful to raise questions about authority (qua title) when humans are no longer in the picture as legal functionaries? Arguably, the question is not about the authority of the robots or machines or the technologies employed in managing the actions of humans; it is about the authority of the humans who have put in place, or who have retained and adopted, such governance arrangements. However, while this might work well enough when the relevant humans are still in office and when humans remain in control (albeit in the background), what if we reach a point where the humans are just part of the history? What if, even if humans wished it, there could be no going back to rule-based or human-centred forms of governance? If this were the context, then law as we know it would certainly be redundant and so, too, would be the concept of legal authority.[11]

Taking stock, the baseline view of the authority of law is deeply problematic. It has no convincing answer to those who challenge the authority of the apex constitutional rules; and, this is the case whether the question pertains to the title of lawmakers and regulators to make and apply the primary rules of the legal system or to their title to adopt technical measures or technologies for regulatory purposes. However, once we entertain the prospect of governance by machines or technological management, the question is not so much whether the authority of the law can be grounded in the apex rules of

---

[11]   See, Bayamlıoğlu and Leenes (n 5); and see, further, the discussion in 13.4.

a particular legal system, but whether it is any longer meaningful to ask such a question.[12]

12.4 CONCLUDING REMARKS

For those who raise (intra legal system) questions about the 'authority' of particular legal officials or other public decision-makers, the traditional Westphalian view offers a limited answer to what is a very limited question. Once the challenge is to the authority of a particular legal system (or of law itself) rather than to the authorisation for a particular person or act within the legal system, the traditional view has no answer. Information technologies present one kind of challenge because it is not clear which legal system, if any, has the best claims to authority in relation to agents who act in cyberspace. However, anticipating our discussion in the next chapter, the more radical challenge comes from technologies that promise to 'do governance' better than humans and rules. Why should we defer to rules and to human decisions when machines and technological measures can do better? Westphalian legal systems might be better than some alternatives, but they are a long way short of perfection. If they are now outperformed by technologies, the basis for their authority and for our respect seems to be lost.[13]

---

[12] We might note here the tendency to commend autonomous systems, not on the basis of their 'authority', but as 'trustworthy'. However, once humans are out of the picture, we might wonder whether conceiving of trustworthy autonomous systems is any more meaningful than conceiving of authoritative autonomous systems. See, further, 13.4.

[13] Compare the direction of the discussion in Ryan Abbott, *The Reasonable Robot* (Cambridge: Cambridge University Press, 2020) Chapter 7.

13. Rethinking respect for law

13.1 INTRODUCTION

Having addressed the question of the authority of law, we now turn to the question of respect for the law. This, we have stipulated, will be taken as raising questions about why we should defer to authorised decisions or comply with the rules or decrees simply because they are 'the law'.

For cyberlibertarians, cybercitizens rightly challenge the authority of national legal systems, and rightly question why they should respect Westphalian law. Now, it might be argued that respect per se has been done no favours by cyberspace and netizens. For example, a decade ago, in their book, *The Offensive Internet*, Saul Levmore and Martha Nussbaum highlighted concerns about the way in which online anonymity seemed to encourage a level of incivility and offence that one would not expect to encounter offline where those acting in such a manner could be identified.[1] Since then, it has become all too easy to point to a culture of online disrespect for others—indeed, the Internet has brought us a whole lexicon of disrespectful acts, such as 'flaming', 'trolling', and 'doxxing'—as well widespread disrespect for IP laws such as copyright and trade marks (witness, for example, illegal peer-to-peer file-sharing and the thousands of websites that trade in counterfeit designer goods). However, it is specifically a lack of respect for the law that is at issue.

What is at issue is the attitude that Joel Reidenberg detected amongst the 'Internet separatists',[2] acting as if the rule of law has no application to their online activities. Equally, what is at issue is Yahoo's famous refusal to accede to the order of the Parisian court in the LICRA case.[3] What is at issue is Mark Zuckerberg's well-publicised reluctance to appear before parliamentary

---

[1]   Saul Levmore and Martha C. Nussbaum (eds), *The Offensive Internet* (Cambridge, Mass.: Harvard University Press, 2010).

[2]   Joel R. Reidenberg, 'Technology and Internet Jurisdiction' (2005) 153 *University of Pennsylvania Law Review* 1951. See, section 5.2.1, above.

[3]   The story has been told many times but, for one of the best renditions, see Jack Goldsmith and Tim Wu, *Who Controls the Internet?* (Oxford: Oxford University Press, 2006) Ch 1.

committees concerned about Facebook, fake news, disinformation, and data privacy issues.[4]

So, whether we focus on the attitude of cyberlibertarians who deny that the writ of legal authority extends to cyberspace, or the disrespect of the Internet separatists, or the attitude of the big tech CEOs, we have a direct challenge to traditional demands made for the authority of and respect for the law. In all these instances, the question is: why should we recognise the authority of your rules simply because they are presented as the law; why should we respect the requirements and prohibitions of your rules simply because they are presented as the law?

Disruptive though these questions provoked by cyberspace are, they are still posed within the traditional paradigm of governance by humans and governance by rules. In this part of the book, the question is: if we move away from governance by humans and by rules to governance by technologies, how does this impact on our traditional questions about authority and respect for the law? If we do move to a more technological mode of governance, we come to a second wave of challenges to traditional thinking about law, authority, and respect. Here, the main challenge to the authority of law and respect for the law is not so much a failure by citizens to comply with the legal rules, or a problem about knowing which set of rules is authoritative, but the replacement of law as governance by (inferior) humans with a superior form of technological governance.

As we noted in the previous chapter, if we accept that the question of authority has been answered satisfactorily, this might or might not anticipate and shape our answer to the question of respect. Where the case for authority rests simply on validation by the apex rule of the legal system, there is still much work to be done. However, if a more demanding validation has been applied, this might go a long way to answering the question that we now have about respect for the law. Accordingly, when we sketch the baseline view for respect, we will find two positions, one more demanding than the other.

Briefly, the less demanding view is that we should respect the law because it achieves some degree of order (it is better than the lawless Wild West); and, by contrast, the more demanding view is that we should respect the (moral) law because it is guided by a vision of an order of *just* governance. The problem with the former response is that the order achieved by law might be defective in all sorts of ways as a result of which the demand for respect has to be rela-

---

[4]   See. e.g., Lauren Feiner, 'Mark Zuckerberg turns down UK parliament request to answer questions about fake news and data privacy on Facebook', CNBC, 7 November 2018: available at https://www.cnbc.com/2018/11/07/mark-zuckerberg-declines-uk -parliament-invite-to-discuss-privacy.html (last accessed 6 March 2021).

Rethinking respect for law 203

tively weak and conditional. The problem with the latter response is that much of what passes for law conspicuously falls short relative to any ideal of justice added to which the concept of justice is itself heavily contested, as a result of which we are being asked to respect a form of law that simply is more hypothetical than real.

To this traditional debate, we now have to add in the view that we humans should be so concerned about governance by machines, by technology, that we should rethink the reasons that we might have for respecting the law. Unlike *Westworld*, or any other technology-managed environment in which humans act, the key feature of law is not so much that it is better than disorder or that it aspires to do justice, but that it is an essentially human enterprise. The law might well be imperfect but the simple fact that the legal enterprise is governance by humans of humans, using rules as the primary regulatory instrument, is what merits respect.[5] This, it will be contended, is the relevant sense in which law should be characterised and preserved as a 'human-centric' enterprise.

That said, while there might be no sense in which we should respect governance exclusively by machines, in what sense might we respect law where technologies are employed in various ways by humans to support and to perform legal functions? What needs to be respected here is not the machines themselves; it is not as though we have to rethink our relationship with machines and treat them as though they were humans. Rather, the basis for our respect goes back to the institutional framework of law, to a new coherentist mission guided by the idea of a triple licence that authorises the use of regulatory technologies. We have to go back, in other words, to those ideas of legality, the rule of law, and legitimacy, that we have rethought in the earlier parts of the book. In that light, it is not so much law as the enterprise of subjecting human conduct to the governance of rules that should command our respect; it is law as a human-centric enterprise of governance that is guided by new coherentist ideals that demands our support and respect.

In this chapter, we start by sketching the thinking associated with the two baseline views (one viewing law as order and the other aspiring to law as *just* order) that feature in the traditional debate about respect for the law. We then describe how the prospect of governance by technologies disrupts that debate and how a 'human-centric' view of law takes shape. This leads to some

---

5   Compare Dilan Thampapillai, 'The Law of Contested Concepts? Reflections on Copyright Law and the Legal and Technological Singularities', in Simon Deakin and Christopher Markou (eds), *Is Law Computable?* (Oxford: Hart, 2020) 223, at 225, arguing that 'copyright law works because it tacitly tolerates a degree of infringement and permits an ever-shifting line between free [i.e., fair] and non-free uses of copyright materials.' According to Thampapillai, the danger of governance by technologies is that 'it threatens to perfect an imperfect system' (ibid.).

reflections on the deeper disruption—not just to the particular debate, but to the centrality of governance by humans—that is presaged by technological governance.

13.2 THE BASELINE VIEWS

Why should we respect (authorised) decrees and decisions simply because they represent the law? Traditionally, two rival answers are given to this question.

One view, assuming a legal positivist conception of law, relies on prudential reasons; and, the other view, assuming a legal idealist conception of law, relies on moral reasons. While the former view does not claim any special moral status for the law, and while it does not claim that law is perfect, it does argue that it is better than the alternative, namely a lawless Wild West or an unpredictable tyranny. The prudential case is that, because the order and calculability given by law is an advance on the alternative, our default position should be to support it and be positively disposed towards it—hence, we should accept the authority of law and respect its prohibitions and requirements. By contrast, the latter view does make some connection between law and morality, and the case for authority and respect is squarely put on moral grounds: to defer to the authority of law and to respect its provisions by compliance is to support a morally guided practice and to do the right thing.

In some contexts, each of these rival views might have some plausibility. However, in communities that are secular, where citizens are used to forming their own judgements (prudential and moral, individual and collective), and where 'ethics' is widely thought to be 'just a matter of opinion', these views come under strain.

Consider, for example, the plausibility of the prudential and legal positivist view during the time of the Covid-19 restrictions on freedom of movement and association. In the United Kingdom, where the government's response was clearly open to question, the former Supreme Court Justice, Jonathan Sumption, was reported as saying that 'people should make their own decisions in the light of their own health and that the law should be a secondary consideration for them'.[6] In such a setting, it is tempting to introduce a proviso

---

[6] C.J. McKinney, 'Coronavirus laws a "secondary consideration", says Sumption', *Legal Cheek* (14 September 2020): available at https://www.legalcheek.com/2020/09/coronavirus-laws-a-secondary-consideration-says-sumption/ (last accessed 16 September 2020); but, for the context in which these remarks were made (and, especially, for reservations about the legality of the restrictions) see, Jonathan Sumption, *Law in a Time of Crisis* (London: Profile Books, 2021) Ch 12. Similarly, Sumption has suggested that people should make their own decisions about whether or not to assist family or friends with assisted suicide (although, in this case, the reasons

that licenses citizens, in exceptional circumstances, to back their own prudential judgements so long as they submit to whatever legal penalties there might be. At the same time, the rival moral view lacks plausibility in communities that are secular, morally pluralistic, and/or morally sceptical. Here, the case for authority and respect amounts to an argument that we should be positively disposed towards officials who are trying to do the right thing (or to act justly relative to their own lights). Again, though, the default will be put under stress unless a conscientious objection clause is recognised. The problem is that, in the traditional debate, we find that the rival views either overclaim (and are then simply rejected as unreasonable) or they underclaim (by allowing too broad an exception) and compromise the proposition that the law is determinative.

13.2.1 The Legal Positivist/Prudentialists' Response

The setting for our first response is that of a community that views law and morals as independent spheres. Like planets that occupy the same universe but orbit independently of one another, law and morals are always separate and distinct although there will be cases where they come quite close to one another. If law is to be respected in such a community, this is not to be understood to be an appeal to good morals (although, no doubt, the moral high ground will be taken by those who demand respect if the opportunity presents itself).

This is not to say that law is not valued in this community of legal positivist prudentialists; and, indeed, by and large, they might happily comply with legal rules. Nevertheless, to use HLA Hart's terminology,[7] the internal aspect of those who comply for prudential reasons is not the same as the internal aspect of those who comply for moral reasons. The question is: what is it about law so conceived, the positive requirements of which will quite possibly conflict with an individual's sense of their (at any rate, short-term) self-interest, that reasonably commands respect?

In the 1970s, EP Thompson shocked some fellow left-leaning intellectuals when he declared that the rule of law, the rule of rules, was an unqualified good.[8] What Thompson meant was that the rule of rules was a better option than the alternative, where that alternative was the arbitrary rule of the powerful. At least, with the rule of rules, the powerful would be constrained by their

---

for breaking the law would be a matter of conscience rather than prudence): see Joshua Rozenberg, *Enemies of the People?* (Bristol: Bristol University Press, 2020) 97–98.

[7] HLA Hart, *The Concept of Law* (Oxford: Clarendon Press, 1961).

[8] EP Thompson, *Whigs and Hunters: The Origin of the Black Act* (New York: Pantheon Books, 1975) at 266.

own rules; and, given a reasonable warning of what the sanctions would be for breach of the rules, the less powerful would have a chance of avoiding unanticipated penalties and punishments. In this way, Thompson echoed not only Lon Fuller—who argued that the procedural constraints of his idea of legality would tend to discourage the exercise of arbitrary power[9]—but also Judith Shklar, who had already highlighted the virtues of legalism in preference to the lawlessness of both fascist and Stalinist regimes.[10]

Similarly, we might hear echoes of this line of thinking in Alain Supiot's commentary on the replacement of law with governance, the flattening of relevant considerations for governance, and the decline of respect for law.[11] Once the 'law' ceases to offer any resistance and is used merely as a tool, those who are subjected to its instrumentalism no longer have any reason to pledge their allegiance to it.

While a persuasive case for preferring the rule of rules to the arbitrary rule of the powerful can be made, the reasons for taking a favourable view of the law are essentially prudential (appealing to the self-interest of those who would otherwise be subjected to the arbitrary governance of the powerful). Contingently, in particular contexts or particular circumstances, the law might have some appeal to those who are disposed to look for moral reasons to respect it. Nevertheless, this is all somewhat different from valuing the law intrinsically. In this first response, insofar as we have a reason to respect the law,[12] it is because the alternative (a kind of rule-less Wild West) is judged to be less attractive relative to both our individual and collective self-interest.

13.2.2 The Legal Idealist/Moralists' Response

The context for our second response is an aspirant moral community, its members not only committed both collectively and individually to doing the right thing, but also sharing a view as to the guiding principles for the community. Such principles might be founded on a religious code or credo, as in the

---

[9]   Lon L. Fuller, *The Morality of Law* (New Haven: Yale University Press, 1969).

[10]   Judith N. Shklar, *Legalism* (Cambridge, Mass: Harvard University Press, 1964).

[11]   Alain Supiot, *Governance By Numbers* (trans by Saskia Brown) (Oxford: Hart, 2017).

[12]   Compare Joseph Raz, *The Authority of Law* (Oxford: Oxford University Press, 1979) Ch 13. Raz's position is (i) that, because (so he contends) there is no general obligation to obey the law, this cannot be the basis for an attitude of practical respect for the law, but (ii) it is nevertheless permissible (optional) for a person to adopt an attitude of respect for the law (in a way analogous to friendship) which then gives reasons for obeying the law (other things being equal).

Thomist tradition.[13] Equally, though, the picture might be entirely secular.[14] In such a context, the law, as a direct translation of the moral law, would necessarily command respect.

Where the life and times of a community are fairly static, where little changes from one generation to the next, where there is little communication or interaction with other communities, the moralists' picture might be sustainable. However, in the world as we know it in the present century, one of the many disruptive effects of emerging technologies is to the conditions that sustain the moralists' picture. When the context for community life changes rapidly, when the application of the guiding principles is moot, it is the task of the law to take a position, a position with which some members might (as the community would see it) reasonably disagree. For example, developments in modern biotechnology have provoked huge challenges for the law—not least in provoking new debates about the interpretation of human dignity[15]—as it is compelled to arbitrate between religious and secular views and between the ethics of prohibition and the ethics of permission.[16] Nevertheless, in this context, respect for the law signifies that, such disagreement notwithstanding, a positive attitude towards legal prescriptions should be maintained.

Moreover, modern moral communities might be even more pluralistic than this. There might be disagreement not only about the application of guiding principles to particular hard cases but also about which principles should be treated as guiding. Where the reference standards or values for doing the right thing are themselves contested, the law faces a greater challenge because the best attempt at accommodating moral disagreement might mean that very few

---

[13] The leading example in modern jurisprudence is John Finnis, *Natural Law and Natural Rights* (Oxford: Oxford University Press, 1980).

[14] For such a picture, see Deryck Beyleveld and Roger Brownsword, *Law as a Moral Judgment* (London: Sweet and Maxwell, 1986; reprinted Sheffield. Sheffield Academic Press, 1994).

[15] See, e.g., Deryck Beyleveld and Roger Brownsword, *Human Dignity in Bioethics and Biolaw* (Oxford: Oxford University Press, 2001); Tim Caulfield and Roger Brownsword, 'Human Dignity: A Guide to Policy Making in the Biotechnology Era' (2006) 7 *Nature Reviews Genetics* 72; Roger Brownsword, 'Human Dignity, Human Rights, and Simply Trying to Do the Right Thing' in Christopher McCrudden (ed), *Understanding Human Dignity* (Proceedings of the British Academy 192) (Oxford: The British Academy and Oxford University Press, 2013) 345; and 'Developing a Modern Understanding of Human Dignity' in Dieter Grimm, Alexandra Kemmerer, and Christoph Möllers (eds), *Human Dignity in Context* (Baden-Baden: Nomos; Oxford: Hart, 2018) 299.

[16] See, e.g., Roger Brownsword, *Rights, Regulation and the Technological Revolution* (Oxford: Oxford University Press, 2008); and 'Regulatory Coherence—A European Challenge' in Kai Purnhagen and Peter Rott (eds), *Varieties of European Economic Law and Regulation: Essays in Honour of Hans Micklitz* (Cham: Springer, 2014) 235.

or even no one in the community actually supports the (compromise) position that is adopted. Once again, though, to demand respect for the law is to demand that all members of the community continue to view the law and its prescriptions in a positive light.

Crucially, in this picture, the members of a moral community respect the law not only when, by their lights, legal prescriptions guide correctly towards doing the right thing but even when it is either unclear or controversial whether they are guiding in the right direction. Looking back, the fact that those who are responsible for making the law are attempting in good faith to maintain the community's moral commitments is sufficient reason to treat the mere fact that this is the law as a good reason for respecting the institution, respecting its officials, and respecting its prescriptions; and, looking forward, the consequences of not respecting the law might be to undermine the moral aspiration of the community. For the legal enterprise to command our respect, to appreciate why the law really matters, it must be conceived of as an integral part of the practice of an aspirant moral community.[17] So viewed, the legal enterprise does not need to align perfectly with the moral law, but it must represent a good faith and serious attempt to do the right thing.[18] Taking this view, the reason why the law should be respected is not because it is the perfect articulation of the moral law but because it is an enterprise guided by moral aspirations. Communities that fully commit to the law are making a moral, not a prudential, declaration.

Accordingly, as this sketch would have it, respect for the law is largely a matter of respect for moral aspiration and integrity. Respect for the authority of legal officials is respect for persons who are trying to do the right thing, and respect for their rules and decisions is respect for an enterprise that is predicated on translating moral pluralism into provisional regulatory positions and determinations.

So much for the traditional opposition. However, once the possibility of governance by technology is introduced into this debate, it disrupts both the 'alternatives' to law (namely, disorder and injustice) as well as the choice that we face—rather than the traditional choice between different forms of governance by rules, we now have a choice between governance by humans with rules and governance by technologies. Our next step is to consider how we might rethink respect for the law in these disrupted circumstances.

---

[17] Here, readers might detect some echoes from Alon Harel, *Why Law Matters* (Oxford: Oxford University Press, 2014).

[18] This is the thrust of the legal idealist position argued for in Deryck Beyleveld and Roger Brownsword (n 14).

13.3 RETHINKING RESPECT

In this part of the chapter, we start by elaborating on the way in which the traditional debate is disrupted by the prospect of superior governance by technology and then we consider the significance of law being a human-centric enterprise, not just run for the benefit of humans but run by humans.[19]

13.3.1 The Debate Disrupted

The disruption brought about by governance by technology impacts on both sides of the traditional debate. On the one side, the prudential case for law is challenged by technologies that promise to outperform humans and rules in achieving order. It is no longer enough to argue that law, albeit less than perfect, is preferable to a lawless and disordered Wild West. Governance by technology claims that it can put in place a near perfect form of order. On the other side of the traditional debate, governance by technology also promises to outperform the aspirant moral order of law. Whether we are thinking just about order, or about just order, the argument for the machines is that they can outperform the human enterprise of law; what we should be deferring to is the judgement of the machines.

To be sure, there will be a debate about whether governance by technology can live up to its promise. If we assume that it can, the traditional debate—which sets one version of human governance against another—is displaced by a quite new debate about authority and respect where the choice is between either governance by humans and rules or governance by technologies.

If the choice is to be made on prudential grounds, the choice seems to be between imperfect order and perfect (or near-perfect) order; and, if we are to push back against the latter, it has to be on the apparently unpromising basis that we believe our self-interest (whether as an individual or as a member of the collective) is better served by imperfect order. If the choice is to be made

---

[19] Compare Recital 10 of the European Commission's proposal for a Regulation on AI, COM(2021) 206 final (Brussels, 21.4.2021), which provides:

> Artificial intelligence should not be an end in itself, but a tool that has to serve people with the ultimate aim of increasing human well-being. Rules for artificial intelligence available in the Union market or otherwise affecting Union citizens should thus put people at the centre (be human-centric), so that they can trust that the technology is used in a way that is safe and compliant with law, including the respect of fundamental rights.

Should we interpret this Recital as arguing for human-centric applications in the sense of being intended to benefit humans or as arguing for self-governance by humans? On the face of it, the Commission is focusing on the former. While this is well intended, arguably, it misses the key point about human-centric governance.

on moral grounds, and if we are to push back against governance by technology, it seems to be on the unpromising basis that we think that we do the right thing by backing our own moral judgements against the more perfectly realised moral order of the machines.

That said, in both cases, and particularly the moral case, we might protest that the technological performance simply cannot be compared with the human performance.[20] There might be some functional similarities, but the performances are fundamentally different. In that light, we come to see that a key feature of the traditional debate about the authority of, and respect for, the law is that it is predicated on a context in which the enterprise of subjecting human conduct to the governance of rules is an essentially human enterprise that uses rules as its regulatory tools.[21] Once we take humans and rules out of the picture, this is a very different context and, concomitantly, a very different debate. In this context, while we can still ask whether we should defer to the machines, arguably, it no longer makes sense to conceive of law in terms of authority (this being characteristic of human relations) and respect (this being characteristic of situations in which the option of non-compliance is available).

13.3.2   Law as a Human-Centric Enterprise

Imagine a community that now not only has at its disposal a range of technologies that can be deployed for regulatory purposes but also an appreciation that such tools might be more effective than rules. This is a community that has come to realise that, far from being a regulatory challenge, technologies can be a regulatory opportunity. In other words, this is a community in which Law 3.0 is already part of the conversation. However, where the functions of law are automated, we are being asked to respect an enterprise that takes humans out of the loop.

From a prudential perspective, the automation of legal functions, the replacement of human officials with machines, might seem risky relative to one's interests. Teething problems are to be expected and over-reliance on the technology might leave both individuals and communities ill prepared for situations in which there are technological malfunctions or breakdowns. Without

---

[20]   See, e.g., Robert Sparrow, 'Why machines cannot be moral' (2021) *AI & Soc*, available at https://doi.org/10.1007/s00146-020-01132-6; and, Hubert Etienne, 'The Dark Side of the "Moral Machine" and the Fallacy of Computational Ethical Decision-Making for Autonomous Vehicles' (2021) 13 *Law, Innovation and Technology* 85.

[21]   Compare Emre Bayamlıoğlu and Ronald Leenes, 'The "Rule of Law" Implications of Data-Driven Decision-Making: A Techno-Regulatory Perspective' (2018) 10 *Law, Innovation and Technology* 295, esp at 309 et seq.

reassurance about the reliability and resilience of the technology, it is unclear whether one should prefer, so to speak, a West Coast regulatory approach with its aspiration of total technological management that will guarantee perfect control and compliance or the traditional East Coast approach where compliance is far from perfect, and where detection and enforcement is also far from perfect.[22] In this light, we might recall Samuel Butler's *Erewhon*,[23] where the Erewhonians—concerned that their machines might develop some kind of 'consciousness', or capacity to reproduce, or agency, and fearful that machines might one day enslave humans—decided that the machines must be destroyed. For the Erewhonians, the East Coast style of regulation was judged to be the better bet.

Similarly, from a moral perspective, it is unclear whether submitting to governance by smart machines is doing the right thing. If we value human discretion in the application of rules, we might worry that, with automation, this is a flexibility that we will lose.[24] Moreover, to the extent that the morality inscribed in machines tends to be utilitarian, this will be unattractive to those moral constituencies that oppose such reasoning. As with the prudential rejection of governance by machines, conserving governance by rules, made by humans and administered by humans, might seem to be the morally indicated option.

In the influential writing of Mireille Hildebrandt, we find this kind of picture of law, with on the one side 'legality' (due process and justice) being valued against mere 'legalism' (mechanical application of the rules) and, on the other, governance by rules being valued against rule by technologies.[25] Accordingly, although Hildebrandt shares the common convention that, when we speak about the law, we refer to 'an institutional normative order',[26] in her distinctive thinking, we find: that legal standards are co-produced (reflecting a commitment to participatory and inclusive democratic practices); that the 'mode of existence' of modern law, with printing technology providing its infrastructure, is in the form of texts (statutes, codes, precedents, and so on); that legal texts are open to interpretation and contestation (in courts) before

---

[22] Seminally, see Lawrence Lessig, *Code and Other Laws of Cyberspace* (New York: Basic Books, 1999). Compare, Roger Brownsword, 'Code, Control, and Choice: Why East is East and West is West' (2005) 25 *Legal Studies* 1.

[23] Samuel Butler, *Erewhon* (London: Penguin, 1970; first published, 1872).

[24] For some pertinent examples, see Robert Veal and Michael Tsimplis, 'The integration of unmanned ships into the lex maritima' [2017] LMCLQ 303.

[25] Mireille Hildebrandt, *Smart Technologies and the End(s) of Law* (Cheltenham: Edward Elgar, 2015). See, too, Mireille Hildebrandt and Kieron O'Hara (eds), *Life and the Law in the Era of Data-Driven Agency* (Cheltenham: Edward Elgar, 2020).

[26] Hildebrandt (n 25), at 143.

their application in individual cases; and that these features, in combination, enable law to serve more than the demand for certainty by responding to the demand for individual justice and for legitimate purposes.[27] By contrast, where order is controlled by technological regulation, we find a very different story. First, technological regulation is not 'controlled by the democratic legislator and there is no legal "enactment"'; second, the design of technological devices might be such as to 'rule out violating the rule they embody, even if this embodiment is a side-effect not deliberately inscribed'; and, third, 'contestation of the technological defaults that regulate our lives may be impossible because they are often invisible and because most of the time there is no jurisdiction and no court'.[28] Stated shortly, Hildebrandt's concern is that smart machines will enhance the power of, and expand the possibilities for, technological regulation in a way that crowds out the features that we value in law. To which we might add that, once we lose what we value in this picture of law, we lose the basis for our respect.

However, to play devil's advocate, suppose that we radically revise our conceptual thinking so that we come to view the law as an expert system, not so much an assembly of philosopher kings as an assemblage of smart machines that can out-calculate, out-compute, and out-perform even the most intelligent and wisest of humans. If this is the relevant picture of the law, would it not be crazy for humans to back their own judgements against the machines? Yet, this is exactly what some would propose. Here, it is the essential humanity of the law that is valued; it is self-governance of humans by humans that is celebrated, albeit that the relevant rules and decisions might be expressions of inferior judgement. Like a see-saw, the dialectic between those who argue for respect for human but imperfect law and those who are discontent (with its imperfections) will move up and down but, as the weight of discontent increases, we might come to think that the law to be respected by humans is after all the law of the machines; even humans will come to realise that, relative to governance by humans, it is governance by machines that is better than the alternative.

Stated shortly, the prospect of Law 3.0 and governance by smart machines has disrupted a debate in which, on the one side, we are invited to respect the predictable order of the legal positivist vision of the law as being preferable to unpredictable disorder. That invitation now also looks in the opposite direction at the all-too-predictable order of technological management. Thus, the case for respect is that the law finds the right balance between predictability and flexibility and, crucially, leaves humans in control. Meanwhile, on the other

---

[27] Ibid., at e.g., 154–155.
[28] Ibid., all at 12; and, see too the summary at 183–185.

side of the traditional debate, where we are invited to respect the aspirant just order of the legal idealist vision of the law, we have to consider the possibility of governance by smart moral machines. Again, the case for respect seems to turn on our valuing the essential humanity of the law notwithstanding that it might fail to match the technologies in realising its aspiration for just order. On both sides of the debate, if we are to resist governance by technologies, the bottom line is that human aspiration and attempt is more important than technological achievement. So, when we say that law should be human-centric, we seem to be echoing the cyberlibertarians in saying that it is human self-governance that we truly value.

13.4 LAW DISRUPTED: THE END OF LAW—AND MUCH ELSE TOO?

In our discussion of authority and respect, we can detect three waves of disruption. First, technologies (particularly, cybertechnologies) disrupt the Westphalian nation-state model of legal authority and, at the same time, provoke renewed questions about why we should respect the law (qua rules made by other humans); second, technologies impact on the traditional jurisprudential debate about legal authority and respect for the law by offering an ostensibly superior form of governance to that of subjecting human conduct to the governance of rules; and, third, to the extent that we embrace governance by machines and technological management, the meaningfulness of the debate itself is radically disrupted. In particular, this third disruptive wave impacts on a raft of concepts that are meaningful when the context is governance by humans and by rules but not so once the context is governance by technology—and, moreover, not so even though we might persist in trying to transplant the language of one context to the other.[29]

If we had a scale to measure the strength of technological disruption to law, this third wave would be right at the top of the scale. Moreover, it introduces far too many questions for this particular book. Let me, therefore, simply sketch an indicative agenda of questions that are prompted by this wave of disruption.[30]

First, how far do the conceptual ideas and the questions that accompany governance where humans are still the authors of regulatory measures remain meaningful once humans are out of the regulatory loop? How far do the con-

---

[29] Compare the general thesis in Alasdair MacIntyre, *After Virtue* (London: Duckworth, 1981). Concepts that are meaningful in a particular context might lose their meaning (even though the linguistic references remain) once that context has changed.

[30] Here, I am drawing on Roger Brownsword and Han Somsen, 'Law, Innovation and Technology: Fast Forward to 2021' (2021) 13 *Law, Innovation and Technology* 1.

ceptual ideas and the questions that accompany governance where it is rules that are the instruments of choice remain meaningful once that context changes to governance by technologies?

Second, at what point should we say that governance is no longer an essentially human enterprise? How deep and how broad must be our reliance on machines and technologies? How difficult must it be to identify accountable humans? Should we treat governance as crossing from human to technological when this is recognised de jure? Or, when there is no longer a willingness by human reviewers to override the decisions made by machines, is de facto reliance sufficient?

Third, is it helpful to try to transplant the language of authority, respect, trust, justice, and so on that is characteristic of human governance to governance by machines?

Fourth, do we now face a Copernican revolution in our conceptual thinking, reworking the ideas (such as transparency, causation, explanation, justification, and so on) that stand behind human-centric self-governance? Or, as we intimated in an earlier chapter, are there some elements of our conceptual thinking—for example, our concepts of justice and desert, equity, trust, accountability, and responsibility—that we wish to retain? While we might be the first to insist that unequal justice is not justice,[31] we might be the last to accept that it is our ideals rather than our practice that needs to be transformed.

Fifth, if we are to re-centre our thinking, where do we now centre it? Do we centre it in the conceptual schemes associated with new technologies, or possibly in some fusion of human-centric and technology-centric thinking?[32]

Sixth, should we now view the law (qua governance by rules) as just one kind of patterned order? To be sure, an order that emerges from humans who are self-consciously following rules is a distinctive kind of order; and, as traditional jurisprudence emphasises, the internal attitude of those who are following the rules is distinctive.[33] Nevertheless, if the predictability of order is the key characteristic, then (given the unpredictability of human responses to rules) legal order is hardly the paradigm. Rather, the paradigm is technologically secured order.

Seventh, closely related to the previous point, should we now rethink the baseline view that there is a sharp distinction between the laws of nature and

---

[31] Compare Jerold S. Auerbach, *Unequal Justice* (Oxford: Oxford University Press, 1976) at 12: 'In the United States justice has been distributed according to race, ethnicity, and wealth rather than need. This is not equal justice.'

[32] Compare Chris Reed, Keri Grieman, and Joseph Early, 'Non-Asimov Explanations—Regulating AI Through Transparency' (2021) *Nordic Yearbook* (forthcoming).

[33] Classically, see HLA Hart (n 7).

the laws of humans? On both sides of the distinction, the mediation of technologies might be seen not only as significant but as disruptive of the distinction. This prompts the thought that the relevant field of inquiry is the governance environment in which humans act—an environment comprising both normative and non-normative signals with the latter including the unmediated laws of nature as well as technologically mediated and managed features.

Eighth, although we have suspended doubts about the superior performance of machines and technological management, a significant number of humans surely will push back against this kind of governance. They will contest the claim that machines do governance better than humans. Given such resistance, why should we assume that the third wave of disruption will take place? Perhaps, it will always remain on the horizon.

Finally, should our working assumption be that, in the bigger picture, most communities will adopt a mode of governance that relies on both humans and technologies? Indeed, this might appeal as the optimal mode of governance, a happy conjunction of humans and machines. In this picture, the outliers will be, at one end of the spectrum, the few communities (such as the fictitious Erewhonians)[34] that either reject governance by machines and hold on firmly to governance by humans and rules and, at the other end of the spectrum, the communities that embrace a brave new world of technological governance.

13.5   CONCLUDING REMARKS

Our reflections on the demand that we should recognise the authority of the law (simply because it is the law) and respect its directives and decisions (simply because they are the law) have provoked two rounds of rethinking.

First, our baseline thinking about the institution of law sets a bar that now seems far too low for the plausibility of such strong demands for recognition and respect. If law is no more than governance by rules—whether those rules are guided by traditional principles (as in Law 1.0) or serve regulatory policies (as in Law 2.0) or are also supported and substituted by technical measures (as in Law 3.0)—this simply is not good enough; in some contexts, the alternative might be worse but this is not universally so. If law is governance by rules guided by a quest for *just* order, this seems to improve the case for recognition and respect. However, if Rome burns while we are debating what justice demands, the case for recognition and respect still comes up short. If the institution of law is to command recognition and respect, it has to be a regime of governance (whether by rules or by rules in conjunction with technical measures) that is infused with the spirit of new coherentism, demanding that

---

[34]   Samuel Butler (n 23).

emerging technologies meet the criteria for the triple licence. If that is the kind of governance that represents the institution of law, any alternative that neglects the protection and maintenance of the global commons is certainly to be rejected.

Having arrived at the idea that the demands for recognition and respect are convincing only if law is institutionally committed to new coherentist thinking, a second round of rethinking is provoked. What if governance by machines (putting humans out of the loop) in conjunction with technological management can do better in serving the new coherentist agenda? To be sure, this might not be comparable to governance by humans with rules,[35] but what if this form of governance does better in protecting and maintaining the global commons, in maintaining the integrity of the community's fundamental commitments, and in finding acceptable accommodations of citizens' interests? On the face of it, it would be irrational for humans to reject such a form of governance—at any rate, it would be so provided that we assume that it would stick to the coherentist agenda and operate in a way that is centred on serving human interests and needs.[36] Nevertheless, if such a regime of governance were to be instated (and could not be recalled or reversed), we would then face a torrent of questions about the concepts that have organised our thinking about law and regulation, about human relations, and about the tools of governance. Not least, we would need to rethink our idea of law as an essentially human enterprise and, with that, whether it is any longer meaningful to conceive of (let alone to question) the authority of law or respect for law, or even law itself (other than as an historical artefact).

If we hesitate to embrace such a radical change to both our thinking about, and practice of, law, we need to resist the momentum behind governance by smart machines, lest we find ourselves irreversibly in a place that we humans do not want to be. In an ideal world, this would be the moment to take time out—time out to ask ourselves precisely that question: where do we want to be, what kind of technological societies do we wish to inhabit, do we want a world of imperfect self-governance or a world of benign technological governance? In our times, sadly, the world is far from ideal; nevertheless, these are key questions for our times.

---

[35] Compare, e.g., Lyria Bennett Moses, 'Not a Single Singularity' in Deakin and Markou (n 5) 205.

[36] Of course, the machines might have other plans for humans. See, Nick Bostrom, *Superintelligence* (Oxford: Oxford University Press, 2014).

PART VI

Rethinking the law school

14. Teaching law

14.1 INTRODUCTION

The law school in which I took my first steps as an academic lawyer was housed in an elegant Victorian property. There was a small lawn at the front of the building. One day, all the staff and students gathered on the lawn for a group photograph, rather like a group assembled for a wedding photograph. There were no more than 100 of us. Thirty years later, at the turn of the century, there were the best part of 2,000 students in the same law school plus about 70 members of staff. The law school had moved buildings; and it would have taken several lawns for a group photograph to be possible.

During that period much changed. As one of my colleagues remarked, all the lines went steadily upwards—undergraduate student numbers, post-graduate student numbers, staff numbers, teaching income, research income, international student numbers, and so on. The culture of the law school also changed from one that was student-centred and teaching-led to one that was expected to have a 'business plan' and be research-led. In line with this change, debates about the curriculum, which in the 1970s were fiercely contested, died a death as research performance became an institutional priority and the principal pathway to promotion.

By the turn of the century, too, the technologies of teaching and research were changing in ways that hinted at the transformation that would soon be under way. In the 1970s, visitors to the law school would find staff in the building and students in the law library (where, as I indicated in the Preface, seats and books would both be in short supply). Fifty years later, even if the functioning of law schools was not impeded by a pandemic, visitors would not find too many of the academic staff (those absent being otherwise engaged with their research) and the student population would be more widely dispersed. Thanks to modern technologies, staff can do most of their research and writing without having to be physically on campus, and online teaching looks like being a large part of the future.

Once upon a time, there might have been robust debate about what should be taught in law schools but there would have been little discussion about where it should be taught (where else other than on the campus?) and about how it should be taught (face-to-face through lectures and tutorials, and with books (such as textbooks and case-books) as well as primary source materials and law reviews). Similarly, there would have been little to discuss about what should be researched—it was, of course, 'the law' that was to be researched.[1] However, new technologies not only present new options for teachers and researchers, but they also present new questions about what should be taught and what should be researched.

Accordingly, if our law schools are to be fit for purpose in the present century, they might not need to change their commitment to educate students to think like lawyers, but they will need to rethink what that commitment involves as well as rethink their practice in delivering legal education.[2]

In this chapter, our rethinking of the law school will work on two axes: the first is the axis of what is taught and the second is the axis of how legal education is delivered. The baseline model teaches a Law 1.0 curriculum and it delivers it by traditional face-to-face lectures, seminars, and tutorials with students. In principle we could rethink this model along one or both of the axes. We might rethink the curriculum (so that it reflects Law 2.0 and Law 3.0 thinking); or we might rethink the traditional mode of delivery, shifting (as with online dispute resolution) to an online model (online legal education); or we might shift along both axes.

In the short term, we can expect some law schools to stick with the baseline model (offering an expensive 'Rolls Royce' option); others to stick with the traditional baseline curriculum but deliver it through online platforms (widening access to legal education); and vanguard law schools to rethink both their curriculum and how they deliver their teaching. In the longer term, it is hard to know how this will play out. Some law schools will see themselves as

---

[1] Implicitly, this meant that the research focus and agenda was dictated by Law 1.0. See, Roger Brownsword, 'Maps, Critiques, and Methodologies: Confessions of a Contract Lawyer' in Mark van Hoecke (ed), *Methodologies of Legal Research* (Oxford: Hart, 2011) 133.

[2] Speaking to the situation in the US, compare Mark Fenwick, Wulf A. Kaal, and Erik P.M. Vermeulen, 'Legal Education in the Blockchain Revolution' (2017) 20 *Vanderbilt Journal of Entertainment and Technology Law* 351, at 355–356 (footnotes omitted):

> The curriculum of US law schools has only marginally changed over the last thirty or more years. Yet as law firms increasingly embrace Legal Tech, the new economy and platform technologies, law schools of the twenty-first century will recognize the new reality and adapt to new demands. Such adaptation will likely entail incorporating AI into the classroom…. Curricular innovations may include coding for lawyers…. With curriculum changes, adaptation to changes in technology, and new teaching methodologies that lend themselves more to technological adaptation, the law schools of the twenty-first century should be able to equip twenty-first-century lawyers with the necessary skillsets to operate effectively in the new world of disruptive innovation that is emerging so rapidly.

220 *Rethinking law, regulation, and technology*

serving the needs of legal practitioners; others will see themselves as offering a liberal education that might or might not be a pathway into legal practice.[3] At the same time, while new technologies might be applied in ways that broaden access to both legal services and to law school education, they might also be applied in ways that reduce the need for so many lawyers. With the right conjunction of circumstances, the lines in the law schools might continue to move upwards; but, in different circumstances, the law schools might all but disappear or be absorbed into other parts of the university.[4]

We can start with the curriculum. Following some general remarks about the different understandings of the law school mission (of what it means to think like a lawyer) and the way in which this will be reflected in the design of the law school curriculum, we offer an extended example of rethinking what we teach, employing a Law 3.0 frame, and using the law of contract as the case in point. After that, there are some further short reflections on how we teach and who we teach. In the next chapter we will assess the implications of new technologies for law school researchers.

14.2   WHAT WE TEACH: THE CURRICULUM

What kind of 'lawyers' do we want our students to become? In all law schools, the mission is likely to remain that of producing graduates who are able 'to think like lawyers'.[5] However, the baseline understanding of this mission, as a Law 1.0 mission, is very different from the understanding that will guide thinking in what I anticipate will be the vanguard law schools. In these law schools, the mission will be read through the lens of Law 2.0 and Law 3.0. These different understandings will translate into quite different curricula.

---

[3]   In John N. Adams and Roger Brownsword, *Understanding Law* (London: Fontana, 1992), we tried to encourage a more liberal approach by highlighting the various questions that one might ask about the practice of law as opposed to those 'questions of law' that we debate *within* the practice itself. In other words, this introduction to law was designed to encourage students to think outside the box of Law 1.0. That said, technology did not feature in that introduction, neither in the background nor the foreground. Compare Fenwick et al (n 2) at 361 (rethinking legal education 'requires out-of-the-box thinking for lawyers who were trained during law school and during their entire careers to think inside the box').

[4]   For some very interesting reflections on how this all might develop, see William N. Lucy, 'Law School 2061' (2022) *Modern Law Review* (forthcoming).

[5]   For some much earlier reflections on the law school mission, see Roger Brownsword, 'Teaching Contract: A Liberal Agenda', in Peter Birks (ed) *Examining the Law Syllabus: The Core* (Oxford: Oxford University Press, 1992) 42.

14.2.1 The Baseline Model

In the world of Law 1.0, teaching students to think like lawyers means that students are trained to analyse 'the legal position' in relation to a particular set of facts, that position being determined by the application of a limited set of rules, standards, and principles (primarily, found in constitutional, legislative, and case-law materials). Where the application is straightforward, thinking like a lawyer is not particularly challenging. However, where the application is not straightforward, the exercise is more challenging, and it is when students are instructed to engage with these harder cases that the law schools begin to differentiate between their students—by reference to how skilful they are in handling and applying the materials. The sign of a first-class lawyer is that they are able to argue a case for the apex court equally compellingly regardless of whether they are acting for the appellant or the respondent.[6]

To train students to think like Law 1.0 lawyers, the traditional law school curriculum will feature the core law subjects, their general principles and more particular rules. These are the principles, it will be recalled, that Frank Easterbrook argued should be focal in legal thinking and in recognising new legal subjects.[7] Having studied the core principles of law, students will then be invited to select some 'optional' courses, some of which build to some extent on the core (e.g., commercial law, insurance law, medical law, labour law, and so on) but many of which are constituted by large legislative schemes (e.g., intellectual property law, company law, tax law, environmental law, competition law, and the like). Whereas much of the study of the core subjects will direct students to their casebooks, their reading beyond the core will tend to be in the statute books.

To the extent that students are critically engaged with the legal material, it is a fairly limited exercise. In relation to the cases, appeal court cases typically present a choice between two lines of precedent, or more than one interpretation of the cases, or between following a clear precedent and going with the merits. Whichever choice the court makes, it is easy pickings to criticise the decision for its failure to make the alternative choice. Similarly, if the issue is about the interpretation of a constitutional document, a statute, or a contract (or some other commercial paper), the courts will face a choice between a literal

---

[6]   Needless to say, many apex court justices are themselves experts in this respect. See, for an illuminating discussion, Bob Woodward and Scott Armstrong, *The Brethren* (New York: Simon and Schuster, 1979) (concerning the work of the US Supreme Court, and particularly the skills of Justice Douglas, for a period during the 1970s).

[7]   Famously, see Frank H. Easterbrook, 'Cyberspace and the Law of the Horse' (1996) *University of Chicago Legal Forum* 207; and, see Roger Brownsword, *Law 3.0: Rules, Regulation and Technology* (Abingdon: Routledge, 2020) Ch 11.

reading and some more purposive or contextual reading. Whichever choice is made, the court is open to criticism for its failure to take the other option. The game varies a bit from one area of law to another but, basically, thinking like a smart lawyer means that one is proficient at playing this game.[8]

That said, the overarching concern in Law 1.0 is with the 'coherence' of legal doctrine. The ambition is to maintain the integrity of the body of legal doctrine by ensuring that its signals are clear and non-contradictory. While this is in line with a procedural ideal of legality, it not only means that Law 1.0 conversations feature some extraordinary attempts to reconcile the clearly irreconcilable, and to smooth over obvious distortions of relevant principles, but it also means that there is no external standard of legitimacy. So, when the great common lawyer, Karl Llewellyn, instructed his students at Columbia to put their ethics into a state of temporary anaesthesia, this was right in line with the Law 1.0 paradigm (even though Llewellyn was to be a major critic of the idea that the cases and the rules simply decide themselves).[9] According to Law 1.0's conception of doctrinal coherence, what makes a decision 'right' is that it can be internally justified. The fact that the decision might be out of line with some external ethical standard is irrelevant.[10]

This is not all. In a Law 1.0 curriculum, one question that will not be asked in relation to the core legal principles is whether they are fit for purpose. Insofar as these principles have a purpose, it is largely a corrective one: restoring parties to a baseline position that reflects a relatively settled understanding of which interests are to be recognised and how they are to be ordered.[11] In a more dynamic society, what might make such principles fit for purpose is their application in the service of regulatory policies, particularly economic objectives. Somewhat confusingly, this kind of consideration is likely to surface when assessing and interpreting the big legislative schemes of the optional courses. However, it will not come into its own until the curriculum is rethought to reflect a Law 2.0 (regulatory) mindset.[12]

---

[8]   See, further, Roger Brownsword, 'Whither the Law and the Law Books: From Prescription to Possibility' (2012) 39 *Journal of Law and Society* 296.

[9]   For Llewellyn's introductory lectures at Columbia, see his classic book, *The Bramble Bush* (New York: Oxford University Press, 2008) [original edition 1930].

[10]   Of course, much more could be said about whether the ethics is external to the body of doctrine or whether it is implicit in doctrine and, thus, internal. Compare, Ronald Dworkin's theory of adjudication in his well-known book, *Taking Rights Seriously* (rev ed) (London: Duckworth, 1978).

[11]   On the criminal side, the principles are less about compensation and restoration but about just punishment. However, the baseline position, disturbed by the crime, is the same.

[12]   Compare Hugh Collins, *Regulating Contracts* (Oxford: Oxford University Press, 1999) at vi:

14.2.2 The Law 2.0 Curriculum

The mission of a law school that is committed to a Law 2.0 approach might still be expressed as being to teach students to think like lawyers, but regulation and policy is now centre stage. Students might still be introduced to law through the traditional principles of what Law 1.0 treats as the core law subjects. However, it will be regulation that is front and centre, and those big legislative schemes that dominate many legal subjects will be interrogated from a regulatory perspective.

The questions that now arise are not about the coherence of legal doctrine—or, at any rate, not doctrinal coherence as understood in Law 1.0. As Edward Rubin aptly observes, we live in the age of modern administrative states where the law is used 'as a means of implementing the policies that [each particular state] adopts. The rules that are declared, and the statutes that enact them, have no necessary relationship with one another; they are all individual and separate acts of will.'[13] In other words:

> Regulations enacted by administrative agencies that the legislature or elected chief executive has authorized are related to the authorizing statute, but have no necessary connection with each other or to regulations promulgated under a different exercise of legislative or executive authority.[14]

In the modern administrative state, the 'standard for judging the value of law is not whether it is coherent but rather whether it is effective, that is, effective in establishing and implementing the policy goals of the modern state'.[15] By contrast, the distinctive feature of Law 1.0 'coherentism' is the idea that law forms 'a coherent system, a set of rules that are connected by some sort of logical relationship to each other'[16]—or 'a system of rules that fit together

---

> Lawyers may learn from the social sciences what kinds of purposes can be pursued productively by legal regulation and how those objectives can best be achieved. Or, to put the point the other way round, lawyers can learn how legal regulation can easily become counter-productive, ineffective, and inefficient. Contract lawyers have not bothered much with these issues in the past, being content rather to attempt to describe principles of good conduct based upon political and moral theory, and then to assume that rules with these purposes have their intended effects.

[13] Edward L. Rubin, 'From Coherence to Effectiveness' in Rob van Gestel, Hans-W Micklitz, and Edward L. Rubin (eds), *Rethinking Legal Scholarship* (New York: Cambridge University Press, 2017) 310 at 311.

[14] Rubin (n 13) at 311.

[15] Rubin (n 13) at 328.

[16] Rubin (n 13) at 312.

in a consistent logically elaborated pattern'.[17] Moreover, within the modern administrative state, the value of coherence itself is transformed: coherence, like the law, is viewed as 'an instrumental device that is deployed only when it can be effective'.[18] In a concluding call to arms, Rubin insists that legal scholarship needs to 'wake from its coherentist reveries';[19] and that legal scholars 'need to relinquish their commitment to coherence and concern themselves with the effectiveness of law and its ability to achieve our democratically determined purposes'.[20]

Although questions about the effectiveness and legitimacy of regulatory interventions are not new, technologies have made these questions more acute; and new technologies often take the eye for the way in which they challenge regulators to keep the law connected. In order to pursue these questions, there is a good deal of regulatory scholarship (much of which is focused on making regulation work), but there is also an open invitation here to reach out to other disciplines, such as sociology, behavioural economics, politics, and philosophy, for guidance. So, when we say that law schools are now more integrated into the social sciences and the mainstreams of academia,[21] this is an indication of the Law 2.0 agenda driving an engagement with other disciplines.

14.2.3 The Law 3.0 Curriculum

There might be more than one focus for a Law 3.0 curriculum; there might be several ways in which such a curriculum is structured and organised; and, there might also be different views as to its interdisciplinarity.[22]

---

[17] Rubin (n 13) at 313.

[18] Rubin (n 13) at 328.

[19] Rubin (n 13) at 349. For scholarly concerns that include but also go beyond coherentism, see Roger Brownsword (n 1).

[20] Rubin (n 13) at 350; and, compare the seminal ideas in Hugh Collins (n 12).

[21] See, e.g., Fiona Cownie, *Legal Academics* (Oxford: Hart, 2004); and Dawn Oliver, 'Teaching and Learning Law: Pressures on the Liberal Law Degree' in Peter Birks (ed), *Reviewing Legal Education* (Oxford: Oxford University Press, 1994) 77.

[22] Compare Fenwick et al (n 2) at 381:

> For law students, the growth of multidisciplinary teams in the technology-based society and economy means that they will be required to work closely not only with accountants or fiscal advisors but also and ever increasingly with engineers, designers, and architects. Crucially, lawyers and legal advisors will find themselves operating as a bridge between the diverse range of actors who must now work together in dealing with increasingly complex challenges....
>
> Specifically, law schools need to enable their students to work in interdisciplinary teams with software engineers. It is essential for law students to gain a greater appreciation of the means by which code can be utilized and integrated in legal contexts.

Adopting a narrow focus, a Law 3.0 curriculum might be designed to train students to think like a regulatory and technologically minded lawyer. Graduates would be ready to participate in a conversation that always asks whether our rules, with their particular content, are fit for regulatory purpose and, at the same time, whether rules as such (rather than technical or technological measures) are fit for our regulatory purposes. This curriculum would in some ways resemble that for Law 2.0 but it would highlight the potential for regulatory solutions that rely on technologies other than rules.

By contrast, a Law 3.0 curriculum that adopts a broader focus would span all three conversations: Law 1.0, Law 2.0, and Law 3.0. The central objective of the curriculum might be to prepare students for a regulatory world in which technical solutions are at least as important as rules. However, graduates from such a law school would also understand, and have the capacity to engage in, other law conversations with their own logic and focus. The thinking at such a law school would be that while Law 1.0 is fine for those who want to do Law 1.0-type things, Law 3.0 is where we are. It follows that, at minimum, students should understand that Law 3.0 represents the bigger picture for their studies so that, when they engage in Law 1.0 conversations, they appreciate exactly where they are relative to co-existent Law 2.0 and Law 3.0 conversations.

To some extent, the structure and organisation of the degree programme might follow from the focus. For example, assuming a three-year degree programme as standard, a law school that adopted a broader focus might teach Law 1.0 thinking in Year 1, Law 2.0 thinking in Year 2, and Law 3.0 thinking in Year 3.[23] However, rather than teaching the three conversations consecutively, they might be taught concurrently and pervasively from the start. In other words, in all subjects, in all years, students would be engaged in three-way conversations.[24]

Given the interest in Law 3.0 in coding, both text-based and non-text-based, a natural question is whether it would be part of the Law 3.0 curriculum that students should also be trained in science and technology subjects. When genetic coding was in the spotlight, we might have thought that biotechnology

---

[23] For example, compare the structure of the Law (Law and Technology Pathway) LLB programme at the University of Surrey, where the majority of the law and technology modules are offered in the third year: see https://www.surrey.ac.uk/undergraduate/law-law-and-technology-pathway#structure (last accessed 29 July 2021).

[24] Compare Julian Webb, 'Information Technology and the Future of Legal Education: A Provocation' (2019) 7 *Griffith Journal of Law and Human Dignity* 72 (arguing, inter alia, that information technology is too important to be treated as merely an optional or peripheral interest for law students; rather, Webb contends, the relationship between law and technology must be understood and problematised pervasively, across the curriculum).

should be part of the Law 3.0 curriculum. Nowadays, the question might be whether lawyers should be trained to code like data scientists.[25] These questions invite further discussion.[26] There is an obvious danger here that the Law 3.0 curriculum falls between several stools, trying to do too much within the compass of a three-year programme. There is also a danger that, rather as with law and language degrees, joint programmes do not reflect the language or the technologies (and coding) that needs to be in the spotlight. Undergraduate law students cannot do everything and it might be that the law schools should leave the lab work to the scientists and stick with the library and a curriculum that is more about regulation and governance than the technological details.[27]

14.3 RETHINKING THE TEACHING OF CONTRACT LAW

According to Brett Frischmann and Evan Selinger, 'No existing contract theory explains or justifies our current electronic contracting law and architecture, at least in a manner that accounts for techno-social engineering.'[28] Although this reflects a US view of contract theory and focuses on consumer contracts, it is an appropriate cue for a Law 3.0 framing of contract law.

Taking this cue, imagine a law school that is committed to a Law 3.0 curriculum; imagine that it starts by giving its students a general introduction to the Law 3.0 landscape—to the characteristics of principles-guided Law 1.0, regulatory Law 2.0, and technology-sensitised Law 3.0; and, imagine that this general backcloth is always present as students are introduced to particular fields of law which are now brought into the foreground.

---

[25]   Compare Fenwick et al (n 2).

[26]   Compare Mark Findlay, *Globalisation, Populism, Pandemics and the Law* (Cheltenham: Edward Elgar, 2021) at 146. Speaking about teaching 'legal analytics' together with the idea that 'legal education should contain components of computer science, algorithmic literacy, and big data computation', Findlay remarks that for 'those who believe legal education is a critical free-thinking discipline, not necessarily compatible with the technological experience...there is cause for unease about the quality of educational experience for student and teacher alike that will emerge.'

[27]   Compare Joshua AT Fairfield, *Runaway Technology* (New York: Cambridge University Press, 2021) at 280 (on the problems caused by 'the modern trend of training lawyers to eschew legal narrative and analogical reasoning and focus instead on armchair empiricism (the current fad is for "legal empirical studies") or rationalism (usually in the form of the law and economics movement).... Lawyers have done a great disservice in abandoning their task of crafting cooperative fictions that helps us work together and stay alive, in exchange for the almost entirely unacknowledged meta-narratives of verificationist science.').

[28]   Brett Frischmann and Evan Selinger, *Re-Engineering Humanity* (Cambridge: Cambridge University Press, 2018) at 311.

In this law school, there might be one or more modules on transactions, or contracts. While some courses might map the law of contract to the backcloth, others might focus on just one part of the legal landscape: for example, while a course that focuses on teaching students to think like a Law 1.0 lawyer, or on the general principles of the law of contract, might look very much like a traditional contracts module, a course that is focused on regulatory Law 2.0 thinking might look rather like modern modules on consumer protection law. There is more than one way of translating the vision of a Law 3.0 curriculum to contracts; and, before long, we can assume that each law school will develop its own model and, with that, its own course materials to support its curriculum.

For the sake of illustration, let us imagine that a law school, having already introduced its students to the landscape of Law 3.0, frames its teaching of contract law by placing it within what it terms the 'context for transactions'. Having elaborated its contextual framing and explained how legal rules and principles as well as transactional practice and technologies fit in, it opens two particular lines of inquiry. First, as new transactional technologies become available and are taken up, there is the question of whether we should focus, like Law 1.0 'coherentists', on applying the rules and principles of the existing body of doctrine or whether we should think about such matters in a more Law 2.0 'regulatory-instrumental' way. Second, getting to the leading edges of the field, there is the question of what we should make of the possibility of regulatory restrictions or requirements being, so to speak, 'designed into' the emerging technological platforms or infrastructures for contracts. In other words, there is the question of what we should make of Law 3.0 'technological management' of transactions. We can speak briefly to the contextual framing and then to the two lines of inquiry that we have highlighted.

14.3.1 Contract Law and the Context for Transactions

The first question is to ask how the law of contract fits into the 'context for transactions'—a context that goes beyond the paper rules of law to include the norms that actually guide contractual practice as well as the application of transactional technologies. We can start with some short remarks about the general idea of a 'contextual' approach to the governance of transactions, and then we can pick out three salient contextual features: namely, the doctrinal, the transactional practice, and the transactional technologies.[29]

---

[29] With a focus on transactions, 'globalisation' would also be a salient part of the context; and, in other areas, the Anthropocene would be an obvious feature to highlight. Compare Findlay (n 26), in which both globalisation and climate change are salient in a discussion, inter alia, of AI, machine learning, blockchain, and the platform economy.

14.3.1.1 The general idea of the context for transactions

As an undergraduate in the mid-1960s, my introduction to the law of contract was in the context of an embryonic modern consumer marketplace emerging from the years of post-War austerity and fuelled by credit. In that context, the law of contract, with its commitment to freedom and sanctity of contract, coupled with an undemanding concept of consent, found itself in something of a crisis.[30] Evidently, the law licensed the use of standard form terms and conditions (which consumers did not read, would not understand, and played no part in negotiating) and, in particular, it licensed suppliers (of cars, fridges, televisions, and the like) to rely on standard term exemption clauses that put the risks of fitness, quality, and safety on the purchaser. In that context, it was said, quite rightly, that some corrections to the law of contract needed to be made; and, in due course, the necessary legislative changes were made.

These days, I would expect the conversation to be rather different. Nowadays, if we detect a crisis in the consumer marketplace, we will say, in the manner of Law 2.0, that the regulatory environment is not fit for purpose; and we will know that an effective response to the problem is likely to involve more than a tweak to the law of contract (or even a bespoke piece of legislation such as the Consumer Rights Act 2015). To get the regulatory environment right, it might also be necessary to make reforms in competition law, in credit law, and criminal law as well as changes in the technical standards for consumer goods and services; and, it might be necessary as well to make changes to the regulatory agencies and, crucially, to take steps to change the business culture of those who supply goods and services in the consumer market.

Once having started to teach the law of contract, I soon became aware of the seminal work of Stewart Macaulay[31] and Ian Macneil.[32] Their insights into the real world of transactions came as quite a shock. How, though, were such contextual commentaries to be fitted into my lecture narrative that started with offer and acceptance and ended with remedies? Clearly, so long as the main story that we tell as teachers of the law of contract is the traditional, Law 1.0, doctrinal story, there is a problem. Accordingly, we need to start with the idea that the field of interest is transactions (whether deep in the business world or in the consumer marketplace or in the emerging peer-to-peer shared economy); and, concomitantly, we need to understand that it is the governance

---

[30] For some recollections and reflections, see Roger Brownsword, 'Fundamental Questions: *Suisse Atlantique* Revisited' in Paul Mitchell and Charles Mitchell (eds), *Landmark Cases in the Law of Contract* (Oxford: Hart, 2008) 299.

[31] Stewart Macaulay, 'Non Contractual Relations in Business: A Preliminary Study' (1963) 28 *American Sociological Review* 55.

[32] Ian R. Macneil, *The New Social Contract* (New Haven: Yale University Press, 1980).

of transactions that is our focus. Importantly, we should not assume that the signals given by the law of contract necessarily are dominant in any particular transactional setting. There is a lot of noise in and around transactions; and, in some environments, such as those studied by Macaulay, the signals given by the law of contract might be very weak indeed. Similarly, we know that in our everyday experience as consumers, whether offline or online, the legal signals are often much less prominent than the suppliers' particular custom and practice, their concern for their trading reputation, and the side arrangements that have been made for guarantees and warranties. We find ourselves, as Macneil points out, in a web of social relations.

So, the first lesson in contract law does not start within the law of contract itself (whether with offer and acceptance or with remedies) but with the context for transactions, with the normative and technological environments in which transactors operate. The law of contract sends signals to transactors, but it is just one element in the regulatory environment. If we start here, the question then is: how wide should we go in drawing the boundaries of the context, and what should we highlight as the significant features of the context?

14.3.1.2 Three significant features of the context for transactions
Having said that the Law 1.0 principles of contract law, as expounded in the many textbooks on the subject, have to be set in context, what are the key features of this context?

First, there is the larger doctrinal context. In the style of 'law in context' that was pioneered at the Warwick Law School in the 1970s, teaching does not stay within the traditional doctrinal silos. According to William Twining, the paradigm for this approach was Patrick McAuslan's course (and book) on 'land use'. Here, we find that a range of legal principles and rules is brought to bear on the governance of land use—some of it Law 1.0 principles (such as the principles of reasonable use that guide the law of nuisance, or the principles that govern restrictive covenants in real property law), some of it entirely Law 2.0 regulatory (such as the law of land use planning and development or the various legislative attempts to tax planning gain). So, for example, if transactions (or, to take a narrower focus, transactions on platforms) is our topic, we might start with the principles of the law of contract but we would also need to be aware of the potential relevance of whatever other bodies of law (such as the criminal law, or competition law, or labour law) provide signals to transactors. While this is challenging, it means that students who spend a lot of time studying the law of contract do not make the mistake of thinking that the regulatory environment for, say, platform services in the shared economy is constituted solely by the law of contract.

Second, there is the actuality of transactional practice. The point is that we should recognise not just the de jure but also the de facto context for transactions. This enables the locating of the law of contract in a signalling environment that includes just the kind of norms (the 'living law') that Macaulay and Macneil identify in their work. From this perspective, we see that transactions, like interactions, take place in an ocean of normativity and that the legal norms are just one island. While students might object that this attaches too little importance to the law, it is a necessary correction lest students assume that the formal legal rules and principles are focal for all sectors of the business community. Moreover, unless we understand business culture and practice, we might misread the reaction of transactors to not only the formal rules of law but also the new options that are made available by developments in transactional technologies (such as blockchain and smart contracts). Understanding what transactors do in practice is at least as important as the law in the books and the technological options that are available.[33]

Third, in addition to the formal law and the informal norms recognised by transactors, we have the technical measures and forms of technological management that are implicated in the governance of transactions. For example, at an automated car park of the kind that English contract lawyers first debated in *Thornton v Shoe Lane Parking Ltd*,[34] the lights at the entrance to the car park might have signalled to motorists whether or not they were permitted to enter, but the architecture of the car park and the presence of the barrier at the entrance were non-normative signals of what was physically possible. Similarly, in modern online environments, unless users click to agree to the terms and conditions for accessing a website, it will not be possible to access the site. Many prospective users do click. Arguably, though, the problem here goes beyond contract law treating the click as a sufficient indication of consent. As Brett Frischmann and Evan Selinger suggest:

> The choice architecture [for online consumer contracts] retains minimal decisional autonomy in simple take-it-or-leave-it fashion, but the fiction of actual choice only contributes to gradual creep of the human-computer interface from websites to apps to smart TVs to smart homes and beyond.[35]

In short, in transactional situations, there is a risk that humans start behaving like automatons: whenever a smart device can only be accessed and operated if consumers click on 'I agree', consumers do just that.

---

[33] Compare the excellent discussion in KEC Levy, 'Book-Smart, Not Street-Smart: Blockchain-Based Smart Contracts and the Social Workings of Law' (2017) 3 *Engaging Science, Technology, and Society* 1.

[34] [1971] 2 WLR 585.

[35] Frischmann and Selinger (n 28) at 80.

Even if humans are not reduced to automatons, if transactional processes are increasingly automated (employing a suite of emerging technologies, such as blockchain, that will support 'smart' contracting), and if transactional technologies are designed to limit the practical options (the practical liberties) available to the parties (even to remove humans from the transactional loop), the regulatory work is not being undertaken by the rules of the law of contract, indeed not by rules of any kind. In this future world of transactions, the regulatory environment is radically different and we might want to teach students about the law of contract in a way that highlights inter alia the relationship between normative and practical liberty by explicitly framing the law in this increasingly technological context.[36]

14.3.2 Should We Think like 'Coherentists' or 'Regulatory-Instrumentalists'?

Having elaborated the doctrinal, practical, and technological features of the context for transactions, we can focus on two particular lines of inquiry. The first asks how we should engage with new transactional technologies. Should we be thinking like Law 1.0 coherentists or should we be taking a Law 2.0 regulatory approach? The second asks what we make of Law 3.0 initiatives. We will speak to the first line of inquiry in the present section and then consider the second line of inquiry in the next section.

14.3.2.1 Coherentism as the default

Reflecting a Law 1.0 mindset, a concern with formal coherence runs through much of the law of contract (particularly where common law and equitable doctrines are juxtaposed) as well as through critical commentaries on the state of the law. As we have said, in the middle years of the last century, the disjunction between the classical principles of contract law that are applied to commercial contracts and their modified application to consumer contracts was one example of incoherence. However, English law is now beset by a further crisis of coherence in relation to the interpretation of commercial contracts—albeit a crisis that has not been provoked by new technologies as such.

While a European regulatory regime for consumer contracts, including for online consumer contracts,[37] took shape, UK law relating to business contracts remained broadly classical. However, it reflected a tension familiar in the US

---

[36] Compare, Roger Brownsword, 'Law, Liberty and Technology', in Roger Brownsword, Eloise Scotford, and Karen Yeung (eds), *The Oxford Handbook of Law, Regulation and Technology* (Oxford: Oxford University Press, 2017) 41.

[37] See, Roger Brownsword, 'The E-Commerce Directive, Consumer Transactions, and the Digital Single Market: Questions of Regulatory Fitness, Regulatory

jurisprudence between the formalism associated with Williston and the contextualism (and protection of reasonable expectations) associated with Corbin.[38] At the turn of the century, starting fairly modestly—in *Mannai Investments Co Ltd v Eagle Star Life Assurance Co Ltd*[39] and *Investors Compensation Scheme Ltd v West Bromwich Building Society*[40]—the seeds of a modern contextualist approach were sown. Initially, contextualism was limited to correcting errors that had clearly been made in the drafting of contracts, but it soon established itself as the standard approach to the interpretation of commercial contracts,[41] before then being proposed as the appropriate approach to the implication of terms,[42] and (in the much-discussed *Yam Seng* case) as a vehicle for introducing a (contextually indicated) requirement of good faith in contracts.[43] In this way, contextualism challenged long-standing doctrines concerning the literal interpretation of contracts, a restrictive approach to implied terms based on necessity, and of course the adversarial ethic that underwrites such features of contract law.[44]

For a while, it seemed that contextualism would become the default approach for all commercial contract disputes. However, in a series of landmark cases—notably *Marks and Spencer plc v BNP Paribas Services Trust*

Disconnection and Rule Redirection' in Stefan Grundmann (ed), *European Contract Law in the Digital Age* (Antwerp: Intersentia, 2018) 165.

[38] See, e.g., Lawrence A. Cunningham, *Contracts in the Real World* 2nd ed (New York: Cambridge University Press, 2016) 6–8.

[39] [1997] 3 All ER 352.

[40] [1998] 1 All ER 98.

[41] See, e.g. *Rainy Sky v Kookmin Bank* [2011] UKSC 50.

[42] *Attorney General of Belize v Belize Telecom Limited* [2009] UKPC 11.

[43] *Yam Seng Pte Limited v International Trade Corporation* [2013] EWHC 111 (QB). There, Leggatt J said that what good faith requires 'is sensitive to context' (para 141); that the core value of honesty might require more or less disclosure depending on the context; and that in 'some contractual contexts the relevant background expectations may extend further to an expectation that the parties will share information relevant to the performance of the contract such that a deliberate omission to disclose such information may amount to bad faith' (para 142). More recently, the gist of these remarks was repeated in *Sheikh Tahnoon Bin Saeed Bin Shakboot Al Nehayan v Kent* [2018] EWHC 333 (Comm), where Leggatt LJ said that 'relational' contracts 'involve trust and confidence but of a different kind from that involved in fiduciary relationships. The trust is not the loyal subordination by one party of its interests to those of another. It is trust that the other party will act with integrity and in a spirit of cooperation. The legitimate expectations which the law should protect in relationships of this kind are embodied in the normative standard of good faith' (para 167).

[44] For discussion of this direction of doctrinal travel, see Roger Brownsword, 'The Law of Contract: Doctrinal Impulses, External Pressures, Future Directions' (2014) 31 *Journal of Contract Law* 73.

Company (Jersey) Limited[45] (on implied terms); and *Arnold v Britton*[46] and *Wood v Capita Insurance Services Ltd*[47] (on interpretation)—the Supreme Court has pushed back against what was becoming the new orthodoxy. In this most recent case law, we find a reaction against expansive implication and interpretation of terms, particularly in carefully drafted commercial contracts.

Taking stock, we can say that contract law today sits on two fault lines. First, the tension between a formalist and contextualist approach to business contracts has not been resolved (although a 'unified' approach, treating both text and context as relevant, is touted as having responded to the problem).[48] Second, although consumer protection has been outsourced to regulatory agencies, contract law still has some responsibility for protecting vulnerable parties. Here, as Stephen Waddams has recently argued, we find that, the commitment to sanctity of contract notwithstanding, the courts have employed a variety of techniques and doctrinal devices to decline to enforce contracts that unfairly burden one party or unjustly enrich the other.[49] For those who value coherence in contract law, this is not a happy state of affairs; and, anticipating our upcoming discussion,[50] if (for the sake of 'congruence') we have to align technological effects with effects indicated by contract law, the uncertain state of contract law does not help us to do this.

14.3.2.2 The significance of the distinction relative to new transactional technologies

Although coherentism centres on the internal consistency of doctrine, it has an extended manifestation in a tendency to apply existing legal frameworks to new technological innovations that bear on transactions, or to try to accommodate novel forms of contracting within the existing categories.[51] We need only recall *The Eurymedon*[52] and Lord Wilberforce's much-cited catalogue of the

---

[45] [2015] UKSC 72; confirmed in *Wells v Devani* [2019] UKSC 4, para 28 (Lord Kitchin).

[46] [2015] UKSC 36.

[47] [2017] UKSC 24.

[48] As Lord Hodge put it in *Wood v Capita Insurance Services Ltd* [2017] UKSC 24 at para 13: 'Textualism and contextualism are not conflicting paradigms in a battle for exclusive occupation of the field of contractual interpretation.' See, too, in defence of the coherence of the law, Zhong Xing Tan, 'Beyond the Real and the Paper Deal: The Quest for Contextual Coherence in Contractual Interpretation' (2016) 79 MLR 623.

[49] Stephen Waddams, *Sanctity of Contracts in a Secular Age* (Cambridge: Cambridge University Press, 2019).

[50] In 14.3.3.2.

[51] See, further, Roger Brownsword, 'After Brexit: Regulatory-Instrumentalism, Coherentism, and the English Law of Contract' (2018) 35 *Journal of Contract Law* 139.

[52] *New Zealand Shipping Co Ltd v A.M. Satterthwaite and Co Ltd* [1975] AC 154.

heroic efforts made by the courts—confronted by modern forms of transport, various kinds of automation, and novel business practices—to force 'the facts to fit uneasily into the marked slots of offer, acceptance and consideration'[53] or whatever other traditional categories of the law of contract might be applicable.

Consider, for example, the view that online shopping sites are functionally, contextually, and normatively equivalent to offline shopping environments. Might it not be argued that it is the differences rather than the similarities that now need to be accentuated? In particular, as Ryan Calo emphasises, purchasers in online environments are technologically 'mediated consumers', approaching 'the marketplace through technology designed by someone else'.[54] Thanks to this technology, prices can be changed minute by minute and customer by customer; and the particular vulnerabilities of consumers can be identified and exploited.[55] Even if there is nothing new in shopping environments being designed to influence purchasing decisions, in online environments this art is taken to a whole new level of technological sophistication. If there is to be a legal correction for any unfairness arising from these vulnerabilities, how should it be made?

Recalling our discussion in Chapter 3, one approach is to seek out a creative solution by reworking the principles of Law 1.0; and, it would certainly be a mistake to underestimate the flexibility of the principles and concepts that are characteristic of contract law.[56] Equally, though, it would be a mistake to overestimate how far the courts can go with a Law 1.0 approach. Law 1.0 is what it is: coherentist thinking seeks to correct individual relations back to a settled baseline; it is not geared for resetting the baseline itself, for either recognising new interests or striking new balances of interest.[57] To do the latter, we need to think in a Law 2.0 regulatory way.

Already, in some jurisdictions, consumers deal in what are heavily regulated marketplaces; here, some regulatory adjustment might be called for. This might be politically contentious, but it is at least regulatory business as usual. In other jurisdictions, where consumers have to look to the principles of con-

---

[53]   Ibid. at 167.

[54]   Ryan Calo, 'Digital Market Manipulation' (2014) 82 *The George Washington Law Review* 995, 1002.

[55]   For discussion, see Ariel Ezrachi and Maurice E. Stucke, *Virtual Competition* (Cambridge, Mass.: Harvard University Press, 2016).

[56]   A point emphasised in Eliza Mik, 'The Resilience of Contract Law in Light of Technological Change' in Michael Furmston (ed), *The Future of the Law of Contract* (Abingdon: Routledge, 2020) 112.

[57]   Compare the discussion in Roger Brownsword, 'Three approaches to the governance of decentralised business models: Contractual, regulatory and technological' in Roger M. Barker and Iris H-Y Chiu (eds), *The Law and Governance of Decentralised Business Models* (Abingdon: Routledge, 2020) 51.

tract law for the protection of their interests, this is a big ask—particularly if it is the courts who are asked the question. If what the online marketplaces need is a new deal for consumers, a deal that instates either new interests or a more acceptable balance of interests, then a regulatory response is required.

That said, once we start thinking in regulatory terms, and where new technologies offer new instruments for assessing and managing risk, we have taken a significant step towards a radically different approach, a Law 3.0 approach, to the governance of transactions.

14.3.3 What Should We Make of Technical Solutions and the Technological Management of Transactions?

If we work with a broad understanding of the context for transactions, we will note that some of the regulatory burden is now borne by technical measures and technological management. One of the questions raised is whether it is desirable to shift the burden from rules (such as those of the law of contract) in this way. In this part of the chapter, we can sketch how the elements of a technocratic regulatory approach might be applied to transactions and what we might then make of this.

14.3.3.1 How would technological management be applied to transactions?

In the field of transactions, we have public regulators who lay down the background rule framework for various kinds of private transactors (both commercial and consumer, as well as both suppliers and those to whom they supply). To some extent, public regulators might also rely on technical measures and technological management in order to regulate the conduct of transactors, especially in markets where there is an imbalance of power that is a matter of public concern, or where there is a public interest in changing consumer behaviour (for example, to make consumption 'greener', or to switch payments away from cash to digital). However, much of the governance will be left to the transactors themselves in the terms and conditions upon which they contract but also in their own reliance on technical measures or technological management. So, for example, commercial providers might rely on tools such as digital rights management (to protect their IP rights) or AI (to place their adverts more effectively, or to respond more sensitively to their customers' preferences and interests) or smart contracts (to streamline the administration of carriage of goods by sea);[58] and, at the same time, consumers might rely on

---

[58] See, on the last-mentioned, Paul Todd, 'Electronic Bills of Lading, Blockchains and Smart Contracts' (2019) 27 *International Journal of Law and Information*

236   *Rethinking law, regulation, and technology*

tools (such as reputational scoring systems or price comparison sites) to make more informed choices in dealing with commercial providers or in the share economy.[59] If the use of such tools raises concerns, public regulators might again be called on to make an intervention—which, in a Law 3.0 world, might involve new rules or some technical or technological correction.

In the transactional context so outlined, humans are still very visibly the transacting parties. However, according to some commentators, contract lawyers should start to imagine a world of automated transactions, where commerce is, so to speak, a conversation conducted by machines, and where (as Richard Ford foresaw some decades ago) digital assistants would take care of our consumer needs.[60] Instead of H2H, whether B2B or B2C or P2P contracts, we have transactions that are M2M. In that world, humans have been taken out of the transactional loop, leaving it to the technology to make decisions that humans would otherwise be responsible for making. Possibly, humans will still be treated as being somewhere on the loop by treating the machines as agents transacting on behalf of human principals, neither H2H nor M2M but, as it were, (H)M2(H)M. That said, precisely how the law in general, and the law of contract in particular, will engage with that future is difficult to know.

On the face of it, once such automated systems are up and running, humans (whether as suppliers or as consumer contractors) largely drop out of the picture; technological management takes over. Now, the technology not only manages the 'ordering' and the supply of goods and services to the consumer's needs, but it also manages whatever risks or problems might arise. For example, if the

---

Technology 339; and, the Law Commission's consultation on Digital Assets: Electronic Trade Documents (Summary of Consultation Paper) (https://s3-eu-west-2.amazonaws .com/lawcom-prod-storage-11jsxou24uy7q/uploads/2021/04/6.7434_LC_Digital -assets-consultation-summary_web3.pdf) p 3:

> We think that this legal position [not recognising that there can be 'possession' of electronic documents] is archaic, inefficient, and wholly unsuited to an increasingly digitalised world. Allowing for electronic versions of trade documents could lead to significant cost savings and efficiencies, together with improvements in information management and security. It could also make the sector more resilient to the type of restrictions on movement and human-to-human contact that were imposed in response to the COVID-19 pandemic. With the development of technologies such as distributed ledger technology over the past decade, this vision of paperless trade has become increasingly feasible. However, the law continues to lag behind.

[59] Compare the application of new tools to regulate the use of unfair terms in consumer contracts: see, Hans-W. Micklitz, Przemyslaw Palka, and Yannis Panagis, 'The Empire Strikes Back: Digital Control of Unfair Terms of Online Services' (2017) 40 *Journal of Consumer Policy* 367.

[60] Richard T. Ford, 'Save the Robots: Cyber Profiling and Your So-Called Life' (2000) 52 *Stanford Law Review* 1576.

scheme of technological management is designed to be consumer-friendly, it will not be possible for the supplier to be credited with the payment unless the goods or services are supplied in accordance with the order and with specified standards. Conversely, if the design is supplier-friendly, the technology will ensure that consumers pay for the ordered goods and services before they are supplied. At the root of such an arrangement, there might be a transaction, very much like a traditional contract (and to which the traditional law of contract might apply) that commits the parties to a certain protocol of technological management; or, it might be that there are background rules that prescribe the design features for systems of this kind. In this latter case, there are rules about the features of transactional technologies; but these are rules that are directed at designers and manufacturers, not at transactors. It is a new world; but, before long, it might be the world in which students find themselves as consumers; and, if this is so, students might reasonably ask how precisely the law of contract connects to this world.

14.3.3.2 What should we make of technological management?

Where it is public regulators who rely on technological management, we will need to be satisfied that it is authorised by, and in accordance with, the rule of law. To this extent, the channelling of conduct by technical measures or by technological management must meet the criteria of the triple licence, whether we are dealing with transactions or crime and security. Moreover, once the rule of law and the triple licence are applied to private governance, the same applies to the use of technical measures or technological management by the transactors themselves.[61]

Suppose, for example, that digital products are supplied under contracts that require users to act in accordance with the intellectual property rights of the suppliers. Now, suppose that, instead of relying on the protection of the contractual terms and conditions, the suppliers simply code in their intellectual property rights—given the coding, it is not possible for the product to be used other than in a way that complies with the relevant rights. Thus far, we might not have serious concerns about the switch from contract to code. However, if the contract or the code were to give the supplier more protection than intellectual property law recognises, this would be a problem. While a legal challenge might be mounted against the contract, the coding of products—which might not be transparent and which would be restrictive of practical liberty—might be more worrying. In both cases, though, we should insist that the actions of the suppliers should be compatible with the rule of law.

---

[61] For our rethinking of the rule of law, see Chapter 5; and for our rethinking of legitimacy and the triple licence, see Chapter 6 above.

238   *Rethinking law, regulation, and technology*

One of the questions that a community might address in its version of the rule of law is whether the results of the use of technical measures or technological management by transactors needs to be congruent with the law of contract. If the matter is explicitly addressed and provided for by the community, the question of congruence (which we touched on earlier in the book)[62] should not be problematic. However, if the matter has not been explicitly addressed and provided for, the co-existence of technological management (such as the use of blockchain and 'smart contracts' to automate payments) with the rules and principles of contract law that the courts would apply (to different effect) could raise some very tricky issues. Divergence between the effects produced, on the one hand, by technological codes and, on the other, by the formal code of contract law might or might not be problematic.[63]

14.3.4   Contract Law 2022

From start to finish, a legal education in the 2020s should focus on Law 3.0, on its three overlapping conversations, on its polycentric nature, and on its increasingly technological complexion. This is not legal education as we have known it; this is not teaching the law of contract as it has been taught to generations of law students; but Law 3.0 is not law as we have known it. Unless law teaching catches up, unless Contract Law 101 is replaced by Contract Law 2022, law students will fall ever further behind.

14.4   HOW WE TEACH AND WHO WE TEACH

To wrap up these reflections about rethinking the teaching side of law schools, we can say a few words about the second axis of our rethinking, that is, about how teaching is delivered, and then about the implications for who is to be admitted and taught.

The analogue model of law school teaching was to give lectures (laying out the basic Law 1.0 principles) and then follow up those lectures with small group discussion (largely based on hypotheticals that teased out the leeways within doctrine and encouraged students to develop the art of reasoning like a lawyer). One of the key messages was that students should always read the cases (not just potted summaries) and similarly they should read the law

---

[62]   See 8.4.2 above.

[63]   See, especially, Roger Brownsword, 'Automated Transactions and the Law of Contract: When Codes are not Congruent' in Michael Furmston (ed), *The Future of the Law of Contract* (Abingdon: Routledge, 2020) 94, and 'Political Disruption, Technological Disruption, and the Future of EU Private Law' in Mateja Durovic and Takis Tridimas (eds), *New Directions in EU Private Law* (Oxford: Hart, 2021) 7.

review articles and comments as instructed (and, again, not rely on textbook summaries). Attending lectures and tutorials was not hugely inconvenient (but students did need to be physically present as per the timetable); but life in the law library could be frustrating because there would be too many students chasing after too few copies of the cases and the key articles.

Repeating our prefatory remarks, as law schools expanded their student populations, hard-copy library collections (really intended for researchers or practitioner reference) came under severe pressure. Students got up to all sorts of ploys in order to access the source material. The problem was alleviated by smarter library practices that, in effect, made the teaching collection available only on a short-loan basis and, very importantly, by the arrival of photocopying facilities which meant that the law library was transformed from a reading room to a copying room.

In the present century, the digitization of legal materials has further transformed the law school. Students are now able to access pretty much all the materials that they require through their smart devices. There is no longer a resource problem. Access to the key materials is no longer a challenge; use of the law reports and law reviews is no longer rivalrous.

During the pandemic, law schools have been compelled to operate online. Teaching has been delivered remotely and off-campus. Some law teachers will have liked it; others will have disliked the lack of face-to-face interaction. Students, too, will have given the experience mixed reviews: while some might like the flexibility, others will think that it is a second-class service and, what is more, many will feel that it fails to deliver the kind of social interaction that universities promise. Having made the effort to translate offline teaching materials to online formats, it would be surprising if the law schools all wanted to revert fully to offline teaching. Whether or not lectures and classes will follow the materials to online environments remains to be seen. In all probability, the various pressures from stakeholders in legal education will result in a period of hybrid teaching, blending both offline and online elements.

Cutting across this picture of each law school finding its own pathway through the new range of delivery tools, there is the possibility that events might be overtaken by rapid mergers and acquisitions—such that, just as with law firms, smaller and medium-sized law schools are taken over by larger players, and we end up with a sector that is dominated by a handful of mega law schools. Already, there is a wealth of online legal materials just waiting to be curated, gated, and exploited. If this happens, it will be a handful of law schools that dictate not only how law is taught but, in all probability, what is taught.

Putting this possibility to one side, the way in which students are taught in law schools might also impact on who those students are. Some prospective students might prefer online delivery, others prefer offline; some might be able to afford only remote access. In principle, though, law schools could offer their online modules to far more students than they can accommodate in the physical setting of the law school. Indeed, as in some other parts of the world, law schools in the UK could make a huge leap in widening access by opening their doors (or, more accurately, opening their programmes) to all those who have minimum entry qualifications, and by using the end of first-year examination as a major filter in relation to who is permitted to proceed.

14.5   CONCLUDING REMARKS

In debates about the delivery of legal services, there is a view that fewer lawyers, but lawyers who are technologically enabled, could actually operate more effectively in meeting legal needs. Similarly, it might be thought that fewer law academics, with the right technological support, could deliver a legal education to more students. However, this presupposes that we are all agreed as to the kind of legal education that is to be delivered. Once we rethink law, regulation, and technology, this is one of the things that is actually far from clear. As with the delivery of legal services, new technologies certainly provide new opportunities for the delivery of legal education, but these same technologies raise fundamental questions about the law school curriculum. Until these questions have been addressed, it is unclear what a Law 3.0 law school should look like. Moreover, if we are to stick with the idea that law teaching in our universities should be 'research-led', we also need some clarity about the research trajectory to be taken by legal scholars as technologies intrude on the legal and regulatory processes.

15. Researching law

15.1 INTRODUCTION

Famously, in the United States, about two-thirds of law professors are 'PhD professors'. This might seem unremarkable when, nowadays, most UK universities insist on their academic staff having a PhD qualification; so, typically, UK law professors will have a PhD in law. However, the sting is that the law professors in the United States have their PhDs in non-law subjects, for example, in disciplines such as economics, history, and philosophy. This difference is reflected in the research undertaken by academic lawyers in the common law world and by the kind of legal scholarship that is valued.

According to Rob van Gestel, Hans Micklitz, and Edward Rubin, while 'Americans often view European legal scholarship as old-fashioned and inward-looking due to its continued engagement with doctrine,...many Europeans see American [legal] scholarship as amateur social science that has lost contact with the realities of legal practice and judicial institutions.'[1] To this, we might add that some Europeans also share the American view of legal scholarship on our side of the Atlantic—indeed, one of the claims in this book is that we spend too much time having doctrinal Law 1.0 conversations.[2] No doubt, it is the case, too, that some legal scholars in the United States (and, especially, some practitioners[3]) share something of the European view concerning American legal scholarship—for example, Joshua Fairfield recalls that in his early career, he often was advised 'to include a few tables or a line of mathematical pseudocode to increase the so-called sexiness of a piece and

---

[1]   Rob van Gestel, Hans-W. Micklitz, and Edward L. Rubin, 'Introduction', in Rob van Gestel, Hans-W. Micklitz, and Edward L. Rubin (eds), *Rethinking Legal Scholarship* (New York: Cambridge University Press, 2017) 2.

[2]   For a balanced assessment of the merits and weaknesses of doctrinal scholarship, see Jan M. Smits, 'What is Legal Doctrine?', in van Gestel, Micklitz, and Rubin (n 1) 207.

[3]   As in the familiar complaint that academic lawyers do little to assist judges in their practice, see Harry T. Edwards, 'The Growing Disjunction Between Legal Education and the Legal Profession' (1992) 91 *Michigan Law Review* 34.

thereby its chances of publication'.[4] Quite rightly, Fairfield sees little virtue in using the language of neoclassical economics in order 'to obscure the mind-bendingly obvious so that it appears more publishable'.[5]

Responding to these transatlantic perceptions of legal scholarship, van Gestel, Micklitz, and Rubin argue that such preconceptions and oppositions need to be set aside. Rather, they see legal scholarship on both sides of the Atlantic as sharing a joint challenge. Thus,

> If legal scholarship becomes too much separated from practice, legal scholars will dig their own grave. If legal scholars, on the other hand, cannot explain to other disciplines what is academic about their research, which methodologies are typical for legal research, and what separates proper research from mediocre or poor research, we will probably end up in a similar situation.[6]

Putting this in the terms of our rethought legal landscape, where Law 1.0 is the paradigm, lay people might wonder what academic lawyers find to research and scholars in other disciplines might wonder in what ways legal researchers significantly advance our knowledge and understanding. For both lay persons and scholars, there is surely little mystery about the law. There are rules; people want to know about the legal position, and, although the rules do change from time to time, things move pretty slowly. Granted, academic lawyers need to be up to speed with the latest developments in the law but, other than updating the standard texts, what more is there to do? That is a very good question and we cannot find a very satisfactory answer until we move beyond Law 1.0. However, as van Gestel, Micklitz, and Rubin caution, we need to be careful that as we move away from legal doctrine and practice we do not become subsumed in another discipline, digging ourselves out of one grave only to dig ourselves into another.

The argument in this book is that lawyers need to move beyond Law 1.0 so that they can engage in the conversations of Law 2.0 and Law 3.0. Those conversations offer a rich agenda of research questions. In order to answer some of those questions, lawyers might need to recur to other disciplines, but the reconstituted field of law, regulation, and technology enables lawyers to make a distinctive contribution in their own right to our knowledge, understanding, and practice of governance in the twenty-first century.

---

[4]   Joshua A.T. Fairfield, *Runaway Technology* (New York: Cambridge University Press, 2021) at 154.

[5]   Ibid. As we will indicate in the next section of the chapter, the environment for legal research is not ideal; and, the ground rules for getting work published are part of that environment. Nevertheless, Fairfield's own scholarship is testament to the opening up of the research agenda once we move beyond Law 1.0.

[6]   Van Gestel, Micklitz, and Rubin (n 1) 2–3.

Accordingly, in this chapter, we will begin to rethink legal research and scholarship as we step outside the box of Law 1.0, rethinking what we research and how we research.

15.2 WHAT WE RESEARCH AND WHAT WE SHOULD RESEARCH

These introductory remarks suggest that, in our rethinking of legal research we need to find the basis for a new partnership between legal scholars. Scholarship in the tradition of Law 1.0 still has a place, but the new direction in legal research has to come from the conversations of Law 2.0 and especially now Law 3.0. In this part of the chapter, we can speak a little more to the proposed partnership; to the new research agenda; to our ability to defend the partnership and its agenda against the familiar complaints that legal research is not scientific, or that it is 'political', or of no practical significance; and to the possible extension of the agenda to include 'ethics' and the 'ethification' of the governance of technologies.

15.2.1   A New Partnership

At the law school where I started my academic career (the same law school that I mentioned in the last chapter), the teaching and research of legal doctrine dominated. Effectively, Law 1.0 was the only conversation. However, when criminology was housed within the law school, this introduced the language and logic of different disciplines; and, as the years went by, and as criminology was joined by socio-legal studies, the complexion of the law school changed as did its conversations. Nevertheless, there remained a divide between the doctrinal and the non-doctrinal (theoretical) wings of the law school. In some respects, the friction between the two sides was quite productive; and, there was a time when some really progressive and significant research was done. But, this was not galvanised by a unitary vision within the law school, by a vision that could explain the contribution made by both doctrinal and theoretical legal scholarship. So, while plurality and fragmentation can be productive, law as a discipline needs a narrative that justifies and explains how the different varieties of its scholarship fit together.

As we have seen, on one side of the Atlantic, in the historic home of the common law, a great deal of legal scholarship and law review writing continues to be in the tradition of Law 1.0. Even authors who have a PhD (where the thesis will often focus on a nice question of law, for example on the doctrinal concept of relational contracts or the idea of lawful act duress) work in this tradition. By contrast, on the other side of the Atlantic, the law reviews simply are not interested in this kind of question and analysis. If an academic is writing about contracts, the doctrines that are focal will be subjected to a critique that goes beyond traditional coherentism, particularly by drawing on economic or philosophical theories.

While, in the United Kingdom and in Europe more generally, rethinking legal scholarship has always been up against the resistance of Law 1.0 doctrinal scholarship (in which academic lawyers will have invested a huge amount of their time—for example, you do not become an expert in Dutch private law overnight), in the United States, there is probably less resistance. Nevertheless, on both sides of the Atlantic, there has been support for a number of initiatives, including the critical legal studies movement, women and the law, law and literature, and law and autopoiesis, the prospectus for each of which has involved a radical rethinking of legal scholarship.[7] However, these are not initiatives that have been geared to bring together law school scholars; particularly in the case of critical legal studies, the law school establishment with its doctrinal preoccupations was the target.[8] Moreover, these were not initiatives that were provoked by technological developments or by a self-consciously regulatory perspective. This is important because it is these provocations that are critical not only to forging a new research agenda in law but also to developing an agenda around which a partnership of legal scholars can be built.

15.2.2 The Law 2.0 and Law 3.0 Research Agenda

Once we have Law 2.0 in our sights, the leading questions about regulatory effectiveness and regulatory legitimacy invite scholarship that can draw on lines of inquiry and insights from other disciplines. In the case of regulatory effectiveness, the insights from sociology, psychology, and behavioural economics are relevant; and in the case of regulatory legitimacy, we might look to philosophy and economics.

Taking a further step away from Law 1.0, Law 3.0 presents another research agenda. Recalling the discussion in the earlier part of the book about new fields, frames, and focal points, there is no need to be imperialistically prescriptive about the particular lines of research that should now be pursued. Nevertheless, there are urgent questions to be addressed. As the exercise in rethinking that has been undertaken in this book clearly highlights, Law 3.0 is

---

[7] For a helpful overview, see van Gestel, Micklitz, and Rubin (n 1) 4–15; and, for an indication of how legal researchers in European law schools view their own research orientation (humanities, social sciences, or practical), see Mathias M. Siems and Daithí Mac Síthigh, 'Why Do We Do What We Do? Comparing Legal Methods in Five Law Schools Through Survey Evidence' in van Gestel, Micklitz, and Rubin (n 1) 31.

[8] Compare Richard Michael Fischl, 'Some Realism about Critical Legal Studies' (1987) 41 *University of Miami Law Review* 505.

Researching law 245

an opportunity to put lawyers in the vanguard. Lawyers can and should lead in relation to the rethinking of the rule of law and, concomitantly, the legitimate applications of new technologies. Lawyers should lead, too, in developing the questions of new coherentism and the institutions, both nationally and internationally, for new coherentist regulatory purposes.

Five years ago, I proposed six questions for a rethought research agenda. Namely:

1. How should we conceive of the 'regulatory environment'?
2. How are the values of the 'rule of law' to be applied where technologies are used as regulatory tools?
3. What is the significance for liberal values of states using technological management as a means of social control and channelling?
4. What is the significance of the complexion of the regulatory environment?
5. Within the larger framework of the regulatory environment, what do we now understand about the effectiveness of law?
6. To what extent can we expect the signals that comprise the regulatory environment to be coherent?[9]

Subsequently, including in the present exercise in rethinking law, regulation, and technology, I have started to answer some of these questions.[10] If, as proposed in this book, we rethink the field of legal scholarship in a way that introduces technology as being of interest both as an object of law and regulation but also as a tool for governance, and if we frame our thinking in terms of Law 3.0 (as three co-existent conversations, or practices, or paradigms), then we have the makings of some answers to some of the questions. However, in this book, we have highlighted further questions and proposals in relation to the rule of law and legality, we have addressed much more explicitly the question of how we do the law jobs (LawTech and RegTech do not appear, as such, on the earlier agenda), and, we have introduced new lines of inquiry about the authority of and respect for the law. Most importantly, two major projects have crystallised: first, there is the 'legitimacy project'; and, second, there is the 'governance choice'. It is no overstatement to say that both projects relate directly to the future of humanity.

In the earlier set of inquiries, there is a question about the effectiveness of law; and, the direction of travel in the rethought regulatory environment is

---

[9] See Roger Brownsword, 'Field, Frame and Focus: Methodological Issues in the New Legal World' in van Gestel, Micklitz, and Rubin (n 1) 112, at 124–125.

[10] Principally, in Roger Brownsword, *Law, Technology and Society: Reimagining the Regulatory Environment* (Abingdon: Routledge, 2019) and *Law 3.0: Rules, Regulation and Technology* (Abingdon: Routledge, 2020).

246 *Rethinking law, regulation, and technology*

towards more effective regulatory interventions. However, the counterpoint to this has to be a concern with legitimacy. What I have proposed in this book is that we need to be much clearer about the different levels of interest that are at issue when we make decisions about the permissibility of particular technologies or their applications. There are different levels of interest within each particular community, but all humans share a common interest in the protection and maintenance of the global commons. Communities need to do better in engaging with new technologies but, most importantly, there needs to be a more focused and effective cosmopolitan engagement.

The second project invites lawyers to confront the choice between governance by humans with rules and governance by technologies. For each particular community, this is a choice to be made. It is unlikely to be presented initially in the sharp binary terms in which it has just been put. Initially, technologies will insinuate themselves into regulation and governance, and this might happen without prior public debate and approval (without an explicit social or community licence). However, once communities wake up to the changes taking place in the practice of governance, they will want to debate their direction of travel. Have they gone as far as they want with technology? Do they want to go back? Or, do they want to proceed? These are huge decisions, and they are potentially destabilising (possibly compromising the commons). In this context, this book is a wake-up call to legal scholars; it is urging that we should not sleepwalk into an unwanted world of technological governance.

15.2.3 Defending the Research Agenda

What should we say to those who might accuse the proposed agenda of Law 3.0 research (here, taking Law 3.0 as encompassing the three co-existing conversations of Law 1.0, Law 2.0, and Law 3.0) as being 'unscientific', 'political', and of no practical significance?

To start with 'unscientific', we can concede that research in the Law 1.0 tradition is not scientific. Moreover, to avoid any misunderstanding, we should emphasise that Law 1.0 is not an enterprise or a project that aspires to be scientific but then fails to make the grade; to the contrary, it is by intent not scientific; it is interpretive and imaginative.[11] Elsewhere within the partner-

---

[11] Compare Paul W. Kahn, 'Freedom and Method' in van Gestel, Micklitz, and Rubin (n 1) 499. At 521, Kahn says that he tells his students that there are three rules: (i) their opinions do not count; (ii) 'there is no right answer to any question'; and (iii) 'legal interpretation is not a matter of predicting how any particular case will come out.' Readers who think that there are too many hostages to fortune in these ground rules might prefer Joshua Fairfield's (n 4) robust defence of legal fiction and analogy coupled with his head-on assault on 'science' (predicated on logical positivist philosophy).

ship, though, researchers are working on understanding and explaining how governance works (and does not work). In Law 2.0, these inquiries are every bit as 'scientific' as we find in the social sciences; and, the inquiries in Law 3.0 are every bit as 'scientific' as we find in the biosciences, data science, and so on. Legal scholarship is no longer a science-free zone.

The charge that legal research is 'political' typically focuses on the interpretive work undertaken in Law 1.0, where, as Paul Kahn puts it, the 'absence of method leads critics to claim that interpretation is only a pretext for the imposition of the personal values of judges and scholars'.[12] If judgement is not objective, it must be a matter of personal value and opinion only. Given the propensity of that last statement to collapse under the weight of its own epistemic demands, we do not need to worry about that particular criticism. Moreover, to the extent that the objection is just another version of the 'unscientific' charge, there is already a robust response in place. Nevertheless, the Law 3.0 research agenda does present another opportunity to clarify the relationship between law and politics. In each community, there will be some understanding about the kind of conversation that it is legitimate to have in the courtroom and that it is legitimate to have in government circles and in the legislative process. Undeniably, Law 2.0 conversations take place within political institutions, and it would be extraordinary if we were to insist that those conversations should not be 'political' (in the sense of being appropriate conversations to have in political institutions). On the other hand, we might say that such conversations are not appropriate for the courtroom;[13] and, to that extent, law and its researchers should not be political. Ultimately, we need guidance in the rethought concepts of the rule of law, of legitimacy, and of the constitution as to which kind of considerations and practices are appropriate in Law 1.0, in Law 2.0, and in Law 3.0 conversations. There might be some kinds of considerations and practices that, being inappropriate tout court, we condemn as 'political'; and there might be some kinds of considerations and practices that we judge to be inappropriate in certain conversations—we might judge in other words that there is a time and a place for being 'political'. Whatever the case, we need to clarify the matter and get on with the urgent business of saving the world and its human communities—which leads us to the third objection to the proposed research agenda.

The idea that a Law 3.0 research agenda is of no practical significance should be dismissed out of hand. To be sure, it might not be judges and traditional legal practitioners who are assisted in their work by legal scholars,

---

[12] Kahn (n 11) at 502.
[13] Compare the famous critique in JAG Griffith, *The Politics of the Judiciary* (4th ed) (London: Fontana, 1991).

248   *Rethinking law, regulation, and technology*

but the stakes are much higher. If we do not get our research act together, the prospects for all humans are seriously reduced. This is the time for lawyers to show that they can make a practical difference—and, what is more, make a difference for the good of all humans.

15.2.4 Extending the Research Agenda

One of the features of the evolving relationship between law, regulation, and technology is the way in which 'ethics' is viewed—and, in particular, the 'ethification' of the governance of emerging technologies as both law and technology hitch ethics to their enterprises. In this context, it might be argued that it is essential to research this matter if we are to see the bigger picture of governance.

From the perspective of Law 1.0, thinking like a lawyer involves thinking inwards, not outwards to technology, and not outwards to ethics. Ethics, as (extra-legal) normative guidance to individuals who are concerned to do the right thing, is simply irrelevant to the application of law—in the previous chapter, we recalled Karl Llewellyn's remark that students will only learn to think like lawyers if they put their ethics into a state of 'temporary anesthesia'.[14] That said, of course, many legal and equitable principles might be seen as vehicles for ethical thinking that has been doctrinally absorbed.

Lawyers taking a Law 2.0 regulatory approach view ethics rather differently; ethics is now salient and significant, but problematic. Particularly as new technologies attract ethical debate, it becomes important for regulators to take into account the ethical views of their communities. To some extent, this could be seen as an aspect of negotiating the social licence for a technology, but it might also speak to community values. If regulators neglect to do this, there is likely to be a degree of regulatory failure whether because the regulatory position is not accepted as legitimate or is not effective or both. However, even with consultation, regulators might find that ethics is challenging because there is a plurality of views in the community. If ethics spoke with one voice, things would be relatively straightforward; but, in many communities, and especially where ethical debate has been provoked by emerging technologies, we find new expressions of ethical division and a sharpening of ethical difference.[15]

---

[14]   Karl N. Llewellyn, *The Bramble Bush* (New York: Oceana Publications, 1951) 101.

[15]   See, e.g., Roger Brownsword, 'Stem Cells and Cloning: Where the Regulatory Consensus Fails' (2005) 39 *New England Law Review* 535, and 'Ethical Pluralism and the Regulation of Modern Biotechnology' in Francesco Francioni (ed), *Biotechnologies and International Human Rights* (Oxford: Hart, 2007) 45.

When the conversation moves on to Law 3.0, ethics remains a challenge. However, just as the legal community is contemplating partnering with the tech community to develop solutions to regulatory problems, we find tech not only articulating its own ethical codes but also working on encoding ethics in the design of its products and processes. This 'ethification' of governance that is characteristic of Law 3.0 invites further inquiry.[16]

15.3 HOW WE RESEARCH AND WITH WHOM WE RESEARCH

Typically, researchers in UK law schools work in an environment that is geared to serve the university's general research strategy and vision. The environment is not specifically modified or crafted for *legal* research. As a result, the signals about whether research is a matter of individual choice or institutional requirement, about what kinds of research (e.g. inter-disciplinary, funded, blue-sky, impactful, and so on) are valued, and about where to publish and what to publish, cascade down from the leaders of our universities. Moreover, these signals are fortified by various kinds of performance indicators, especially the indicators given by national research assessment exercises.

Because the research environment is not created specifically for law researchers—for many of whom it is simply sustained periods of time rather than expensive equipment or large teams of research assistants that are the most important resource—it tends to have a distorting effect on research activity. Generally, the law community has resisted bibliometric measures of the quality of its research outputs, but it is otherwise constrained by university (now business) plans and priorities and by the way that public money is made available for research through the Research Councils. There is much that could be said about this (and, we might start by asking whether the present practices and systems are fit for purpose if we aim to support legal research that is original and significant[17]), but this is not the place. Here, our question is whether,

---

[16]   See, e.g., Niels van Dijk and Simone Casiraghi, 'The "Ethification" of Privacy and Data Protection Law in the European Union: The Case of Artificial Intelligence' Brussels Privacy Hub, Working Paper Vol 6, No 22, May 2020; available at https://brusselsprivacyhub.eu/publications/BPH-Working-Paper-VOL6-N22.pdf (last accessed 14 May 2021).

[17]   In this context, it would be helpful to know how many of the 'deliverables' that result from Research Council funding for 'law' projects are submitted to the UK's national research assessment exercises (the REF); and, it would be even more interesting to know what percentage of those outputs that REF Law panels judge to be of world-leading quality (i.e., judge to be four-star outputs) can be attributed, directly or indirectly, to Research Council funding.

given our rethinking of law, regulation, and technology, academic lawyers should be rethinking how they research and with whom they research.

To state the obvious, the tools that academic lawyers now use for their research are quite different from the tools that I used as an early career researcher. Just as law students have gone from pen and paper (possibly, manual typewriters) together with hard-copy resources to word processors, digital devices, and electronic resources, the same applies to legal researchers—and, in both cases, the pandemic has accelerated the tendency to study and research in online environments. While this might seem obvious, we should not forget that this has all happened quite recently—a fact of which I am frequently reminded when I receive requests via ResearchGate[18] for articles written in the 1980s or 1990s which were never in a digital format.

Typically, today's tools make it easier for researchers to access relevant materials quickly. For researchers who are working on Law 1.0 questions, this is beneficial and, to some extent, there will also be benefits for Law 2.0 researchers. However, the question is how we should go about research where we are thinking in a Law 3.0 way. Technology has driven our research agenda, but does it also drive the way in which we do our research? For some the answer will be that it does because we, lawyers, need to get into 'labs' to work closely and routinely with technological colleagues and research partners. Some will believe that it is through intensive interactions of this kind that we will get the synergies that come from a combination of disciplinary perspectives. Others might think that legal researchers should still operate at some distance from the technologies because the fundamental governance questions are not of a technical nature. Moreover, while we might aspire to be renaissance researchers, how realistic is it to expect lawyers to be experts in each new technology as it comes onto the legal and regulatory radar?

As for the closely related question of with whom legal researchers should work, Law 3.0 research projects invite collaborative networks or teams of interdisciplinary researchers.[19] Whether or not these teams are led by lawyers is perhaps not a capital question. However, it is imperative that the non-lawyers

---

[18]   https://www.researchgate.net.

[19]   See, e.g., Thibault Schrepel and Vitalik Buterin, 'Blockchain Code as Antitrust' (2021) *Berkeley Technology Law Journal* (forthcoming); Simon McCarthy-Jones, 'The Autonomous Mind: The Right to Freedom of Thought in the Twenty-First Century' (2019) 2 *Frontiers in Artificial Intelligence* article 19 at 13 (proposing 'interdisciplinary conversations between lawyers, neuroscientists, psychologists, philosophers, and those working in the technology industries'); and, David Freeman Engstrom, Daniel E. Ho, Catherine M. Sharkey, and Mariano-Florentino Cuéllar, *Government by Algorithm: Artificial Intelligence in Federal Administrative Agencies* (February, 2020) at 8; available at https://papers.ssrn.com/sol3/papers.cfm?abstract_id=3551505 (last accessed 10 April 2021).

Researching law 251

in these groups understand the contribution that the lawyers can make and do not regard them as useful only for the advice that they can give on particular Law 1.0-type questions.

There is one other point. It used to be said that legal scholarship, Law 1.0 research, is typically sole scholarship. I am not sure how far that is borne out in practice—for example, texts for legal practitioners will often bring together a team of authors. At all events, once legal scholars move beyond Law 1.0 questions to engage with the research agenda of Law 2.0 and Law 3.0, collaboration is likely to be the rule rather than the exception.

15.4 CONCLUDING REMARKS

As we said in the previous chapter, the expectation in university law schools is that teaching will be research-led. At the same time, the expectation is that the research that is undertaken will align with the university's business plan and priorities. This might be a good time to rethink the law school but, so long as law schools operate in a way that is designed to meet the university's targets, we can expect resistance to proposed changes that will impact negatively on relevant income streams. For sure, new technologies will disrupt the traditional practices of our law schools; some rethinking is inevitable; but, if history is to judge the rethinking as a success, law school leaders need to have a clear vision of what their intellectual project has to be.

To conclude on another autobiographical note, as a teenager, I was advised by a local lawyer that, while going to university with a view to making a career in law was a good idea, going to university to study law was a thoroughly bad idea. The purpose of going to university, I was advised, was to become a 'civilised' person. Although I did not follow this advice, it surely was sound. For, so long as the law schools centre their teaching and research on a Law 1.0 mission, they do disconnect themselves from what it takes to be civilised. Thinking outside the box of Law 1.0 is a considerable challenge, but the opportunities for those law schools that succeed in doing so are enormous. With the right teaching mission and the right research agenda, with the right reconnection to civilisation, law can become much less of a silo or an outlier and, instead, one of the intellectual hubs of the university.

16. Concluding remarks

According to the Secretary-General of the United Nations,

> Increasingly,…the decisions that shape the public's every day experience are found not in legislative codes but software codes and are made not by elected officials in parliaments, but by scientists and innovators in private settings. Their choices will resonate for generations to come.
>
> And, increasingly, the overriding question for the United Nations has become: how can we ensure that the voices and concerns of those who may be significantly affected by new technologies are heard, even if they are developed on the other side of the globe and their effects and consequences are not yet evident?[1]

This is a wake-up call to the world and, in this book, it has become a wake-up call to lawyers in particular.

After thousands of years of gradual technological development, technological innovation and application has gone into a different gear. The acceleration in technological development has required considerable human adjustment and it has brought with it a mixed bag of benefits and harms. The disruptive impact of these developments on both societies and economies is well known; but, the disruption also extends to our traditional thinking about law, about how we practise, teach, and research law, and about our attitudes towards the law.

The thrust of this book has been that, whether we are technophiles or technophobes, we need to rethink law, regulation, and technology but, above all, we need to rethink governance by an assemblage of laws, regulations, and technological measures. This is now the way that we should view the legal landscape.

Nevertheless, some persons (both lawyers and non-lawyers) might decline the invitation to rethink law, regulation, and technology. Where such persons form groups, they will continue to think about law in traditional Westphalian terms, their ideas about respect for the law will also be traditional and they will gear their practical conduct to that conception of law as a rules-based human enterprise. This might lead to there being pockets of resistance to rethinking law as attempts are made to conserve or to put such a traditional conception

---

[1] *UN Secretary-General's Strategy on New Technologies*, September 2018, available at https://www.un.org/en/newtechnologies/images/pdf/SGs-Strategy-on-New-Technologies.pdf (last accessed 26 April 2021).

Concluding remarks 253

into practice (whether in self-governing micro communities, in law schools that stick to a Law 1.0 curriculum, in research that does not stray beyond doctrinal questions, or in professional practice that puts a premium on face-to-face dealing and human functionaries). But, of course, the world outside these 'bubbles' will move on, not only widening the gap between the technological actuality of governance and the conception of law within the bubbles, but also presenting challenges to the viability of such communities.

By contrast, where it is accepted that we need to rethink law, regulation, and technology, there will be two major challenges. One challenge will be simply to keep up with governance as reliance on technological measures intensifies. Whether or not there will be anything like a Moore's Law to cover the speed at which governance by machines and technological management take on the legal and regulatory work, we will have to see; but, simply maintaining a picture of governance that stays connected to the state of the practice will be difficult. The other challenge is to maintain a critical grip on governance. A key role for lawyers will be to help their communities to make decisions about the uses of technology for legal and regulatory purposes. In this book, it has been suggested that a revised understanding of the rule of law in conjunction with the idea of a triple licence for legitimate applications of technologies offers the right kind of approach; but, it has also been conceded that our institutions, both nationally and internationally, are woefully inadequate.

Summing up, in this book, the process of rethinking some very traditional and resilient ideas about law and its relationship with regulation and, especially, technology has begun. To some extent, we are catching up with events; but we also need to be thinking ahead. Technological development is unlikely to stop any time soon. Our tendency to default to technological solutions will intensify. What we begin to see with both LawTech and RegTech is surely just the beginning. Rethinking law, regulation, and technology will not end with the last page of this book; this will be a continuing process of work in progress.

Index

accommodation of interests, regulatory responsibility to seek 100–102
accurate administration, principle of 65–6
adaptive governance 165
additive manufacturing 39
    agencies for 166
    technologies for 28
agencies, legitimacy of 16
Alarie, Ben 106
algorithmic governance tools 105
alternative forms of dispute resolution (ADR) 122, 126–9, 136
Anglo-Saxon jurisprudence 80
anticipatory responsibility 167, 168–9
anti-competitive agreements 136
Arnold v Britton 233
artificial intelligence (AI) 61, 145
    benefits of 148
    government deployment of 105
    IMPACT tool 113
    Internet Courts 129
    judging machines based on 137
    justice delivery system 129
    predictive tools in the criminal justice system 143
    for reduction of false negatives 143
    regulator of 108
    risks posed by 176
    smart tools to guide decision-making 111
    use of 87, 105, 106
        to assist with official decision-making 111–13
        to clarify the legal position I 107–8
        to clarify the legal position II 108–9
        to enforce one's legal rights 110–11
        to exercise one's legal powers 109–10

for improving compliance with mandatory legal rules 115–16
for making official decisions 113–15
Asilomar Conference on Recombinant DNA 41
asylum seekers 74
auditing responsibility 167, 173–4
authority of law
    baseline view of 195–6
    Basic Norm 196
    rethinking of 194–5, 197–200
automated justice system
    expectations, criminal justice, and automation 146–8
    from humans being 'in the loop' to being 'out of the loop' 148–50
    use of predictive algorithms 147
automated process of dispute resolution 129–30

balance of interests 93, 133, 177, 235
Beshada v Johns-Manville Products Corp. 125
big data, significance of 144–5
bioscience 247
biotechnologies 36, 38, 46, 169
blockchain technology 231, 238
    transactions based on 119
    use of 110, 130, 132
body worn cameras/videos (BWVs) 148
border crossing and migration control 74

care.data initiative 81
Carmarthenshire County Council v Lewis 123
carriage of goods by sea 235
Case of S. and Marper v The United Kingdom 145

Charter of Fundamental Rights of the European Union 170
Cheung, Anne 48
Citron, Danielle Keats 68
civic order, rational principles of 77
civil justice
    accessibility and affordability of 119
    automated 129
    rethinking of 122, 139
cloud computing services, ecosystem of 49
code, idea of 6
coding of rules 65
coherentism, as the default 231–3
commercial contracts, interpretation of 25
common good, idea of 82
common law 43, 45
    jurisdictions 46, 106
    jurisprudence 106
commons licence 15, 153, 160, 175
community
    fundamental values of 9
    sense of justice of 141
community licence 10, 83, 91, 96, 153, 160, 175
    rule of law and 83–4
community of agents 95, 98
community's fundamental values, regulatory responsibility to respect 99–100
COMPAS risk assessment 112
compensatory responsibility
    attribution of fault and allocation of 124
    rethinking of 123–6
competition law 29, 221, 229
computer-based communications *see* online communications, regulation of
confidentiality, law of 43
conflict of laws 16
congruence, principle of 60, 65, 135–6
consent, concept of 228
consumer contracts 226
    European regulatory regime for 231
    for offline shopping 234
    for online shopping 234
    UK law relating to 231
Consumer Rights Act (2015), 228

contract law 29, 43, 46
    on carriage of goods by sea 235
    in context for transactions 227–31
        features of 229–31
        general idea of 228–9
    Contract Law 2022 238
    electronic contracting law and architecture 226
    Law 3.0 framing of 226
    principles of 227, 229, 231
    regulatory environment of 229
    teaching of 226–38
        approach for 238–40
    for technological management of transactions
        application of 235–7
        channelling of conduct by technical measures 237–8
    thinking like 'coherentists' or 'regulatory-instrumentalists'
        coherentism as the default 231–3
        distinction relative to new transactional technologies 233–5
    US view of 226
conversations, three co-existing 52–5
Copernican revolution 214
court-based adjudication 12, 119
Covid-19 pandemic 176, 204
crime control, valuations of 139
criminal justice system 12–13, 38, 138, 160
    AI predictive tools in 143
    automation of processes in 140, 146
    DNA profiles for 145
    law and regulation of 139
    plea bargaining deals in 139
    rethinking of 140
criminal law
    code of 48
    regulatory themes of 140–46
        dealing with the dangerous 142–4
        regulatory offences 140–41
        using technologies to deter and detect crime 144–6
    rethinking of 140
cross-border

commerce 126
disputes, resolution of 127
cyberattacks 184–5
cybercrime 38
cybercriminals 75
cyberlaw 6, 39, 49
cyberspace, development of 16, 75
cybertechnologies 75, 185, 198, 213
cyber-wrongdoing 49

dangerous people, dealing with 142–4
Data Protection Directive 87
data science 247
decision-making, process of 67, 85, 105, 139
deepfake technology 166
deliberative democracy, principles of 73, 84
digital law 18
digital rights management 5, 51, 79, 235
Directive 95/46/EC 85
disclosure, function of 12, 120
dispute-resolution services 18
disputes
court-centred handling of 11
online dispute resolution systems 12
settlement of 28, 128
dispute settlement and resolution, technologies for 128
distributed denial-of-service (DDoS) attack 184
DNA profiling, use of 38, 144
due diligence 12, 120
due process, valuations of 139

eBay 127
e-commerce 38, 127
product liability claims 129
e-government 130
emerging technologies 14, 34, 42, 55, 80, 166–7, 178, 207
applications of 83
compatibility of 174
governance intelligence in relation to 190
governance of 175, 180
regulation of 162–3
employers' liability 106.

environmental harm, risk assessment for 165
essential design conditions 164–7
differentiated functions 167
technology-specific model 165–6
essential infrastructure, respect for 98–9
ethical EU policymaking, promotion of 170
European Commission 86
European Group on Ethics in Science and New Technologies (EGE) 169–70
Eurymedon, The 233
evidence, gathering of 172
ex ante dispute avoidance 130–36, 150–60
comparing smart prevention with other strategies 158–60
congruence, ideal of 135–6
legal risk management 131
prevention better than dispute
humans are accidents waiting to happen 132–5
promises are made to be broken 131–2
smart prevention and moral aspiration 156–8
smart prevention, community values, and the commons 155–60
true and false positives 153–4

Facebook 30, 202
facial recognition technology, use of 38, 145
fair dispute-resolution procedures 126
fairness, community's ideas of 66
fair warning, principle of 62
fake news 202
fault-based liability, principle of 53
field of law 28–31
Financial Conduct Authority (FCA) 12, 121
first responder, responsibility as 169–70
foci for inquiry 32
foresight and horizon-scanning responsibility 168
framing of rules 31–2
Freedman, Lawrence 185
Frischmann, Brett 226

Fuller, Lon 2, 7, 8, 28, 29, 57–9, 64–5, 68–71, 73, 77, 135, 206

General Data Protection Regulation (GDPR) 148
  Article 22 of 85–8
generality, principle of 60, 66–8
geo-engineering 50, 190
geo-locating technologies 38
global commons 91, 96, 177, 187, 191
  protection and maintenance of 216
  regulatory stewardship for 180, 190
global ID systems 74
global licence, idea of 83, 96
global stewardship 181
global technology governance 181
good faith and fair dealing, obligations of 25, 62
Google Spain case 87
governance
  by humans 17, 59, 203
  by machines 83–8
  by non-normative strategies 58
  replacement of law with 206
  by rules 59, 61–2, 66, 69
  technological modes of 67
  by technologies 61
  Westphalian commitment to 102
Group of Advisers on Ethical Implications of Biotechnology 169

hard law 170–74
Hartian model of a legal system 57
high-tech medicine 24
  see also low-tech medicine
Hildebrandt, Mireille 69, 88, 211–12
Holmes, Oliver Wendell 44
Horizon Scanning Advisory Group 168
horizon scanning programme 168
human
  as accidents waiting to happen 132–5
  social systems 36
human agents
  characteristic of 97
  communities of 99
human conduct, rule-based channelling of 11

human dignity
  commitment to respect for 100
  interpretation of 207
  issue of 94, 99
Human Fertilisation and Embryology Act (1990), UK 163, 173
Human Genetics Commission, UK 164
human genetics, developments in 38
human interventions, to enforce compliance 65
human-machine interaction 114
human rights, respect for 99
humans and rules, de-centring of 19
human species
  biological characteristics and needs of 97
  defined 97
human tribunal 114
hybrid warfare 184

iBorder control strategies 74
information societies 78
information war 185
institution of law, rethinking of 16–18
intellectual property law 29, 221, 237
intelligence gathering 166
intelligent governance 189
intelligent hub 14, 167, 174–5, 189–90, 192
international agencies 15–16, 181–2, 186–7
international legal and regulatory institutions
  international design 188–91
    building on the national and regional hubs 189
    stewardship remit for the agency 190–91
  international relations and agencies 182–8
  rethinking of 180–82
international relations 16, 178, 183–6, 191
Internet separatists 76, 201–2
Investors Compensation Scheme Ltd v West Bromwich Building Society 232
IP rights, infringement of 110

judicial review 176
just governance, order of 202
just punishment, theory of 79–80, 155

knowledge, democratization of 78
Koop, Christel 26

labour law 221, 229
Law 1.0 43–4, 46–7, 123, 135–6, 220, 223, 242
Law 2.0 47–9, 53, 121, 123, 127, 139–40, 145, 174, 220, 242, 244–6
Law 3.0 45, 50–51, 54, 74, 119, 127, 131, 139, 145, 212, 220, 238, 242
  characteristic of 249
  curriculum 224–6
  essential element in living with 175
  framing of contract law 226
  research agenda 244–6
law and legitimacy, rule of 19
Law Enforcement Directive 149
law jobs 104
law, regulation, and technology
  baseline thinking about 25–8
  relationship between 37–41
law school 218
  curriculum
    Law 1.0 253
    Law 3.0 226
  functioning of 218
  mission of 223
  rethinking of 18–19
  Warwick Law School 229
law, teaching of
  contract law 226–38
  curriculum for 220–26
    baseline model 221–2
    Law 2.0 approach 223–4
    Law 3.0 approach 224–6
  technologies of 218
LawTech 11, 12, 21, 104, 120, 136, 245
  development of 120
  use of 106–17
law–technology relationship 43
law, three paths for 43–5
  Law 1.0 43–4, 46–7
  Law 2.0 47–9, 53
  Law 3.0 45, 50–51, 54, 74, 119

legal and regulatory institutions, rethinking of 14–16
legal education
  practice in delivering 219
  technologically enabled 18
legal enterprise, predicates of 8
legalism, ideal of 57, 211
legality
  baseline view of 57–9
  in conjunction with the rule of law 102
  demand for 102
  Fullerian idea of 59–60, 77
  Hildebrandt's conception of 69
  notion of 7–8, 88
  principles of 59
    accurate administration 65–6
    epistemic 60–63
    Fullerian 59–60, 77
    generality 66–8
    practical possibility 63–5
  and reciprocity 68–70
  rethinking of 70
legal materials, digitization of 239
legal ordering 69
legal practitioners, needs of 220
legal research
  agenda for
    defending 246–8
    extending 248–9
    Law 2.0 and Law 3.0 244–6
  approach for 249–51
  new partnership 243–4
  performance indicators of 249
  rethinking of 243
  through the Research Councils 249
  topics of 243–9
legal rules, making of 28
legal scholarship 2, 19, 32, 33, 241, 243, 247
  rethinking of 244
  transatlantic perceptions of 242
legal services
  consumers of 13
  delivery of 240
  provision of 11
Legal Services Board 10
legal thinking, Westphalian 95
legitimacy
  of agencies 16

baseline views of
  internal test 92
  simple balancing 92–4
of law 9–10
rethinking of 90, 94–6
  responsibility to respect
    the community's
    fundamental values
    99–100
  responsibility to seek
    an acceptable
    accommodation of
    interests 100–102
  stewardship responsibility for
    the commons 96–9
social basis of 172
of technological application 90
in Westphalian view of law 92
legitimate governance, principles of 67
Lessig, Lawrence 6
liability
  fault-based 124
  product 125
Llewellyn, Karl 29, 104, 248
Lodge, Martin 26
London bombings (July 2005) 155
Loomis case 112–13, 144
low-tech medicine 24

machine learning 61, 115, 145
  agencies for additive manufacturing
    166
  first responder to 169
managing danger, strategy of 140
*Mannai Investments Co Ltd v Eagle Star
  Life Assurance Co Ltd* 232
*Marks and Spencer plc v BNP Paribas
  Services Trust Company (Jersey)
  Limited* 232–3
McLennan, Alison 34, 165
mens rea
  proof of 48, 140
  requirement of 141
Minority Report 150
monitoring responsibility 173
Moore's Law 253
Moors murderers 142
moral agency 98
  commons' conditions for 99
  development of 98

'moral' development 98
morality, privatisation of 150
moral pluralism 99, 208
Murray, Andrew 197–8

nanotechnology 36, 38, 172
national legal and regulatory institutions
  elaboration of design of 167–75
    anticipatory responsibility
      168–9
    auditing responsibility 173–4
    intelligent hub 174–5
    monitoring responsibility 173
    responsibility as first responder
      169–70
    responsibility for the initial
      intervention 170–73
  essential design conditions of 164–7
    differentiated functions model
      167
    technology-specific model
      165–6
  new coherentism 175–8
  rethinking of 162–4
  societal implications of 169
national legal systems 2, 4, 118, 197, 201
nation-state constitutions and codes 25
nature of law 69
neoclassical economics 242
neurotechnologies 144
new technologies, development of 40,
  140
no-fault compensation schemes 12, 53,
  120, 124
non-compliance, penalties for 60
Nuffield Council on Bioethics 168–70

offenders, rights of 143
offline shopping 234
online communications, regulation of 75
online conduct, codes of 198
Online Court 128
online dispute resolution (ODR) system
  12, 122, 126–9, 136, 219
online intermediaries, role of 4, 30, 49
online shopping 234

Parliamentary Office of Science and
  Technology (POST) 171

patent law, application of 37–8
payment, legal right to 110
plea bargaining deals, in criminal justice system 139
portraits of private persons, unauthorized circulation of 43
post-War austerity 228
practical possibility, principles of 63–5
prerogative power, abuse of 66
Presentence Investigation Report (PSI) 112
privacy right, jurisprudence of 43
privacy, right to 43, 82
procedural integrity, notion of 80–81
processual inclusivity, notion of 80–81
product liability 124–5, 129
proportionality, test of 177
public deliberation and debate, de-centring of 151
public/private partnership, need for 51
public re-enactment of a society's moral code 147
'public welfare' offences 140–41

Reed, Chris 197
RegTech 11, 21, 33, 104, 121, 245
    use of 106–17
regulation, rethinking 26
    the field 33
    focus of inquiry 34–5
    legal framing 33–4
regulatory agencies 26
'regulatory' offences, recognition of 140–41
regulatory reasoning, role of policy in 52
Reidenberg, Joel 76
relative constancy, principle of 60
Renzo, Massimo 97
ResearchGate 250
respect for law
    baseline views on 204–8
        legal idealist/moralists' response 206–8
        legal positivist/prudentialists' response 205–6
    disruption of law 213–15
    rethinking of 209–13
        disruption brought about by governance 209–10

law as a human-centric enterprise 210–13
responsible innovation, idea of 40
rethinking law 104
    field of law 28–31
    foci for inquiry 32
    framing of rules 31–2
rethinking technology 35–7
retribution, philosophical theories of 80
risk and liability, distribution of 45
risk assessment 140
    algorithms 147
    for environmental harm 165
risk communication 140
risk management 13, 84, 140, 153
robot judges, development of 130
rule-based governance 32
rule-breaking, sanction for 59
rule of law 3, 7, 8–9, 17, 57–8, 70, 102, 237–8, 247, 253
    achievements of 88
    and community licence 83–4
    condition of 84
    and governance by machines 83–8
    legality in conjunction with 102
    link with human adjudication 115
    online as well as offline 74–6
    private as well as public 76–9
    processual inclusivity and procedural integrity 80–81
    proposal for extension to the industry 77
    rethinking of 74–82, 245
    and the social licence 84–5
    substantive as well as procedural 82
    and technical measures 79–80
    Westphalian thinking about 72

sanctity of contracts, principle of 50
self-governance 16–17, 33, 172, 198, 216
    of humans by humans 212, 214
self-governing micro communities 253
self-teaching algorithms 150
Selinger, Evan 226
Selznick, Philip 26
Shachar, Ayelet 74
'smart' cities, development of 77
smart contracts 46, 50, 132, 230–31, 235, 238

smart machines 3, 9, 11–12, 17, 19, 21, 90, 109, 130, 137, 148, 211, 216
social licence 10, 90, 153
  idea of 80, 83, 96
  for new technologies 80
  rule of law and 84–5
social technology 35–6
soft law 15, 167, 172–3, 174
state-centric rules, with governance 32
State of Wisconsin v Loomis 112
stewardship remit for the agency 190–91
stewardship responsibility, for the commons 96–9
  agency conditions 97–8
  existence conditions 97
  respect for the essential infrastructure 98–9
Strategy on New Technologies 181
suicide bombers 142, 155
surveillance and identification technologies 38, 60–61
surveillance capitalism 77–8
Synthetic Biology Agency 165–6
synthetic biology, regulation of 165

Tamanaha, Brian 82
technological development 5, 14, 20, 35, 40–41, 47, 71, 79, 114, 160, 165, 244, 252–3
technological governance 5, 17, 202, 204, 215–16, 246
technological innovation 20, 139, 233, 252
technological instruments, use of 80
technological management 19, 21, 50, 51, 59, 61–5, 77, 83–8, 104, 139, 175, 212
  of conduct 11
  strategy of 117
  use of 7, 11, 85
    to guarantee compliance with mandatory legal rules 116–17
    by regulators 110
technological regulation 212

technological tools 11
  to deter and detect crime and determine guilt 144–6
techno-social engineering 226
Thornton v Shoe Lane Parking Ltd 230
tort claims 46, 124
tort law 25, 43–4, 46, 123
trade marks 111, 201
traditional ideas, about the connection between fault, liability, and compensatory responsibility 123–6
transactional technologies 227
  features of 237
transnational governance 33
transnational law, idea of 5, 42
transport technologies 45, 52
triple licence, idea of 90, 96, 203, 237, 253
'true positive' offenders, identification of 151

Uber test-case (UK) 106–7

Warren, Samuel 43
weapons of mass destruction (WMD) 186
web-blocking orders 110–11
Weber, Rolf 48
Westphalian legal systems 75, 200
Westphalian model of law 4, 17, 25, 28, 41, 42, 195
  on legal thinking 95
  on legitimacy 92
Wood v Capita Insurance Services Ltd 233
World Economic Forum 181, 186
World Justice Project's report (2019) 118

Yam Seng case 232

Zuboff, Shoshana 77–8
Zuckerberg, Mark 201